FOUNDATIONS *for* Preaching *and* Teaching

SCRIPTURE BACKGROUNDS FOR 2012

PEGGY EKERDT • JEAN MARIE HIESBERGER • BIAGIO MAZZA

MARY M. McGLONE, CSJ • ABBOT GREGORY J. POLAN, OSB

DENISE SIMEONE • PAUL TURNER

LTP
LITURGY
TRAINING
PUBLICATIONS

Nihil Obstat
Very Reverend Daniel A. Smilanic, JCD
Vicar for Canonical Services
Archdiocese of Chicago
September 3, 2010

Imprimatur
Reverend Monsignor John F. Canary, STL, DMIN
Vicar General
Archdiocese of Chicago
September 3, 2010

The *Nihil Obstat* and *Imprimatur* are declarations that the material is free from doctrinal or moral error, and thus is granted permission to publish in accordance with c. 827. No legal responsibility is assumed by the grant of this permission. No implication is contained herein that those who have granted the *Nihil Obstat* and *Imprimatur* agree with the content, opinions, or statements expressed.

Authors: Peggy Ekerdt; Jean Marie Hiesberger; Biagio Mazza; Mary M. McGlone, CSJ; Abbot Gregory J. Polan, OSB; Denise Simeone, Paul Turner

Table of Contents

Introduction

When you prepare a homily or a catechetical session based on the Sunday Lectionary, you set off a chain of events. You open the Lectionary and meet the Word of God on the page, a Word that is alive, waiting to be spoken and heard in the community. You absorb that Word through prayer and meditation, opening your heart to let it work on you. It touches something within you—your faith in God and your commitment to Christ. There, the Word ignites a fire that eventually opens your mouth to proclaim what you have seen and heard. Although you speak because of an inner need to express what you have experienced, you also speak in order to share the fire. Others who hear your message then let the Word of God dwell in their hearts. It directs their lives and inspires even more people by the thoughts and actions it spreads.

This book will help homilists and catechists perform the early stages of these events. It explains what the scriptures say, but it does something more. It uncovers additional meanings that are hidden within the fabric of the Lectionary. Why does this reading go with that one? Is the psalm really important this weekend? How do these readings fit this season of the year? How has the Catholic Church presented the meaning of the Bible in our catechesis and missionary activity? This resource answers these questions.

This resource is for homilists and catechists. It gives the leaders of your community a common background to assist your meditation and presentation. You don't have to present the readings in the same way, but if you share the same formation, you will help the entire community to meet the Word of God, to feel its challenge, and to put it into action.

Join the chain of events. And let the Holy Spirit be your guide.

—Paul Turner

Advent

Overview of Advent

Advent is a time for looking back at the ancient promises fulfilled in Christ, for seeking to deepen our awareness of his presence, and for looking forward to Christ's return at the end of time. The readings for the first week of Advent in this cycle are remarkable for how they combine those thrusts, seemingly summarizing the focus of the season as they remind us of the eternal fatherhood of God, our dual longing for and celebration of God's presence, and the great unknown of the moment and effects of Christ's return at the end of time.

Advent's liturgies celebrate the season as one of radical hope. That is a mood we can only attain when we take the time Advent offers us to reflect and pray. As we remember the grace of our collective past, Advent calls us to deepen our longing and cry out, "Lord Jesus, come in glory!"

First Readings

Throughout Advent, most of the Old Testament readings come from the book of the prophet Isaiah. In the Year B cycle of Sunday readings, we will hear from Isaiah three times and once from 2 Samuel. These readings follow a progression from the urgent cry, "Rend the heavens and come down" (Isaiah 63:19), to a word of comfort for God's people, the promise that God's Chosen One will care for all the poor, and, finally, God's promise to raise up a Savior from the house of David. Each of these readings contributed in its own way to sustain Israel's hope for salvation and the coming of the Messiah.

Responsorial Psalms

The psalms of Advent correspond beautifully with the messages of the First Readings. In Psalm 80 on the First Sunday of Advent, after crying, "Rouse your power, and come!" (80:3), we beg to see the saving face of the Lord. Responding to Isaiah's words of comfort on the Second Sunday of Advent, we announce the nearness of salvation. On the Third Sunday, we sing with Mary that Isaiah's promises have been fulfilled. Finally, on the last Sunday before Christmas, we proclaim God's kindness and that the throne of his Son will last forever. At the same time, these psalms look forward to the Gospel messages of hoping for Christ's presence and watching for his return.

Second Readings

Advent's Second Readings are chosen from four different letters and underscore the themes of each of the Sundays. What unites them is their unwavering focus on God's promises. From 1 Corinthians, we hear of God's faithfulness. The Second Letter of Peter reminds us that God has promised new heavens and earth. On the Third Sunday, we are told to rejoice because God can bring us to holiness. Finally, Paul calls us to give glory to the God whose mystery we have seen revealed.

Gospel Readings

In the Year A cycle of Sunday Lectionary readings, the Gospel readings mainly come from Matthew's account, and in Year C, they are mostly from the Gospel according to Luke. In this liturgical year, we will hear the Year B cycle of readings, mainly focusing on the Gospel according to Mark. During Advent, however, we will hear from Mark on the first two Sundays, from John on the third, and from Luke on the fourth. The reason for this, as we shall see throughout this year, is that Mark's account of the Gospel is significantly more compact than the others. Mark says less than the others about John the Baptist and has no infancy narrative at all.

The progression of these Gospel readings seemingly reverses our understanding of chronological order. We begin with a focus on Christ's coming at the end of time. After that, we have two presentations of John the Baptist's witness to Jesus, the one who will come after him. Finally, we hear the narrative of the Annunciation in which Mary speaks the words that summarize her life: "May it be done to me according to your word" (Luke 1:38). From beginning to end, the message is clear: the Christ who came will return, and his kingdom will have no end.

First Sunday of Advent
Be Alert! The Messiah Comes

November 27, 2011

Connections to Church Teaching and Tradition

- "God calls lay people to witness and share their faith in the midst of the world. By their Baptism they share in Christ's priesthood and are sealed by the Spirit. They are thus called to holiness, to a prophetic witness in the world, and to a kingly resolve to sanctify the world by their words and deeds" (USCCA, 138).

- "Charity in truth, to which Jesus Christ bore witness by his earthly life and especially by his death and resurrection, is the principal driving force behind the authentic development of every person and of all humanity. Love—*caritas*—is an extraordinary force which leads people to opt for courageous and generous engagement in the field of justice and peace" (CIV, 1).

Isaiah 63:16b–17, 19b; 64:2–7 The prophet Isaiah was writing to the Israelites at a time of national disaster, as they returned to rebuild their community after long years of exile in Babylonia. Isaiah admonished them to remember that God had saved them in the past and would do so again. In return, they must be faithful, crying out to God to lead them to salvation. By confessing their guilt and putting themselves into God's hands, they will know God's presence among them again. As God's people, they must lead lives that are faithful and holy as they fulfill their part of the covenant with God.

The concluding verses are a well known-image: "we are the clay and you the potter: / we are all the work of your hands" (Isaiah 64:8). The message to be ready at all times to put oneself in God's hands is echoed in the Gospel exhortation from Mark: "Be watchful! Be alert!" (Mark 13:33). By remembering the covenant and putting their lives into God's hands in trust, the people of Israel would know the joy of redemption. This Advent, we, too, can place our lives in God's hands and invite him to shape us into faithful followers.

Psalm 80:2–3, 15–16, 18–19 (4) In her writing about this Sunday's psalm, Irene Nowell, OSB, says this refrain calls upon God to make us do two things: return to him and be faithful, and turn our lives around in order to improve our situation. We hear in the psalm how this will happen. We ask God to show compassion to us, be kind to us, protect us, and save us.

Psalm 80 is a prayer of a nation that has been beset by calamity and disaster. Yet, the image in the first stanza of God as the guiding shepherd reminds us that we are not abandoned, but saved. God has saved his people in the past and he will do so again. It remains for us to offer our faithful response by turning toward the God who saves us.

1 Corinthians 1:3–9 Where the Gospel prods us to attention this First Sunday of Advent, the letter from Paul assures us of God's faithful initiative and action. Paul's words, written around 54 AD from Ephesus to the community of believers at Corinth, are assuring to us, too, as we await God's revelation in our lives this Advent. Paul's letters to the Corinthians are characterized by their explanations of how the members of a community of brothers and sisters are to treat one another. A community that acts with love for others is a reflection and a sign to the world of God's love. Such a community is a true witness to Jesus Christ, who gave his very life for all and who showed us the kind of love we are to offer one another through his suffering, death, and Resurrection. As communities, we are called to remind ourselves at Advent to pay attention to how we act in the world; in essence, to be alert every moment for God's reign of peace and justice in order to fulfill Paul's prodding to love. When we do this, we are signs of God's love to the world.

Mark 13:33–37 This passage sounds like the last judgment and end of the world, and indeed it is sometimes referred to as "the little apocalypse." No one knows when the Messiah will come; therefore, Jesus is clear in his warnings to disciples to watch, stay awake, and be alert. These are Jesus' last words to his disciples before the beginning of his Passion.

There are many times in our lives when we are alert and watchful, like when we are cooking something that can burn easily, patrolling on guard duty, hovering over a sick child, or trying to drive and follow directions. We know what it feels like to stay alert because if we don't, we may miss a crucial moment. Jesus does not want disciples to miss the opportunity; he does not want distractions to get in the way of our seeing the presence of God in our midst. Seeing God and knowing that he is present despite perils or hardships gives us hope that God's saving power can be found clearly among his people. We read this passage with anticipation, reminding ourselves that once again we remember that the Messiah comes to save. As we proclaim in the refrain of the psalm, our response is to turn our face to God and be saved.

Connections to Church Teaching and Tradition

■ "The forms and tasks of life are many but there is one holiness, which is cultivated by all who are led by God's Spirit and, obeying the Father's voice and adoring God the Father in spirit and in truth, follow Christ" (LG, 41).

■ "The Word became flesh *to be our model of holiness*" (CCC, 459).

■ "Now, what was once preached by the Lord, or fulfilled in him for the salvation of humankind, must be proclaimed and extended to the ends of the earth,[1] starting from Jerusalem,[2] so that what was accomplished for the salvation of all may, in the course of time, achieve its universal effect. To do this, Christ sent the holy Spirit from the Father to exercise inwardly his saving influence, and to promote the spread of the church" (AG, 3–4).

Isaiah 40:1–5, 9–11   The image in this passage of preparing the way of the Lord and making the path straight is so significant that it is quoted in all four accounts of the Gospel (Matthew 3:3, Mark 1:2, Luke 3:4, John 1:23). In today's Gospel, we hear it in reference to John the Baptist and his role proclaiming God's message of repentance. Like the Baptist, Isaiah delivers God's call and message to the people.

Isaiah, speaking to Israel during her exile, announces in beautifully poetic language that God has forgiven her. He also gives instructions. God's people are to build a highway for God, leveling all the bumps, ruts, and hills that are in the way. They are to walk along the road, proclaiming the Good News of God's salvation, announcing it to all, crying out in a loud voice. We can rejoice because God has forgiven Israel for her sins! Those who were exiled can return home. But in return, they must do their part to fulfill their covenant with God.

Psalm 85:9–10, 11–12, 13–14 (8)   Imagine someone on a dark night shining a flashlight in front of your feet as you are trying to negotiate a path through a forest. Such is the image we proclaim in this psalm today. The last verses suggest that justice will walk before the Lord and prepare the way. The first part of the psalm that we do not hear this Advent is a lament that reminds God of times of past forgiveness. But in the following verses the images are of hope for the restoration of the covenant relationship with God. God's presence can be seen when faithful virtues like justice, kindness, and peace (shalom) are practiced. Those who practice this love give abundant expression to the way of God and prepare the way so the entire world can see God. This kind of light shining on the way is an appropriate symbol to remember as we follow along on our own Advent journey.

2 Peter 3:8–14   The Second Letter of Peter gives us a map of how we ought to live as we await the Lord's coming. This epistle was written to address some issues that the Christian community was having with false teachers who appeared to be denying the Second Coming of the Messiah. Believers were beginning to lose hope and were abandoning their way. The letter reminds listeners that God does not perceive time in the same way that human beings do. Written with the Second Coming of the Messiah in mind, it gives appropriate instructions for us as we prepare ourselves during our Advent journey. We do not know God's ways, but we can hold fast to the belief that this time is a gift from God for us to repent and learn to live holy lives, be ready, and prepare for the day of the Lord's coming. The kinds of people we are to be are those living lives of holiness, devotion, obedience, and faithfulness as we wait for the Lord's Second Coming. The message of this epistle is made all the more critical as we hear the Baptist's call in today's Gospel.

Mark 1:1–8   The first verse of Mark's account of the Gospel starts with this title: "The beginning of the Gospel of Jesus Christ the Son of God." With these beginning verses, Mark lays the foundation for his Gospel. There is no infancy story, nor any announcement to Mary or Joseph. Mark plunges right in with the call of the Baptist, proclaiming a baptism of repentance for the forgiveness of sins. We hear in the passage that many people were coming to John and acknowledging their sins as they were baptized. This is Mark's Good News. This is the mission that disciples are invited to follow.

Many of the men and women we hear about in Mark's account of the Gospel need to be reminded that they are called to follow Jesus Christ and to preach the Gospel to the entire world. Mark gives many examples of people, including disciples, who do not fulfill Christ's mission because they are afraid or have abandoned their role. Even the very end of Mark's account of the Gospel has the women hearing the news of the risen Christ and being afraid to tell anyone. Yet Mark reminds us about one who was not afraid, who did not abandon his role as herald; instead, by his words and actions, he invited other believers to do the same. John the Baptist calls out to us as we continue on our Advent journey, inviting our faithful response to prepare the way of God.

---

1 Acts 1:8.
2 Cf. Lk 24:27.

Connections to Church Teaching and Tradition

- Mary was conceived without sin. She is known by the title, "the Immaculate Conception" (CCC, 490–493).

- God intends to redeem the human race. Although human beings are guilty of sin, God stands ready to forgive and heal (CCC, 410–412).

- God's eternal plan is good. This plan was already in the mind of God at the creation, and it extends to redemption at the end of time (CCC Glossary, "Economy of Salvation").

Genesis 3:9–15, 20   An old Christmas carol proclaimed, *"Nova! Nova! Ave fit ex Eva."* The Latin word *nova* morphed into the French *noël*. It means "good news," but it has come to mean Christmas itself. The rest of that carol's title is a play on words in Latin: *Ave* comes from *Eva*. In Latin, the name of the first woman in the book of Genesis, Eve, is *Eva*. When you twist those letters backward, you get in Latin the word that the angel Gabriel used to greet the symbolic first woman of Luke's account of the Gospel: *Ave*, or, "Hail, full of grace." Today's readings have in mind this contrast between Eve and Mary. Unfair as it is to pin the blame for all sin upon Eve, the point is that Mary became an instrument in God's plan of salvation. Eve foreshadows Mary, who became the mother of the Living One. Where our first parents said no, Mary said yes.

Psalm 98:1, 2–3, 3–4 (1a)   The psalmist praises God for possessing and exercising power. God's power is matched by his kindness and faithfulness. The psalmist personally and Israel collectively have benefited from God's might. Not everyone likes to sing new songs. Most people like the old ones. But sometimes something so wonderful happens that it requires new notes and a new voice. The old songs do not always fit new circumstances. We have to change our tune.

In the Immaculate Conception, God has worked something tremendously powerful and totally new: creating a human being conceived with sin. God had the power to do this, and God exercised this power not just on Mary's behalf, but for the sake of us all. Only a new song can hope to tell the wondrous deeds of God.

Ephesians 1:3–6, 11–12   God chose Abraham, his wife, and their descendants to be a special people for a historic covenant. So, God has chosen the followers of Jesus Christ to be a special people for an eternal covenant. This mystery of God's choice is the subject of an early Christian hymn preserved in the Letter to the Ephesians. We may not feel worthy of this relationship with God, and we are not. However, God makes us worthy. God chose us to be holy and without blemish.

The first covenant was made to an extended family. But in Christ, God has willed to extend the boundaries of this family through a spiritual adoption. This reading especially fits the celebration of the immaculate conception because of our belief that God chose Mary for a special ministry in the history of salvation. God preserved her from sin, making her holy and without blemish for all time. Still, all of us have been chosen "in accord with the purpose of the One who accomplishes all things according to the intention of his will." We do not perform the same role that Mary did, but we each play a part in the great drama of God's good plan for the salvation of the world.

Luke 1:26–38   God's miraculous powers are evident in the announcement Gabriel makes to Mary. She, who is full of grace, will become the mother of God's Son, and her elderly kinswoman has also conceived. Miracle upon miracle appears.

Today's solemnity concerns the earliest miracle of the series: the immaculate conception of Mary. From the moment her parents conceived her, Mary was preserved from all sin. We believe this in part because of the way Gabriel greets her: "full of grace." Gabriel announces that Mary, though a virgin, will become a mother. We commonly call this second miracle of the series the virgin birth of Christ. The words *immaculate conception* refer to Mary, not to Jesus. The miracle of Jesus' virginal conception was preceded by the miracle of Mary's immaculate conception.

As if that were not enough, Gabriel announces yet another miracle. Elizabeth, Mary's relative, a woman advanced in years, has also conceived a son. One reason for this miracle was to reassure Mary that "nothing will be impossible for God." Mary first found the angel's announcement preposterous. How can a virgin conceive? But she had to rethink the news in the light of another miracle. How can an elderly woman conceive? Nothing is impossible for God.

This solemnity celebrates the triumph of God's power. It consoles us in our weakness and sin, in our misfortune and misjudgment. God is more powerful than we are, and God has proven it throughout the course of time, miracle upon miracle.

Connections to Church Teaching and Tradition

■ "Since this mission continues and, in the course of history, unfolds the mission of Christ, who was sent to evangelize the poor, the church, urged on by the Spirit of Christ, must walk the road Christ himself walked, a way of poverty and obedience, of service and self-sacrifice even to death, a death from which he emerged victorious by his resurrection" (AG, 5).

■ "John faithfully echoes the words of Isaiah, words which in the ancient Prophet concerned the future, while in John's teaching on the banks of the Jordan they are the immediate introduction to the new messianic reality. John is not only a prophet but also a messenger: he is the precursor of Christ" (DVI, 19).

■ "As the Spirit of truth will also do, John 'came to bear witness to the light'[1]" (CCC, 719).

Isaiah 61:1–2a, 10–11   Scripture scholars believe that when this passage from Isaiah was written, it was at a time of Israel's lowest experience. The people of Israel had returned from exile to find that Jerusalem had been ruined. Yet it was there in this awful time of pain and loss that the Israelites felt the presence of God. They had been liberated, freed by God, and Isaiah reminds them that they have reason to rejoice at that sign of God's action in their lives. They have not been abandoned.

The year of God's favor announced in the reading gives images of a jubilee year when all debts are forgiven, property is restored to its owners, the land is allowed to lie free of crops so it may rest, and captives are released from prison. It is a time of extraordinary mercy and healing. In recalling these images, the Israelites would have remembered that they were not just the recipients of these wonderful things, but also that they were called to offer them to all.

Luke 1:46–48, 49–50, 53–54 (Isaiah 61:10b)   The Responsorial Psalm for this Sunday uses the verses from Luke's account of the Gospel that Mary sings after her journey to visit Elizabeth. She joyfully proclaims it in response to Elizabeth's greeting to her as the Mother of the Lord. This prayer or song of praise used as the Responsorial is also called a canticle, and we refer to it as the Magnificat. Two other canticles, the Canticle of Zechariah (Luke 1:68–79) and the Canticle of Simeon (Luke 2:29–32) are also found in the first chapter of Luke. All three give praise for God's goodness and salvation.

Mary's canticle speaks especially of God's regard for the lowly (also known as the *anawim*). It is to these who are most in need that God has given favor and mercy. Over the ages, God has shown great tenderness toward those who are most powerless, vulnerable, or forgotten. This characteristic is manifested in the ways that Jesus acted in welcoming the outcasts, the poor, and excluded members of the community. In fact, Jesus' willingness to walk among human beings as one of us is the ultimate action of God's mercy and compassion. Mary's canticle, which she proclaimed to testify to God's grace, is an invitation for us to add our joyful praise and witness to God in this Advent hymn on what is traditionally referred to as Gaudete Sunday (*gaudete* being the Latin word for *rejoice*).

1 Thessalonians 5:16–24   Once again, an epistle for Advent gives us instructions on how we are to act. In this letter written for the Thessalonian community, Paul gives clear images of a person who is faithful to God. The staccato nature of the short sentences has led one scripture scholar to describe these as "shotgun" exhortations of the protocol of living a Christian life. The faithful have been given the Good News by Jesus Christ, and now it is up to disciples to live a worthy life. They must rejoice, pray, give thanks. They must live holy lives.

Paul tells the community members that they must allow the Holy Spirit to be manifested and to test that it is truly from God. If it builds up the community and if it witnesses to Christ, then it is to be retained. If their aim is toward God, the Thessalonians will give joyous witness. If we give witness and live lives such as Paul describes, we, too, will be joyful signs of the light that has come among us in the Messiah's Incarnation. Paul uses clear words and phrases to declare the imperative: always, entirely, without ceasing. In every moment of our lives, in everything that we do, we are called to recognize God's presence among us and to add our testimony to that of the many faithful who have gone before us.

John 1:6–8, 19–28   In this Sunday's Gospel, John tells his questioners that he is not the one, but is the voice for the one who is to come. He is not the light, but he knows he is called to testify to the light. John clearly states who he is not. He wants no confusion over his identity. He knows that the one who is to come after him is the one they have been waiting for, and he is prepared to testify to that. Even later in this Gospel, John makes it clear that he must decrease while the Messiah must increase (John 3:26–30).

The image of John the Baptist in John's account of the Gospel is different from the one we heard from Mark on the First Sunday of Advent. Mark and Luke identify John's baptism of sinners as a baptism of repentance for the forgiveness of sin. The baptist in John points clearly to the coming baptism by Christ that will purify disciples.

---

1 Jn 1:7; cf. Jn 15:26; 5:35.

Connections to Church Teaching and Tradition

- Mary is the Mother of Christ and the Mother of the Church (CCC, 963–975).

- "Despite all this, then, humanity is able to hope. Indeed it must hope: the living and personal Gospel, *Jesus Christ himself, is the "good news" and the bearer of joy* that the Church announces each day, and to whom the Church bears testimony before all people" (CL, 7).

- "In the Church's Liturgy, in her prayer, in the living community of believers, we experience the love of God, we perceive his presence and we thus learn to recognize that presence in our daily lives. He has loved us first and he continues to do so; we too, then, can respond with love. God does not demand of us a feeling which we ourselves are incapable of producing . . . since he has 'loved us first,' love can also blossom as a response within us" (DCE, 17).

2 Samuel 7:1–5, 8b–12, 14a, 16   The words in Samuel are like a great epic sketch of the history of God's promise. David wants to build a house for God, but instead God responds that he will build the house: "I will fix a place for my people Israel; I will plant them so that they may dwell in their place" (7:10). God promises David that this house and kingdom will be firm forever. We hear the fulfillment of that promise in today's Gospel story of Mary's obedience.

The house of David also means the household, family, or relations of David. David's salvation does not come alone as an individual or even as a king. Rather, it comes in community, among people who are in relationship with one another. In God's decision to tell David that it is he who will build the house, God expanded the relationships within the house. In our relationship to God as daughters and sons, we find that we are locked in an embrace with all people who are sons and daughters, making us all sisters and brothers. This family relationship will be all the more emphasized by Jesus' image of how we treat our brothers and sisters.

Psalm 89:2–3, 4–5, 27, 29 (2a)   Psalm 89, a royal psalm, includes prayers for the king because it is through him that the people of God are blessed. Therefore, how the king behaved as a servant of the Lord was significant, and often prophets approached the king, calling upon him to change his behavior to be more faithful to his royal heritage. Psalm 89 laments over the suffering of the king, possibly because of his defeat and disgrace in battle. Yet in the verses we hear on this Advent Sunday, we hear no laments, but only praise for the God of the covenant.

The opening line announces the theme of God's faithfulness over all time. Terms like *forever* and *all generations* convey the lasting depth of the covenant and reflect God's continual promise to David's house. Seen in light of a possible military loss, it is certain that despite defeat, God's love for David does not change. This Sunday, we sing praise and proclaim the faithfulness of God for the entire world to know.

Romans 16:25–27   Found at the end of Paul's epistle, these verses are a doxology or a benediction, a hymn of praise and glory to God. This reading echoes connections to the other readings in images of the endless mystery of God to be proclaimed to all nations. Paul emphasizes that all Jews and Gentiles now share in the promise of salvation fulfilled in Jesus Christ. In proclaiming this gracious and generous message of covenantal relationship and compassion to all, it will become known to the world that God is indeed faithful. While this message may seem impossible to some, to others this Good News of Jesus Christ will be seen as the fulfillment of the enormous capacity and power of the Lord.

Luke 1:26–38   The revelation in this Sunday's Gospel must have seemed inconceivable to Mary. It was impossible for her to conceive a child and impossible for her barren cousin Elizabeth to bear a child. Yet, she believed: "Nothing will be impossible for God" (Luke 1:37). God has promised salvation to his people, and it has begun with these two women with their willingness to accept impossibly good news.

We are entering the final week of Advent, our final preparation for the celebration of the Incarnation: God's willingness to walk among humanity. In telling Mary's story on this last Sunday, the Church highlights her response to the overwhelming power of God's Spirit. In her acceptance and trust of God's promise, Mary responded as a faithful servant of the line of David. There had been no kings in the Davidic line for over five centuries since the Babylonian exile, yet God is faithful and has found a way to allow the Son of the Most High to inherit David's throne.

Mary's simple statement of obedience did not come without fear or anxiety or challenge, yet it came: "Behold, I am the handmaid of the Lord. May it be done to me according to your word" (Luke 1:38). As in the psalm, we hear images of the eternal and a kingdom with no end. Mary has responded as a faithful disciple and, because of her willingness to allow God to enter into her very self, God's salvation will be seen upon the earth.

Christmas

Overview of Christmas

While the secular world may observe Christmas as a season starting right after Thanksgiving and lasting until Christmas Day, the Catholic Church observes Christmas as a season that starts with vespers on December 24 and that will last this year through the feast of the Baptism of the Lord on Monday, January 9.

Christians have celebrated this feast since the fourth century, choosing the date as an alternative to the Roman celebration of the unconquered sun, and using the feast to combat the Arians, who denied that Christ was fully divine. Since then, the Christmas season has grown to be one of the most important feasts that we celebrate as a Church. "Next to the yearly celebration of the paschal mystery, the Church holds most sacred the memorial of Christ's birth and early manifestations. This is the purpose of the Christmas season" (GN, 32).

Because December 25 falls on a Sunday this year, the longest possible season of Advent is followed by a shortened Christmas season, with the feast of the Holy Family transferred to Friday, December 30, and the feast of the Baptism of the Lord transferred to Monday, January 9.

First Readings

Most of the First Readings in this season come from the prophet Isaiah, whose exaltation can hardly be contained as he proclaims what God will accomplish for the people. The message is both particular to his people and universal. Christians have interpreted these proclamations of salvation through the Chosen People as prophesies about Christ.

On January 1, the solemnity of Mary, the Holy Mother of God, we hear a blessing from Numbers. It is particularly appropriate for the beginning of the new year and the annual World Day of Peace.

Responsorial Psalms

Like Isaiah's theology, the psalms we sing for Christmas interpret Israel's prayer in the light of Christ. As in Advent, we recall that the covenant is eternal. Even more than that, with such phrases as "the LORD . . . comes to rule the earth" (Psalm 96:13) and "he shall rule the world with justice" (96:13), we celebrate the universality of salvation in Christ.

Most of all, when we sing, "Sing joyfully to the LORD, all you lands" (98:4) and "The LORD is king; let the earth rejoice!" (97:1), we express the joy of Christmas. These twenty-five-hundred-year-old hymns offer a wonderful alternative to much of contemporary Christmas music.

Second Readings

The core message of the Christmas season's Second Readings can be culled from the opening line of Hebrews, which we hear in the Mass during the Day on the solemnity of the Nativity of the Lord: "In times past, God spoke in partial and various ways to our ancestors through the prophets; in these last days, he has spoken to us through a son" (1:1). Each of the readings emphasizes a distinct dimension of the mystery of the Incarnation. On the solemnity of the Nativity of the Lord at the Masses at Midnight and at Dawn, Titus proclaims the universality of salvation and God's mercy. On the solemnity of Mary, the Holy Mother of God, in Galatians, we find Paul's only mention of the Mother of God, the person through whom God acted in the fullness of time. Finally, on the solemnity of the Epiphany of the Lord, Ephesians reiterates the revelation that everyone is called to be a copartner in the promise of Christ.

FOUNDATIONS FOR PREACHING AND TEACHING © 2011 Liturgy Training Publications.

Gospel Readings

Our Gospel readings this year take us through the Christmas narratives. By paying close attention to the readings, we discover that Matthew and Luke, the only two evangelists who recount the events of Jesus' birth, relate very different details. We begin and end the season with Matthew. At the Vigil Mass on Christmas Eve, Matthew's genealogy emphasizes that Jesus is a son of the covenant. Interestingly, Matthew includes four "outsider" women through whom God worked to save the people. The story of the Magi, which we hear on the solemnity of the Epiphany of the Lord, also emphasizes the universal significance of Jesus' birth, as another set of "outsiders," this time foreigners, are called to visit the newborn king.

The Lucan narrative, which we hear during the Mass at Dawn on the solemnity of the Nativity of the Lord, focuses more on the shepherds and Mary, representatives of the lowly and poor, the first to collaborate in and benefit from the coming of the Savior. At the Mass during the Day on the solemnity of the Nativity of the Lord, we hear the prologue to John's account of the Gospel describe Christ as the Eternal Word who took flesh to dwell among us. In simple stories and mystical theology, these Gospel readings lead us to contemplate again the mystery of Emmanuel, God-with-us.

Generations Have Waited

Connections to Church Teaching and Tradition

■ "Conversion is the change of our lives that comes about through the power of the Holy Spirit. All who accept the Gospel undergo change as we continually put on the mind of Christ by rejecting sin and becoming more faithful disciples in his Church. Unless we undergo conversion, we have not truly accepted the Gospel" (GMD, 12).

■ "To bring the good news from city to city and especially to the poor, who are often better disposed to receive it, so that it might be proclaimed that the promises of the New Covenant made by God had been fulfilled, this was the special mission for the accomplishment of which Jesus declared that he had been sent by the Father" (EN, 6).

Isaiah 62:1–5   Have you ever tried to hush a singing child or quiet a baby's loud babbling? Sometimes, it seems impossible. Such is the wonderful image of the first reading from Isaiah: I will not be silent, I will not be quiet. We hear this reading every year at the Christmas Vigil Mass. It is a wonderful beginning to a day on which we cannot contain our joy or hold back our praise. Like the generations that waited in hope for the coming of the Messiah, we are all one people as we celebrate on this vigil night the coming of our Savior.

We have heard the songs of Isaiah throughout most of Advent and will continue to proclaim them at all the Christmas Masses. His wonderfully poetic images are meant to allay anxieties and restore hope to a dejected and broken people. Indeed, in the reading for the vigil, the very names that have been used to refer to Israel such as "Forsaken" and "Desolate" will now be replaced with new names: "Espoused" and "My Delight." Israel has long waited for this moment, and Isaiah promises that the wait has not been in vain. Just as the fulfillment of God's promise of a Messiah casts a bright light on this night of darkness, so, too, does a new and loving image offer Israel and all of God's people the prospect of daylight and new life. Isaiah cannot contain his joy and will not be silenced. So, too, are all of God's people invited to join their voices in a grateful song of praise for God's goodness.

Psalm 89:4–5, 16–17, 27, 29 (2a)   Do you hear the echo? We sang parts of this psalm just last week on the Fourth Sunday of Advent. The same refrain: "For ever I will sing the goodness of the Lord" (Psalm 89:2) echoes across the days. We do, indeed, sing out praise for God's faithful response to his people throughout all of history. God's fidelity can be seen in the covenant he made and fulfilled with his people. In light of the promised Messiah, we, too, can sing with all the ages. When we feel defeated, abandoned, disgraced, or alone, these are the times we can hold fast to God's promise made long ago and fulfilled across all the ages, even in our own lives. When we encounter others who feel alone, discouraged, lost, or disheartened, we can offer them the promise of a God who walks beside them, holding them tenderly and treating them with compassion. On this night of the Christmas Vigil we remember the promise and its fulfillment in Christ's birth, and we rejoice!

Acts 13:16–17, 22–25   We began this Advent season hearing Jesus' words to his followers to be watchful and alert. It was a call to pay attention. Now, we hear that call to attention from Paul. In this reading from Acts, Paul calls out to followers of Christ to listen. We want to stay alert to his message. He reminds his listeners of their great link to the exodus event and the establishment of the obedient servant of God in David the king. But he continues with the announcement of the new exodus by John the Baptist. The Baptist's mission is to point the way toward God's mission. Jesus Christ will proclaim the Good News of liberation to everyone, for there is no distinction because all people are one with God and therefore with one another. John the Baptist, like Paul, prepares the way. We, too, are called to prepare the way, bringing the Good News so the Messiah can come again and again into our very lives and circumstances. When the world sees those signs of God's Incarnation, the entire people of the world will proclaim the goodness of God.

Matthew 1:1–25 or 1:18–25   At the Vigil Mass we hear three sections of many names, representing multiple generations each: from Abraham to David, from David to the Babylonian exile, and from the exile to Jesus. The genealogy contains the names of ancestors, men and women as well as followers and sinners. Imagine hearing a confident proclamation of these names and connections. Instead of letting our attention fade with the unfamiliar names, can we surface the images of the many times God has been active in salvation history? These stories of these faithful men and women are like our family history. We hear the story of how it came to be that the Messiah was conceived and protected. The Gospel ends with the story of both Mary's and Joseph's faithfulness and trust in the promises of old. But for their action, the long line would have been broken.

Connections to Church Teaching and Tradition

- Jesus was born into a poor family in a stable, and lowly shepherds were among the first to witness to his birth. "In this poverty heaven's glory was made manifest[1]" (CCC, 525).

- "The primary and immediate task of lay people is . . . to put to use every Christian and evangelical possibility latent but already present in the affairs of the world" (EN, 70).

- "[B]y his Incarnation, he, the son of God, *in a certain way united himself with each man.* He worked with human hands, he thought with a human mind. He acted with a human will, and with a human heart he loved" (RH, 8).

Isaiah 9:1–6 Isaiah, the most famous of Old Testament prophets, lived in the eighth century BC at a time of enormous crisis for the Hebrew people. The northern tribes of Israel had been deported by the Assyrians. This exile shaped Isaiah's prophecy as he both rebuked his people for their fickle ways and encouraged their faithfulness to the Lord. This reading from Isaiah is a song of joy that describes the advent of a king. In Isaiah's day, the meaning of the hymn was filtered through the lens of the Assyrian oppression. The prophet foretold that the chains of slavery, the yoke and pole, would be destroyed with the birth of a child. The child would be from the family of David. This son given to them would become the king whose dominion would be vast and forever peaceful. Today, we as Christians hear and understand this reading through the lens of the joyful Christmas feast and our belief in Jesus as the Wonderful Counselor and Prince of Peace.

Psalm 96:1–2, 2–3, 11–12, 13 (Luke 2:11) The joy of this psalm leaps from the page as it anticipates the elation of a freed people, for when the Lord comes he will save all people from oppression. Then they shall "exult before the LORD." Those who sing this psalm do not have the option of keeping silent. Rather, they receive an explicit set of instructions from the psalmist: Sing this new song for we have reason to rejoice. Trust this news and praise the Lord. Spread the word beyond the next village. Take this word, as missionaries would, to the entire world. Announce his salvation every day for all days to come, for the faithful and constant Lord comes to rule with justice. Finally, the psalm's refrain, "Today is born our Savior, Christ the Lord," is taken from the Gospel according to Luke. Its use with the psalm establishes that the child born in the city of David is both the melody and the lyric of the new song. He is the long-awaited Messiah, the one who will bring justice to all the earth.

Titus 2:11–14 Titus is a short letter that bears the name of one of Paul's colleagues. After a brief stay (Acts 27: –15) in Crete, Paul entrusted the formation of the new faith community to Titus. This was a fledgling community without structure or leadership, so the letter is filled with directions about qualifications for leadership as well as behavioral codes for the entire community. The letter works out of the belief that faithful living begins with belief in Christ, whose coming as man made God present in the world through the power of the Holy Spirit in a new and definitive way. In coming to live among us, Jesus modeled a way of life that to this day challenges presumptions of power and success. In his very person and life, he demonstrates that the things of this world will not satisfy human hearts. Only this will satisfy: "live temperately, justly, and devoutly." On this solemnity, these words still invite us to the real power of faith in Jesus Christ—God-with-us, the Savior of the world.

Luke 2:1–14 Ours is a culture that has made Christmas into an iconic celebration. The secular world has defined Christmas in a way that stands in stark contrast to the message of the Gospel. As the Lucan narrative of Christmas teaches us, the birth of Christ is characterized by simplicity and faith. Luke positions the birth of the Lord in the reign of Caesar Augustus. The historical dates are slightly off, but that is a reminder that his account is not meant primarily as historical fact; it is a Gospel narrative of faith. In this instance, Luke's reference to local government establishes the point that the real Savior of the world is not a human ruler like Augustus. Rather, the Savior came as a child of humble birth and gave his life for the salvation of the world. In Luke's account of the Gospel, it is not the famous, powerful, or wealthy who first hear the Good News. Rather, Luke intentionally writes that the simple shepherds at work in the fields are the first to hear the angels' news. This stands as the evangelist's clear signal that the poor are first in God's favor. As we embrace the work of faith, the work of announcing salvation, we do so not just on Christmas Day, but on all days.

---

1 Cf. Lk 2:8–20.

Solemnity of the Nativity of the Lord (Dawn) December 25, 2011
The Light Shines

Connections to Church Teaching and Tradition

- "No one . . . can approach God . . . except by kneeling before the manger . . . and adoring him hidden in the weakness of a new-born child" (CCC, 563).

- "Listening to the cry of those who suffer violence and are oppressed by unjust systems and structures, and hearing the appeal of a world that by its perversity contradicts the plan of its Creator, we have shared our awareness of the Church's vocation to be present in the heart of the world by proclaiming the Good News to the poor, freedom to the oppressed, and joy to the afflicted" (CU, 5).

- "Christ is the light of nations and consequently this holy Synod . . . ardently desires to bring all humanity that light of Christ . . . by proclaiming his Gospel to every creature[1]" (LG, 1).

Isaiah 62:11–12   Often when people were changed by an encounter with God, they were given a new name. So, too, Isaiah says the city of Zion will be given a new name. Her reputation of being forsaken and desolate will be gone, and instead she will be called "frequented" (62:12). Third Isaiah (55–66), from which this passage is taken, imagines a new dawning of creation. "Lo, I am about to create new heavens / and a new earth; / The things of the past shall not be remembered / or come to mind" (65:17). These passages, most likely written by disciples of Isaiah who carried on his work, speak of the beginning of a new place that welcomes strangers and foreigners. This new city will be frequented and sought out because of her own salvation and willingness to offer that gift to all.

Psalm 97:1, 6, 11–12   Psalm 97 proclaims God as a mighty king triumphantly coming to Mount Zion. The psalm effectively captures the emotion of Isaiah's hope for God's city and Paul's image of baptism in the First and Second Readings. In this message of light, gladness, and thanksgiving, we can almost hear the shepherds in the Gospel reading: "Light dawns for the just; / and gladness, for the upright of heart. / Be glad in the LORD, you just, / and give thanks to his holy name" (97:11–12).

Titus 3:4–7   This passage from Paul to Titus may have been used in the early Church's baptismal rites. The reference to the "bath of rebirth and renewal by the Holy Spirit" (3:5) reminded Titus that he was saved through Christ. Verse 3, the verse immediately before the beginning of the Second Reading, speaks of old vices, while verse 4, which begins the reading, tells of the generosity of God's kindness and love. At the end of this passage, Paul refers to two theological insights that are characteristic of his writing: we are justified by the grace of God and we are heirs who await the promise of eternal life.

Luke 2:15–20   When we hear this passage from Luke, we step into the narrative at the point of the shepherds' response. This scene is the third annunciation story in Luke. The first story is Zechariah's (1:5–10), who, in protesting the possibility of a child, is struck speechless after his son John is born. The second is Mary's, who responds with an act of faith (1:26–38). The third precedes the passage we hear at this liturgy and is made by angels to the shepherds (2:8–14). The shepherds' response to the angels' announcement is immediate: "Let us go, then, to Bethlehem to see this thing that has taken place, which the Lord has made known to us" (2:15). It is significant that the angels chose shepherds, who were seen as unclean, to be the first recipients of the Good News of Jesus' birth. This reinforces one of the main underlying themes of the Lucan narrative, in which the lowly are frequently singled out as recipients of God's blessings and favor. This announcement to the shepherds is in keeping with Mary's Magnificat in the previous chapter: "He has thrown down the rulers from their thrones / but lifted up the lowly. / The hungry he has filled with good things; / the rich he has sent away empty" (1:52–53). Choosing the shepherds as the first recipients of the angels' message is not just significant because of their lowliness, it also relates symbolically to many other scripture passages. Many other Gospel stories and parables relate to the role of the shepherd. Some examples include the story of the shepherd who loses something precious, the story of the woman and the lost coin, and the story of the prodigal son and forgiving father. John images Jesus as the Good Shepherd, willing to lay down his life for his flock (10:11–15) and David, when he was called by Samuel before he came king, was tending sheep. In the Gospel for the Nativity Mass at Dawn, there is a major role for the shepherds who, after hearing the angels' message, go and see the child and then make the message known to the amazement of all who hear it. In fact, the shepherds never stop proclaiming the Good News and glorifying and praising God (2:17–18, 20). Theirs is a wonderful example of living Christmas for us to learn from.

---

1 Cf. Mk 16:15.

FOUNDATIONS FOR PREACHING AND TEACHING © 2011 Liturgy Training Publications.

Solemnity of the Nativity of the Lord (Day)   December 25, 2011

Sing Joyfully to the Lord!

Connections to Church Teaching and Tradition

- ■ "Every disciple of the Lord Jesus shares in this mission. To do their part, adult Catholics must be mature in faith and well equipped to share the Gospel, promoting it in every family circle, in every church gathering, in every place of work, and in every public forum. They must be women and men of prayer whose faith is alive and vital, grounded in a deep commitment to the person and message of Jesus" (OHWB, 2).

- ■ ". . . you have received the Spirit of Christ Jesus, which brings salvation and hope; your lives are a witness of faith" (GMD, 6).

- ■ In Baptism, we are born into new life in Christ (CCC, 1277).

Isaiah 52:7–10   Right at the beginning of the Isaiah reading, we hear a wonderful image of what it means to spread glad tidings. Stand upon the mountain and cry out! Announce salvation, good news, and peace! Sing for joy! God has come to his people to comfort and redeem them. In the face of Jerusalem's destruction and disgrace, God has come with new hope for his people. The writings of the prophet Isaiah were promulgated after the Babylonian exile in the sixth century BC. Some Israelites found themselves in a strange land, driven far from their homeland without any rights or freedoms. Yet some had been left behind. It appears that it is these sentinels or the watchers who now see the restoration of Zion before their very eyes. Those in exile are returning. They understand this joy of salvation and have raised the cry for all nations and all the ends of the earth to hear about their God who has begun this work. This is glad tidings!

Psalm 98:1, 2–3, 3–4, 5–6 (3c)   Perhaps we have experienced the joy of breaking into song (or even excited speech with our words tripping over each other) when something wonderful has happened. The Responsorial Psalm we sing on Christmas Day could be sung by those we heard about in the First Reading, who were being joyfully reunited after exile. In fact, the image of singing and proclaiming to the ends of the earth is contained in both readings. Psalm 98, considered an enthronement psalm, celebrates God as king over everything. The psalm calls attention to God's victory in saving his people. The deeds of God and the faithfulness of the covenant can be seen by all. These flowing verses heard on Christmas seem to bring to a crescendo all that can praise God: songs, harps, trumpets, horns, voices, lands—break into song! We can add our joy, for a Savior who will witness to a life of justice and peace has been born. As we hear in the Gospel, into the darkness a light has come. The light of salvation has dawned, and the rays of that light will reach to the ends of the earth.

Hebrews 1:1–6   If we ever wanted to do a theological reflection about Christ, these opening verses from Hebrews would be a good place to start. God has disclosed himself in his Son, Jesus, who is the Word of God. Christ is divine and he is one with and equal to God. In the past, the prophets revealed God in various but incomplete ways. Our ancestors and the prophets saw fragments or pieces, but now the Son has made God's salvation known again, as we have heard in the previous two readings, to all the ends of the earth. We hear two images for Jesus that are not very common: Jesus is the refulgence of God's glory and the very imprint of God's being. Jesus, the Son of God, is the bright and brilliant light of God, and he is the mark or indication of God's presence. The world has been changed because the Savior has come. It seems an appropriate expression to worship the Messiah along with the angels on this joyful Christmas Day as we proclaim the glad tidings of the Savior's birth.

John 1:1–18 or 1:1–5, 9–14   The Alleluia verse for the Mass for Christmas Day reads: "A holy day has dawned upon us. Come, you nations, and adore the Lord. For today a great light has come upon the earth." It seems a wonderful segue into these opening verses, also known as the prologue, from John's Gospel. Its opening phrase, "In the beginning," reminds us of similar biblical words rooted in Genesis 1:1. The light has emerged and been recognized, and the darkness has been overcome and banished. In rich baptismal imagery, we hear that we can be born again. The great light that has come into the world is God's Word, God's only Son, who came to offer us the chance to be born again as children of God by accepting and believing in his name. The evangelist John weaves together the identity of the Son and the testimony and proclamation of John the Baptist to that identity. This is who he was sent to serve, the one who was greater than himself and who revealed the face of God to the world: "The only Son, God, who is at the Father's side, has revealed him" (1:14). Like John the Baptist, we add our testimony to this witness. The Savior has been born!

Connections to Church Teaching and Tradition

- *"The salvation offered in its fullness to men in Jesus Christ by God the Father's initiative, and brought about and transmitted by the Holy Spirit, is salvation for all people and of the whole person: it is universal and integral salvation"* (CSDC, 38).

- *"We confess together that God forgives sin by grace and at the same time frees human beings from sin's enslaving power and imparts the gift of new life in Christ. When persons come by faith to share in Christ . . . the Holy Spirit effects in them an active love"* (JDDJ, 22).

- *"All daughters and sons of the Church should nevertheless remember that their exalted status is not to be ascribed to their own merits but to the special grace of Christ"* (LG, 14).

Numbers 6:22–27   New Year's Day has been associated with the octave of Christmas, Jesus' circumcision, and the holy name of Jesus given at his circumcision, along with the current emphasis on Mary as the Mother of God. The blessing that Moses receives from God and passes on to Aaron to bless the people highlights the theme of today's feast: God's graciousness. Three times the Lord's name is invoked to protect, to show kindness, and to give peace to the individual and the whole community. Knowing and being able to invoke God's name gave the community a sense of intimacy and connection to God. God graciously chose them and became intimate with them through this special revelation. To invoke God's name gave the community a sharing in God's life. The Hebrew verb translated as *invoke* literally means "to put my name" on them. They were "branded" with God's name, and in their willingness to be so branded, God promised to bless them continually and be gracious to them. Christians believe that, through Mary, his mother, Jesus, the Son of God, became intimate with all people by becoming human and by sharing God's graciousness with all humanity.

Psalm 67:2–3, 5, 6, 8 (2a)   This thanksgiving psalm praises God for the many blessings given to the community. God's graciousness is invoked upon the community with words connected to the blessing of Aaron in our First Reading. God's blessing upon the Jewish community becomes a vehicle of blessing for all nations. God is acclaimed as the ruler and guide of all people. God's blessings and mercy upon Israel will cause all nations to stand up and take notice. The psalmist anticipates that Israel's intimate relationship with God, along with God's rich blessings, will move all nations to affirm God's graciousness. Through Israel, all nations will be blessed. The psalmist prays that through God's blessing upon Israel, all nations will "fear" the Lord; namely, they will have awe and reverence for Israel's God. They, too, will come to know and acknowledge God's graciousness.

Galatians 4:4–7   Paul addresses the Galatians with words that affirm their new status as followers of Christ. In Christ, they are now God's adopted sons and daughters. The focus on sons, indicative of the patriarchal nature of the times, should not distract us from Paul's underlying meaning that, in Christ, we are all mature adopted children of God. How did this come about? At "the fullness of time . . . God sent his Son, born of a woman, born under the law . . ." (4:4). Jesus is both fully God and fully human, who, in becoming human, willingly subjected himself to all human limitations and vulnerabilities. In so doing, Jesus modeled for us how God intended us to live as full human beings, thus freeing us from the limitations of the law. With Jesus' coming, the guidance that Jewish law offered is now offered by the Spirit of Jesus poured "into our hearts." His Spirit in our hearts (through Baptism) enables us to call God "Abba," the intimate "Daddy" who has made us, in Christ, both children and heirs of God's graciousness and love.

Luke 2:16–21   The shepherds and Mary are the focus of this section of the longer narrative in Luke's version of Jesus' birth. The angels had announced to the shepherds the birth of a "savior . . . who is Christ and Lord." The shepherds are told of the sign given to them, a child lying in a manger. The angels confirm that this sign is the manifestation of God's graciousness and love for all humanity. The shepherds hurry to Bethlehem where they are the first to experience God's saving work in the sign of an infant child. They go forth proclaiming the angels' Good News, as well as all they have seen and heard. They are the first evangelizers of God's gracious love. All are amazed by their news, a typical reaction to the adult Jesus' miracles and ministry. Mary reflected on all these things in her heart. She sees, hears, and plumbs the deeper meaning of what is happening around her. In so doing, Mary allows the experiences to connect her more deeply with Jesus' identity and mission. In pondering God's gracious actions swirling around her, Mary becomes a model for disciples. Each new year offers a challenge to all disciples to read the signs of the times and ponder them in light of God's gracious love and saving action in the world. Pondering should move us to action on behalf of others, so that all can see and experience God's gracious love.

FOUNDATIONS FOR PREACHING AND TEACHING © 2011 Liturgy Training Publications.

Connections to Church Teaching and Tradition

- "The church is . . . a *sheepfold*, the sole and necessary entrance to which is Christ.[1] It is also a flock, of which God foretold that he would himself be the shepherd,[2] and whose sheep, although watched over by human shepherds, are nevertheless at all times led and brought to pasture by Christ himself, the Good Shepherd and prince of shepherds,[3] who gave his life for his sheep"[4] (LG, 6).

- "In Christ and in the Church, there is . . . no inequality arising from race or nationality, social condition or sex, for 'there is neither Jew nor Greek; there is neither slave nor freeman; there is neither male nor female. For you are all one in Christ Jesus'[5]" (LG, 32).

- "But the message of reconciliation has also been entrusted to the whole community of believers, to the whole fabric of the church, that is to say, the task of doing everything possible to witness to reconciliation and to bring it about in the world" (RP, 8).

Isaiah 60:1–6   A world transformed—that is how the words of the prophet Isaiah must have seemed to his listeners. To these people, beleaguered and lost in exile, Isaiah's images might have seemed impossible, and yet this might be the hope to which they could cling. God promised, so therefore God will do it. Someday, there will once again be light, glory, and justice. The signs of Jerusalem's overflowing riches, splendor, and radiance will once again be seen by all. All nations shall return to this new vision, not just exiles.

This Old Testament image of all nations flowing together in harmony is confirmed even further in the other readings for Epiphany. Psalm 72 suggests the unification of all nations and rulers as they pay homage to the king who rules with justice and peace and care for the poor. Ephesians puts forth the image of former enemies being seen as coheirs and partners in Christ through the Gospel. Matthew's Gospel passage presents the picture of fulfillment in a shepherd who comes from an insignificant place but who cares for the least of all the world.

Psalm 72:1–2, 7–8, 10–11, 12–13 (see 11)   What kind of king do we honor? What manner of Lord will we celebrate on this Epiphany feast? The Responsorial is clear. He will use God's judgment, not the judgment of an earthly king. He will rule from sea to sea, but he will rule with justice. He will be known to the ends of the earth, but his rule will be one of peace. His reign will be such that other kings, rather than being envious or disturbed by such a ruler, will offer homage and gifts. (We hear the story of how some royal visitors did just that in the Gospel story.) Their nations will not go to war over power, but rather will adore this king. A remarkable image of peace and justice emerges in this psalm. This king will care for the afflicted, the lowly, and the poor. All who have no one else to care for them or rescue them will have this ruler who will hear their cries and will save them.

The image of every nation presents us with one of the central themes of the Epiphany. The Messiah, the Savior of the world, came for all. All boundaries are broken. All types of exclusions have been rendered obsolete. All are promised the salvation that originally appeared to be only offered to Israel. In breaking the bonds of sin, God has revealed himself so abundantly and powerfully that nothing can hold back his grace and mercy. Like a true shepherd, he cares for all people with compassion and faithfulness.

Ephesians 3:2–3a, 5–6   If there was any doubt that Jesus Christ offered his message of salvation to all, Paul makes it clear in his letter to the Ephesians: "It was not made known to people in other generations as it has now been revealed to his holy apostles and prophets by the Spirit: that the Gentiles are coheirs, members of the same body, and copartners in the promise in Christ Jesus through the gospel" (3:5–6). Making people coheirs and partners, members of the same body, is the embodiment of God's plan to unite all peoples. Bringing about this kind of reign of God on earth is even more than the people could imagine. Yet, this is the kind of mysterious plan for universal salvation that is being revealed by the Messiah. To become one with someone who might formerly have been seen as an enemy or outsider, the boundaries of God's grace is exactly what is being promised if believers do their part to bring about God's reign.

Matthew 2:1–12   The passage from Matthew in which we hear about the Magi on every feast of Epiphany quotes the prophet Micah: "*And you, Bethlehem, land of Judah, are by no means least among the rulers of Judah; since from you shall come a ruler, who is to shepherd my people Israel*" (2:6). This story of royal visitors tells of their long journey to find this new king and to bring gifts and pay homage. It also speaks of another ruler who was troubled by this possibility of a new ruler and who later slaughtered innocent children to try to prevent his kingship. But the Old Testament prophecy speaks about a different kind of kingship, not one of riches or majesty that rulers like Herod would envy. Rather, it will be a ruler who will care for the people of God like a shepherd cares for his sheep. Hardly an impressive picture for a king, yet this is the Messiah we celebrate this Epiphany!

---

1 Cf. Jn 10:1–10.
2 Cf. Is 40:11; Ez 34:11 ff.
3 Cf. Jn 10:11; 1 Pet 5:4.
4 Cf. Jn 10:11–15.
5 Gal 3:28 Greek; cf. Col 3:11.

Ordinary Time
in Winter

Overview of Ordinary Time in Winter

The phrase *Ordinary Time* describes the 33 or 34 weeks of the liturgical year that fall outside the Lent/Easter and Advent/Christmas cycles. This year, we will have six weeks of Ordinary Time before the beginning of Lent. During Ordinary Time, the Sunday Lectionary leads us to reflect on the life of Christ, the writings of the apostles, and the unity of the Old and New Testament scriptures.

Now, as we move through Year B of the cycle of Lectionary readings, we will primarily hear from the Gospel according to Mark. The Old Testament readings and psalms are chosen to complement the themes in the Gospel readings. Our readings from the New Testament letters offer semicontinuous selections of key passages from the letters to help us become more familiar with the themes and theology.

First Readings

The First Readings of these weeks put us in touch with some of the great personalities of the Old Testament. We see Samuel discern and accept his call to serve God on the Second Sunday in Ordinary Time. Then we get a glimpse of Jonah's successful preaching on the Third Sunday. The Fourth Sunday's reading from Deuteronomy reminds us of the continuity of God's care, as Moses assures the people that God will send another prophet to follow him. Job's complaint on the Fifth Sunday invites us to confront the problem of innocent suffering. On the Sixth Sunday, Leviticus introduces us to Old Testament legislation about disease, and then on the Seventh Sunday, Isaiah leads us into Lent, promising that God will renew the people.

Responsorial Psalms

The psalms we pray this season seem to fit into two general categories: connection with Jesus' call to participate in the reign of God, and our relationship with and reliance on God. Thus, in Psalm 40, we join Samuel and proclaim our desire to do God's will. Praying Psalm 25, we who would follow beg to learn the ways of God. Psalm 95 reminds us that listening and worship involve our heart.

In praying Psalm 147, we express our awe at the grandeur and the mercy of God. Psalm 32 declares our reliance on God's help and forgiveness, and Psalm 41 reminds us of God's healing action in our lives.

Second Readings

In each of the three cycles of Sunday readings, Ordinary Time begins with selections from 1 Corinthians. In Year B, our readings come from chapters 6–11, and finally from 2 Corinthians. Skipping over some of Paul's major eucharistic themes, these selections present Paul's vision of life in light of the Resurrection. For Paul, this is not a theoretical consideration. The Resurrection has very real impacts for daily life: we are united with Christ and one another, worldly anxieties are transitory, and our only concern should be pleasing the Lord, doing everything in his name.

Gospel Readings

The reading from John's account of the Gospel on the Second Sunday in Ordinary Time, describing John the Baptist's recognition of Jesus, reflects back to the solemnity of Epiphany, and the revelation of Jesus' true identity. At the same time, with the invitation to the disciples, it is a fitting introduction to the coming Sundays, which will present the beginning of Jesus' ministry. From there, we launch into the Gospel according to Mark on the Third Sunday in Ordinary Time. Over the next five Sundays, we hear continuous selections from Mark's account of the Gospel. Here, we are presented with Jesus' proclamation of the kingdom of

FOUNDATIONS FOR PREACHING AND TEACHING © 2011 Liturgy Training Publications.

God in word and deed. Mark 1:14—2:12 paints the portrait of Jesus the preacher, caller of disciples, victor over demons, healer, prayerful person, itinerant missionary, and forgiver of sins. With that whirlwind introduction, we get a good sense of why Jesus' popularity grew so quickly. With Christmas behind us and Lent coming in six weeks, this segment of Ordinary Time invites us to focus anew on the person of Jesus and his call to us.

Connections to Church Teaching and Tradition

■ "The Lord addresses his call to each and every one" (CL, 53).

■ "Therefore, in the life of each member of the lay faithful there are *particularly significant and decisive moments* for discerning God's call and embracing the mission entrusted by Him. . . . Therefore, the fundamental and continuous attitude of the disciple should be one of vigilance and a conscious attentiveness to the voice of God. . . . It is not a question of simply *knowing* what God wants from each of us in the various situations of life. The individual must *do* what God wants" (CL, 58).

■ "The relationship with Jesus, however, is a relationship with the one who gave himself as a ransom for all.[1] Being in communion with Jesus Christ draws us into his 'being for all'; it makes it our own way of being. He commits us to live for others, but only through communion with him does it become possible truly to be there for others, for the whole" (SS, 28).

1 Samuel 3:3b–10, 19   Before Samuel's birth, his mother, Hannah, went to the temple, weeping and praying, begging God to reverse her barrenness. Such was the intensity of her prayer that the priest, Eli, thought she was drunk and chided her for it. When Samuel was weaned, Hannah entrusted him to Eli to serve the Lord. The old priest Eli had proven unworthy of his role, giving his family preference over the Lord.

The biblical author informs us that because Samuel was not yet familiar with the Lord, he mistook the divine voice for that of Eli. It was Eli who realized that it was the Lord who was calling Samuel. Upon hearing the fourth call, Samuel took the step that would be decisive for the remainder of his life: he identified himself as God's servant and attuned his ear to the word and will of God.

Psalm 40:2, 4, 7–8, 8–9, 10 (8a and 9a)   There could hardly be a better psalm to follow the story of Samuel's obedience to the voice of God. As we pray this psalm, we underline the mutuality of our relationship with God. Like Samuel, we proclaim our desire to be found and commissioned by God. Like him, we experience God with us. In a striking reversal of much of the religious thinking of the time, we recognize that God's desire is not for shows of sacrifice. In speaking of the ears God gives, the Hebrew literally says, "ears you have dug for me," reminding us that standing in God's presence is an undeserved gift, and also that we may be holding some attitudes or conceptions that God must burrow through in order to reach us.

1 Corinthians 6:13c–15a, 17–20   The First Letter to the Corinthians introduces us to Paul the pastor calling his people to a deeper and more authentic expression of their Christian commitment. In the process, he also spells out what he sees as the very real consequences of Baptism and the Lord's Resurrection. According to Paul, the baptized have become "members of Christ" so completely that they can be called temples of the Holy Spirit and people who no longer belong to themselves. Their human status has been changed forever. Paul insists that the community, and each member of it, now belongs thoroughly to Christ.

In the face of some who would promote the idea that they are free to do anything they want with their perishable bodies, Paul responds that their bodies, like that of Christ, are destined for resurrection. The meaning of life for disciples is no longer to be historical—understood in terms of the family, nation, or the faith from which they came—but eschatological, formed by the future they are moving toward. All of this is possible because, and only because, they are joined to the Lord and one Spirit with him.

John 1:35–42   In this scene from the Gospel according to John, we find John the Baptist gazing intently at Jesus as he passes by. Rather than address him, John points him out to others, calling him the Lamb of God. John is the only person to call Jesus by that title, and scholars have a variety of opinions about what it implies. The majority say that it is a reference to Isaiah 53, where the suffering servant is led away like a lamb, or that it is a reference to the Passover lamb mentioned in the Passion narrative (19:14, 29, 31). Whatever they thought John meant, two of his disciples responded to that statement by leaving John and going after Jesus.

As events unfolded, Jesus turned and asked the two what they were seeking. Their response indicated that they had not understood what John had said about Jesus. John had already stated that the Lamb would take away the sin of the world, that he had seen the Spirit come down on him and that he was the Son of God. The tongue-tied disciples addressed Jesus as "Rabbi," a term of respect, but surely not of deep faith. All they could ask was, "Where are you staying?" Jesus' response, "Come and you will see," was not only a call to vocation, but a promise that their vision of him would deepen until they understood who he was and why he was worthy of their discipleship.

When taken together, today's readings show us stages of discipleship. From Samuel's introduction to the Lord's voice, we humbly praise the God who has given us ears to hear the Word. The Gospel presents us with the dialogue of growing discipleship as Christ invites us to continue to come to him and to learn to see as he does. Finally, Paul calls us to live our faith by allowing every dimension of our humanity to be infused by the Spirit of God.

---

1 Cf. 1 Tim 2:6.

FOUNDATIONS FOR PREACHING AND TEACHING © 2011 Liturgy Training Publications.

Connections to Church Teaching and Tradition

- "'To encounter . . . Christ means to accept the love by which he loves us first . . . to adhere freely to his person and his plan, which consists in proclaiming and in bringing about the Kingdom of God'[1]" (EIA, 68).

- "*Metanoia* . . . means a change of mentality. It is not simply a matter of thinking differently in an intellectual sense, but of revising the reasons behind one's actions in the light of the Gospel" (EIA 26).

- "We want the joy that we have received in the encounter with Jesus Christ . . . to reach all . . . wounded by adversities . . . all who lie along the roadside, asking for alms and compassion[2]. . . . The disciple's joy serves as remedy for a world fearful of the future and overwhelmed by violence and hatred. The disciple's joy is not a feeling of selfish well-being, but a certainty that springs from faith, that soothes the heart and provides the ability to proclaim the good news of God's love" (*Aparecida*, 29).

---

1 *Propositio* 2.
2 Cf. Lk 10:29–37; 18:25–43.

Jonah 3:1–5, 10 As one of the great comic characters of the Bible, Jonah preached far more effectively than he had ever hoped to do. When we meet him in today's reading, he has already tried to hide from God and has done time in the belly of a whale. That first escapade was a learning experience, in that he discovered that he could not escape the God of creation by fleeing the Holy Land. To his chagrin and the scandal of his shipmates, he realized that God doesn't respect territoriality.

When the rebellious prophet finally did preach to the Ninevites, enemies who had taken over the northern kingdom of Israel and humiliated his people, they repented and God did not destroy them. That infuriated Jonah, who wanted nothing to do with new life for his foes.

Psalm 25:4–5, 6–7, 8–9 (4a) This psalm is the antithesis of what we find in Jonah. The psalmist leads us in a humble plea to learn the ways of God. In the second strophe, we proclaim God's compassion and ask to experience it in our own life. In the last set of verses, we praise God's care for sinners and for all who are humble. We will pray this psalm again in just over a month when it will orient us on our Lenten journey.

1 Corinthians 7:29–31 As in last week's reading, Paul is exhorting his community to live in the light of what is coming, not what has been or is currently happening. This "already/not yet" tension calls the Christian community to creativity. It is impossible to ignore the realities that surround us, and yet, warns Paul, it is entirely too possible to treat them as if they were the ultimate reality. Therefore, Paul cautions against being so caught up in today that we overlook what God has started and will complete.

Mark 1:14–20 This Sunday we begin a time when Mark will dominate our Gospel readings. Mark is often thought to be a companion of Peter and, perhaps, Paul. Although opinions differ, many date his Gospel in the later years of the sixties, a time coinciding with persecution of the Christians in Rome.

Verse 1 of Mark, "The beginning of the gospel of Jesus Christ the Son of God," can be considered the title of the work. The original ending of Mark's Gospel account, "They said nothing to anyone, for they were afraid," indicates that Mark intended his entire narrative, from 1:1 to 16:8b, to remind the community that Jesus' life and death were only the beginning of what God was doing. It was then, and is now, time for the disciples to continue to proclaim the Good News in deed and word. Mark's narrative style is almost the opposite of John's; whereas John specializes in discourses, Mark shows action, quoting relatively few of Jesus' words. Praying with and meditating on the Gospel according to Mark this year can sharpen our vision of Jesus and intensify our awareness of the responsibility of discipleship.

Today's selection is true to the description above. In the first 14 verses of the Gospel, Mark has introduced John the Baptist, Jesus' baptism, and his 40 days in the wilderness. Now, after John is off the scene, Jesus appears and preaches, "This is the time of fulfillment. The kingdom of God is at hand. Repent, and believe in the gospel." Those 19 words will be the only verbal preaching we will hear from Jesus in the first three chapters of Mark's account of the Gospel.

Neither our language nor our religious culture can adequately translate those phrases. The word used here for time, *kairos*, depicts time as intensely meaningful, a far cry from *chronos*, which is time measured quantitatively: a number, hour, or date. What Jesus proclaims here is that this is the *kairos* of the fulfillment of all Israel's hopes. This is a time like no other before it. Jesus then describes the *kairos* of fulfillment as the nearness of the "reigning" of God. As Jesus spoke of the kingdom, he did not refer to a place. When he spoke of God, he did not refer to him as a monarch, but rather as a God so active in the hearts of people that the world was being transformed.

Finally, Jesus calls for repentance, or *metanoia*, and belief. While we translate *metanoia* as *repentance*, the Greek root of that word refers to the eye of the heart. Thus, Jesus is calling forth faith in a thoroughly new vision of life. During most of Ordinary Time in this coming year, we will see how Mark presents Jesus as the expression of God's reign, the one who calls us to new life.

Connections to Church Teaching and Tradition

- "We must ask explicitly: is the Christian faith also for us today a life-changing and life-sustaining hope? Is it 'performative' for us—is it a message which shapes our life in a new way, or is it just 'information'" (SS, 10).

- "We disciples of Jesus recognize that He is the first and greatest evangelizer sent by God[1]. . . . We believe and proclaim 'the good news of Jesus,'[2] . . . we want to listen to Jesus[3] . . . because He is the only Master"[4] (*Aparecida*, 103).

- "The Church offers mankind the Gospel, that prophetic message which responds to the needs and aspirations of the human heart and always remains 'Good News'" (RMI, 11).

- "Fulfilling the prophetic proclamation of the Messiah and savior joyfully announced by the psalmist and the prophet Ezekiel,[5] Jesus presents himself as 'the good shepherd,'[6] not only of Israel but of all humanity.[7] His whole life is a continual manifestation of his 'pastoral charity'" (PDV, 22).

---

1 Cf. Rom 1:3.
2 Mk 1:1.
3 Cf. Lk 9:3.
4 Cf. Mt 23:8.
5 Cf. Ps 22–23; Ezek 34:11.
6 Jn 10:11, 14.
7 Cf. Jn 10:16.

Deuteronomy 18:15–20 Today's reading from Deuteronomy comes from a section that describes positions of public authority in Israel including royal, juridical, and priestly offices (17:8—18:22). The similarity among those three is that they were solidly established, permanent in their position of power, and could easily value the preservation of their status over responding to changing circumstances and the needs of the people. Moses' proclamation that the Lord will raise up a prophet counterbalances that institutionalized power with divine spontaneity.

While the right to hold the other offices was clearly delineated, the people questioned how they would discern the authenticity of a prophet. Moses' response was that the prophet would not be extraordinary, but one from their own kin: one whose teaching would be like Moses' own. The prophet would be "raised up" by God with the authority to speak in God's name, and therefore could command their listening. Finally, Moses warned that no one should take on prophecy without being called nor proclaim anything that was not inspired lest they die (see Jeremiah 28).

Psalm 95:1–2, 6–7, 7–9 (8) This psalm is alternatively characterized as an "enthronement song" or a prophetic exhortation. The opening is surely aptly described as enthronement, beginning with the call to praise, with verses 3–6 extolling God's kingship. Nevertheless, the last verses lead to a strong argument for its prophetic character. The psalm moves from a call to praise and worship to a plea to listen to God's voice. In that, it echoes one of the consistent themes of prophecy: worship is genuinely hard hearted if not accompanied by obedience to God's will.

1 Corinthians 7:32–35 This is a part of a section in a larger section that deals with questions of being married or single. As with the two readings from 1 Corinthians that we have already heard, this reading must be understood in the light of Paul's eschatological vision. As we heard last week, in Paul's mind, the time is running out. Because of that, every aspect of life must be oriented to the Lord.

Regarding the reference to unmarried women and virgins, scholars speculate that some Corinthian women, influenced by the vestal virgins, saw virginity as a way of being "holy in both body and spirit." It is most likely that the phrase is not Paul's own, but a quote from them; Paul does not advocate a division in the human person, but rather sees the person holistically and recognizes the holiness of marriage as well as of celibacy. It should be noted that today's reading, like much of chapter 7, illustrates Paul's assumption about the equality of men and women (see 7:4).

Mark 1:21–28 The city of Capernaum, the center of Jesus' Galilean ministry, borders the northwest side of the Sea of Galilee. At the beginning of Mark's account of the Gospel, this synagogue is hospitable enough for Jesus to participate in the service of readings, prayers, and teaching. While Mark does not give us the verbal content of Jesus' preaching in the synagogue, he presents Jesus' defeat of the demon as an active expression of his teaching. The authority of his proclamation of nearness of the reigning of God is now made obvious in his authority over the unclean spirit.

Mark can hardly say enough about the people's response to Jesus. They were astonished and amazed; they publicized him such that his fame spread through the entire region. While that may sound very good, it fell woefully short of what Jesus called for in his pithy preaching about accepting the coming of the reigning of God. As Mark's account of the Gospel continues, we will witness the struggle of *metanoia* (conversion of mind and heart) as the disciples slowly grow in their faith, while others increasingly harden their hearts to Jesus and his message.

Looking at the message of today's readings, we first hear Moses remind us that God will freely choose servants through whom to speak. The only extraordinary thing about them will be the authority behind their message. Mark then presents Jesus in the line of the prophets rather than the established teachers or authorities. What marks him out is not his repetition of the tradition, but the way he carries out God's will for the good of all creatures. The message seems clear: a heart attuned to God recognizes prophets by the authenticity of their actions.

Connections to Church Teaching and Tradition

- "Having been sent by God to the nations . . . the church, in obedience to the command of her founder[1] . . . strives to preach the gospel to all" (AG, 1).

- "The mission of preaching the Gospel dictates . . . that we should dedicate ourselves to the liberation of people even in their present existence in this world. For unless the Christian message of love and justice shows its effectiveness through action in the cause of justice in the world, it will only with difficulty gain credibility with the people of our times" (JM, 35).

- "'Woe to me if I do not preach the Gospel!'[2] . . . St. Paul addresses . . . a call to walk all paths of evangelization . . . religion must not be restricted 'to the purely private sphere'[3] . . . the Christian message must not relegated to a purely other-worldly salvation incapable of shedding light on our earthly existence[4]" (CSDC, 71).

Job 7:1–4, 6–7   Job is one of the best known characters in the Old Testament. While many speak of the "patience of Job," reading his words proves him to a complainer and debater, a person who did not accept easy explanations for his suffering. The book of Job deals with the question of innocent suffering, trying to move beyond the overly simple belief that the good or evil that befall people are God's reward or punishment for their actions. The story begins as God points out what a good man Job is, to which Satan replies that Job is good because of the rewards he receives, not for genuine love of God. As the tale goes, God allows Satan to test Job. For 40 chapters of poetic argumentation, Job defends himself against friends who assert that he must be guilty of something if he has been so punished. While Job refuses to blame God for his calamity, he nevertheless calls on God to explain why he must suffer so much.

In the end, God denounces Job's friends and their theories of divine retribution, but also teaches Job that he cannot call God to account. While the friends offer sacrifice for their presumption, God restores Job's fortunes, giving him more than he ever had and an additional 140 years in which to enjoy life. In the passage we hear today, Job has just begun his time of trial and is giving a sorry account of the hopeless drudgery of life. In the last line he addresses God, asking God to remember him. That is a typical prayer in the scriptures, usually implying a plea for God's mercy, compassion, or restraint (see Psalms 78:39, 103:14).

Psalm 147:1–2, 3–4, 5–6 (see 3a)   This psalm might well be the song of Job when he was restored. Most poignant, if we take all of Job's sufferings into account, is the idea that the Lord heals the brokenhearted and binds up their wounds. We are reminded of the end of the book of Job in praising God's limitless wisdom, care for the lowly, and the demand that the wicked repent.

1 Corinthians 9:16–19, 22–23   "Woe to me if I do not preach [the Gospel]!" In previous readings from 1 Corinthians, we have seen that Paul interprets the meaning of human life in terms of God's future. In today's selection, Paul describes his understanding of his own vocation. After assuring the community that he was radically free (9:1–14), he now says that he cannot boast about his service of the Gospel because he is obligated to do it. In this, he depicts himself like Jeremiah, called from his mother's womb (see Galatians 1:15).

In fact, he actually describes himself as compelled, and eventually even as a slave (see Romans 1:1, Galatians 1:10). Paul believes that after receiving the call of Christ, his life has but one object: to preach the Gospel. Thus, he feels he must do anything and everything possible to complete that obligation.

Mark 1:29–39   In the scenes we visit today, Jesus continues his intensive activity of healing and casting out demons. The first healing miracle Mark recounts is that of Simon's mother-in-law. Earlier, when Jesus cast out a demon in the synagogue (1:26), the response was that everyone was amazed. When this woman was healed, we hear that she "waited on them," a phrase which can also be translated as "ministered to them." As the word that is also the etymological root of the English word *deacon*, this is the same word that Mark used for the angels' ministry to Jesus in the wilderness. Mark's next use of the word will be in 10:45, where Jesus teaches that the greatest must "serve." Thus, while her waiting on them gives solid evidence of her healing, it also demonstrates her response of discipleship: she who was healed, responded in ministry to others. This goes significantly further than the astonishment of those who heard Jesus' preaching in the synagogue.

As Mark continues his account of Jesus' inaugural activity, his exaggerated vocabulary emphasizes the impact Jesus was having on his contemporaries. The other side of that was Jesus' own sense of being driven to mission. Preaching the Gospel through teaching and healing was the sole purpose of his life: "For this purpose have I come."

---

1 Mt 16:15.
2 1 Cor 9:16.
3 John Paul II, *Message to the Secretary-General of the United Nations, on the occasion of the thirtieth anniversary of the Universal Declaration of Human Rights* (2 December 1978): AAS 71 (1979), 124.
4 Cf. John Paul II, Encyclical Letter *Centesimus Annus*, 5: AAS 83 (1991), 799.

Connections to Church Teaching and Tradition

- "Man's great, true hope . . . can only be God—God . . . who continues to love us 'to the end,'[1] . . . Jesus, who said that he had come so that we might have life and have it in its fullness, in abundance,[2] has also explained to us what 'life' means: '. . . that they know you the only true God, and Jesus Christ whom you have sent'[3] " (SS, 27).

- "Jesus . . . teaches us *filial boldness*: 'Whatever you ask in prayer, believe that you receive it, and you will'[4]" (CCC, 2610).

- "Suffering stems partly from our finitude, and partly from the mass of sin which has accumulated over the course of history, and continues to grow unabated today" (SS, 36).

Leviticus 13:1–2, 44–46   This reading presents the law regarding people with leprosy or other diseases of the skin that were thought to be dangerous. The regulations affecting a person with a skin disease served the dual purpose of protecting others from contagion and expressing the theological belief that maladies were caused by other-worldly powers, be they God or demons. Because of that, only God could heal such infirmities, either directly or through a chosen agent.

The practical result of being judged "unclean" in this way was tantamount to social and religious death. The physical signs of rent garments, an uncovered head and a covered beard were all signs of mourning. The diseased person was not allowed to interact with others, and certainly not to enter the temple. The work of the priest was not to heal, but to judge whether or not the person was afflicted or fully cured. All a victim could do was call on God.

Psalm 32:1–2, 5, 11 (7)   This faith-filled song of penitence and praise rightly belongs in the mouth of anyone who has been healed or forgiven. In connection with the healing theme of the readings, it is interesting that the Church chose to skip verses 3 and 4, which say, "As long as I kept silent, my bones wasted away . . . / day and night your hand was heavy upon me, / my strength withered."

The opening line of the psalm recalls Psalm 1, "Blessed those who follow not / the counsel of the wicked" (1:1), and reminds us that being blessed is not a matter of being sinless, but of being forgiven. While the Church does not teach that there is a connection between sin and sickness, in both we find ourselves turning to the Lord in our trouble and receiving the gift of salvation.

1 Corinthians 10:31—11:1   The context for today's selection from 1 Corinthians is the debate about whether the Christians could eat food that had been part of pagan worship. The question arose because when people made sacrifices, much of the meat offered was later sold in public markets at reasonable prices. For some, it was scandalous or sinful to eat such food, while others felt free to do so because they realized that the idols were meaningless in the face of the one God (see 8:7–13).

Paul speaks of the "glory" of God, which frequently refers to the salvation that comes from God's self-revelation. Thus, when Paul calls the community to eat, drink, and do everything for the glory of God, he is calling them to be sure that all they do is helpful to salvation for themselves and for all others.

Mark 1:40–45   Jesus' last activity in this eventful opening chapter of Mark's account of the Gospel brings him into contact with someone who begs for help. The leper's seemingly simple statement said much more than we might first assume. Because only God or God's chosen one could heal leprosy, people understood such healing to be a sign of the coming of God's kingdom. Thus, in saying, "If you wish, you can," the man effectively proclaimed faith in Jesus' preaching that the kingdom of God was at hand.

This leper was a man whose disease had cut him off from everything. Like Job, from whom we heard last week, and today's psalmist, the man ignored the injunction to remain at a distance and cry, "Unclean!" Instead, he cried out for help. Mark tells us that Jesus was "moved with pity." The word we translate as *pity* expresses profound emotion; it is a word that implies that one is moved from their inmost being—literally, from their guts. In this incident, we meet the Jesus who remains in union with the Father who gives life and wants, as Jesus said, fullness of life for all (John 10:10).

Jesus' healing words and touch show extraordinary solidarity. Jesus himself became unclean by that touch. But, while that legal element did not overly concern Jesus, he did not flaunt the law. Because the man would not be restored to social and religious life without the approval of a priest, Jesus sent him to fulfill what Moses had ordered. Going against what Jesus asked him to do, the man who had received back his very life couldn't help but proclaim the news. Like the psalmist, he exultantly proclaimed what God had done for him.

---

1 Cf. Jn 13:1.
2 Cf. Jn 10:10.
3 Jn 17:3.
4 Mk 11:24.

FOUNDATIONS FOR PREACHING AND TEACHING © 2011 Liturgy Training Publications.

Connections to Church Teaching and Tradition

- "The world which the council has in mind is the world of women and men, the entire human family seen in its total environment. . . . It is the world which Christians believe has been created and is sustained by the love of its maker, has fallen into the slavery of sin but has been freed by Christ, who was crucified and rose again in order to break the stranglehold of the evil one, so that it might be fashioned anew . . ." (GS, 2).

- "God forgives sin by grace and . . . frees human beings from sin's enslaving power and imparts the gift of new life in Christ. When persons come by faith to share in Christ, God . . . effects in them an active love" (JDDJ, 22).

- "The liberation and salvation brought by the kingdom of God come to the human person both in his physical and spiritual dimensions. Two gestures are characteristic of Jesus' mission: healing and forgiving" (RMI, 14).

- "Jesus shows the salvific meaning of his death and resurrection, a mystery which renews history and the whole cosmos" (SCA, 10).

Isaiah 43:18–19, 21–22, 24b–25   In this passage Isaiah writes to comfort his people in exile. He declares that God is changing history: "Remember not the events of the past." Even while this passage clearly recalls the past, it proclaims that what is to come will be like a new Exodus: "In the desert I make a way." But, this new way will be even more marvelous. In Exodus 15:23–27, God taught Moses how to sweeten brackish water and led the people to springs. Now, God will give them nothing less than rivers in the wasteland.

And, lest they forget their unworthiness of all of this, Isaiah makes it absolutely clear that it is all God's free action. This people wearies God is forgiven, not because of their merit, but, as God says, "for my own sake." The new thing, the new free and forgiven status of the forsaken people is a revelation of God's goodness.

Psalm 41:2–3, 4–5, 13–14 (5b)   Our collection of 150 psalms is ordered into five books, each of which ends with a prayer of praise. Psalm 41 is the last of the first book. Interestingly, like Psalm 1, Psalm 41 opens by describing the one who is happy or blessed. In Psalm 1, the blessed one follows the law of the Lord; here, the blessed is the one who has regard for the lowly and poor. Between the first and last psalm of the first book, we have love of God and neighbor. Although this Psalm begins with a beatitude, it is actually a prayer for help—help that the psalmist admits is not fully deserved. In the psalmist's worldview, sin and illness are intimately connected; lack of moral integrity results in lack of physical integrity. By the time we reach the last verses, the penitent psalmist makes a proclamation of faith: those who place all their trust in God will be healed and will bless God for all eternity.

2 Corinthians 1:18–22   In our first selection from 2 Corinthians, Paul refutes a charge that he has been capricious about visiting Corinth. Later, he will say that he did not go there to cause grief. But before he explains his travel plans, he moves from self-defense into a theological proclamation. Paul insists that he is as reliable as the word he preached to them, and that Word was Jesus Christ in whom all of God's promises have been fulfilled. Beyond affirming the absolute yes of God's Word and his own steadfastness, the closing verses of the reading reveal Paul's Trinitarian theology and the anthropology that flows from it. He reminds his readers that it is God who has brought them together in Christ, and it is God who has given them the first installment of the Spirit in their hearts. This would quite likely remind them of the theme of unity and love he expounded in 1 Corinthians 12–13. Thus, as Paul begins what many see as his most personal letter, he calls the community to express the forbearance and self-awareness that should spring from their unity with and in Christ.

Mark 2:1–12   In the beginning of Mark's account of the Gospel, Jesus has been depicted as so successful that people crowd around him, even blocking the door to the house where he stays. As mentioned in the commentary for the Fourth Sunday of Ordinary Time, the crowds originally responded to Jesus' words and deeds with amazement and astonishment. Now, for the first time, people come to Jesus with "faith." Judging by all they did, the friends who brought the paralytic to Jesus had faith that he could and would heal. Jesus' immediate response to that faith was to forgive the man's sins.

Those were audacious words; everyone knew that only God can forgive sin. The scribes correctly understood that Jesus was assuming a divine right. It should come as no surprise that Jesus would intuit their thoughts and respond with a question that would trap them. Because both healing and forgiving were considered divine prerogatives, Jesus' healing activity was a sign that he was acting with God's power (see Isaiah 35:6, Micah 3:6).

While the scribes sulked, the crowds glorified the God who makes all things new. Some were beginning to recognize Jesus as one who made God's healing love and forgiveness present among them. Finally, it should be noted that while Jesus both forgave and healed, he did not link illness and guilt. In fact, when he broached the topic, he contradicted the accepted wisdom about it, denying that victims of calamity or illness were more sinful than others (John 9:2–3, Luke 13:2).

Lent

Overview of Lent

Lent is characterized by themes of Baptism and Penance. As a liturgical season, it has its roots in the second half of the fourth century in Rome. Imitating Christ's days in the desert, it is the only liturgical season that begins on a weekday (Ash Wednesday), an arrangement made necessary by the desire to have 40 days of penitence without including the Triduum or Sundays.

On the Third, Fourth, and Fifth Sundays of Lent, parishes may choose to use the readings from the Year A cycle of readings or the readings from the current cycle, in this case, Year B. The Year A readings highlight baptismal themes and are especially appropriate for the catechumens who will be initiated at the Easter Vigil. The information below will primarily apply to the Year B readings, although scripture backgrounds on both cycles of readings are printed in this resource.

In addition to the scripture readings, Lent's liturgical prayers help us to understand the grace the season offers. The first preface for Lent gives thanks for this joyful season through which we prepare for Easter with renewed minds and hearts. It goes on to recognize that, as we recall the great events of salvation history, God's grace leads us to reverence and service of our neighbor.

First Readings

In addition to reflecting the themes of the Year B cycle of Gospel readings, our First Readings highlight some of the great events of salvation history. We begin with God's covenant promise to Noah on the First Sunday of Lent. Then, on the Second Sunday of Lent, we see Abraham offer everything to God. On the Third Sunday of Lent, the commandments remind us of our covenant responsibility. Listening to 2 Chronicles on the Fourth Sunday of Lent, we recall the cycle of infidelity, exile, and God's redeeming action. Then, on the Fifth Sunday of Lent, Jeremiah promises a New Covenant engraved on the heart. Finally, on Palm Sunday, we hear the song of the servant through whom the New Covenant will be accomplished.

Responsorial Psalms

While the psalms chosen for the Lectionary most directly respond to the First Readings, they also offer us a special Lenten prayer book when taken on their own. Psalm 25, which we hear on the First Sunday of Lent, requests that God be our Lenten teacher. On the next Sunday, we pray for trust, especially in difficult times, with Psalm 116. Psalm 19, which we hear on the Third Sunday of Lent, proclaims the joy God's law offers us. In Psalm 137, which we hear on the Fourth Sunday of Lent, we ask to never forget God's blessings, even when they may seem to be absent. On the Fifth Sunday of Lent, with Psalm 51, we ask for the grace of a clean heart. Finally on Palm Sunday, echoing Jesus' cry from the cross, Psalm 22 admits near despair, but ends with hope. These are prayers of faith put to the test.

Second Readings

In the seasons of Lent, Easter, Advent, and Christmas, the Second Readings often reflect on the other readings, unlike the readings in Ordinary Time. Each of the Second Readings deepens our appreciation of the Sunday theme, and taken together, they represent the early strands of Christology, the understanding of Jesus' identity. From 1 Peter and Romans, we hear that Christ suffered once for all as a sign of God's love. First Corinthians says that the cross seems foolish but demonstrates God's unfathomable wisdom. Ephesians teaches that believers are renewed in him, and the last two selections teach how Christ practiced obedience and humble self-giving.

Gospel Readings

As the Second Readings could be understood to represent the primitive Church's developing reflection on Christ, the Gospel readings of this cycle are an ongoing revelation of Jesus' person and mission. The First Sunday's reading from Mark shows us the very human Jesus being tempted. That is followed by the Transfiguration, the revelation that this Son of Man was also uniquely the Son of God.

On the middle three Sundays of Lent, we will hear from John's account of the Gospel. With the cleansing of the temple, we get the image of Jesus as the new Temple, the place where God and humanity come to meet. In the dialogue with Nicodemus, we are reminded that Jesus is the sign of God's unfathomable love for humanity. The reading from John 12 shows Jesus reflecting on the difficulty and necessity of his mission of suffering and glory. On Palm Sunday, the reading of the Passion draws us again into the dramatic narrative about Jesus, the servant who emptied himself in the total self-giving that brought salvation.

Connections to Church Teaching and Tradition

- By promising never to send a flood again, God makes a covenant with Noah and with all of humanity. This covenant promise will continue as long as the world endures (CCC, 71).

- "In Christ we have been called to a New Covenant and a New Law that fulfills and perfects the Old Law. We also are invited to experience God's love for us and to return that love to God and to our neighbor. Our love of neighbor includes our solidarity with the human community and a commitment to social justice for all" (USCCA, 325).

- "Lent is ordered to preparing for the celebration of Easter, since the Lenten liturgy prepares for celebration of the Paschal Mystery both catechumens, by the various stages of Christian Initiation, and the faithful, who recall their own Baptism and do penance" (UN, 27).

Genesis 9:8–15   *Covenant* is the word that unifies today's readings. We first hear it in the Genesis reading. As the primeval story is told, a flood of devastation has covered the earth and only Noah, seven members of his family, and the animals on the ark have survived. Frustrated and angered by the moral corruption that pervaded the lives of the Hebrew people (Genesis 6:1–2), God found only Noah and his tribe worth saving. Now with the dawn of a dry day, God expresses a change of heart and an eternal promise to Noah and to all creatures. Never again will a flood destroy all creation. This covenant is a sign of mercy as God makes clear that it is love rather than harsh punishment that will mark his relationship with the human family. God will forgive the sins of all people with a divine compassion that steadfastly invites conversion of human hearts. This is the promise of the covenant.

Psalm 25:4–5, 6–7, 8–9 (see 10)   This psalm is an acrostic poem where each verse begins with the successive letter of the Hebrew alphabet. This detail is lost on us as we read, pray, or sing the English translation of this psalm. But what should not be lost on any of us is the psalm's reference to the compassion of the Lord, a compassion made known in the aftermath of the great flood, a compassion that is the source of redemption and model for human relationship. The cry of the psalmist becomes our own prayer: "Teach me your paths." Teach us to be more loving, teach us to know and live your truth. Teach us your compassion and lead us to your justice. And with the psalmist we remember that divine compassion will not falter, will not give up on us. For that is God's promise of old to all generations. God has made his covenant and, in doing so, he shows us the way.

1 Peter 3:18–22   When people gather at a baptismal font with a cross imprinted in its design, or when a funeral liturgy begins with the sprinkling of water from the font and the words "In baptism, our loved one died with Christ," faith's connection between dying and rising is strengthened. For the cross, the sign of our faith, is intimately connected to our Baptism. When we are baptized in Christ—when we go down into the waters—we die to an old way of life and take on new life in the Lord.

That is the message of the reading from the letter of Peter. With a statement of belief (3:18, 22) and a reference to Noah's past redemption (3:19–21), the author reminds the new converts to Christ that when they were baptized, they embraced a spiritual rebirth. They took on the life of Jesus Christ and his redemptive suffering, death, and Resurrection. The cross, a symbol of shame, terror, and agony, had been transformed to a symbol of power and new life. Death had lost its power in the triumph of the cross. This cross that Jesus embraced had become the sign of the New Covenant between God and humanity.

It remains the sign of faith, the covenant we embrace at Baptism and every day beyond. Just as Jesus suffered and died on the cross in order to bring new life to us, we believe that our own suffering will lead to new life. It is our well-founded hope, belief, and promise of the New Covenant.

Mark 1:12–15   It is the First Sunday of Lent, so we know the Gospel will focus on Jesus' time of temptation in the desert and the time of testing that precedes his public ministry. Matthew, Mark, and Luke each describe this desert episode, and this year it is Mark who provides what is the shortest and most direct version of the story. Jesus is driven into the desert by the Spirit and remains there for 40 days. Satan tempts him and angels minister to him. When Jesus hears of John's arrest, an arrest that foreshadows his own, he goes to Galilee. Having successfully faced temptation and surrendered his will to that of the Father, Jesus begins his public ministry. He no longer can stand back but must begin to give voice to the truth within, the truth that begs him to speak of the kingdom of God. With a call to repent sinful ways and believe in the Gospel of eternal justice, Jesus sets out to gather a band of followers. Thus begins the journey that will lead to the cross, a cross that does not mark the end, but the beginning of the mission that will never end and indeed brings us here today.

FOUNDATIONS FOR PREACHING AND TEACHING © 2011 Liturgy Training Publications.

Connections to Church Teaching and Tradition

■ When God asks Abraham to sacrifice his son, Abraham does not cease to trust in God's goodness. Thus, Abraham prefigures God the Father, who will sacrifice his Son for all (CCC, 2572).

■ Our belief in God cannot be separated from our belief in his Son, Jesus Christ, to whom we are to listen (CCC, 151).

■ "The title *Son of God* refers to the truth that Jesus Christ is the unique and eternal Son of the Father. At Christ's baptism and Transfiguration, the Father says of Jesus, 'This is my beloved Son.'[1] To profess Jesus as *Lord* is to believe in his divinity" (USCCA, 85).

Genesis 22:1–2, 9a, 10–13, 15–18   For many people, this story can be disturbing. How could God ask Abraham to kill his son? Even when we take into account that God did not spare his own Son, we can still struggle to reconcile the God of love that Jesus preached with the God who tells Abraham, "Take your son . . . your only one, whom you love, and . . . offer him up as a holocaust." We often read this story, thinking of our own life experiences as parents or children, rather than through the lens of our faith. For this is a story that isn't so much a criticism of the practice of human sacrifice or even a commentary about it. It is an archetypal story of biblical faith. Abraham is put to the test, and he surrenders his entire being and will to God. He is obedient to the command of God, and thus, he is for all people and all time a model of faith and trust. He, too, is a beloved son who follows the command of God, trusting that God will care for him even when he does not understand what he is called to do.

Psalm 116:10, 15, 16–17, 18–19 (116:9)   The title given to this psalm in the *New American Bible* is "Thanksgiving to God Who Saves from Death." The title reminds us that the psalmist is grateful to the merciful Lord who "saved my life" (116:4) and provides a context for the psalm's refrain "I will walk before the Lord, / in the land of the living" (116.9). For who would not choose to walk in the presence of the one who protects and saves? Filled with awe in the presence of the Lord who has "loosed my bonds," the psalmist writes, "I am your servant." It is indeed a psalm of gratitude and pledged faithfulness. God, who rescues his servant from the cords of death, regards the death of his faithful ones as precious. We see a God who cares for humanity in all its frailty, imperfection, and possibility. God loves his people and asks only for obedience in return. Could the words of the psalmist then belong to Abraham and Isaac and to us all? "I will walk before the Lord, / in the land of the living."

Romans 8:31b–34   Again, we come face to face with love that is so big and so generous that nothing can stop it. In a statement that invites comparison to today's First Reading (Genesis 22:16), Paul writes to the people of Rome that absolutely nothing can stop God's love for them, for the gift of a Son exemplifies the ultimate act of love. If God did not spare his own Son, Paul tells the Romans, but handed him over for us all, there is nothing he won't do for us. For this same Son, Jesus the Christ, who died and rose for us, not only won salvation for us, but will ever after intercede on our behalf. It is an interesting aside to consider that Jesus, who is himself God, is our intercessor who sits at the right hand of God. That is something to consider in our own conversations, our own prayer, with God in this Lenten season. Paul's letter suggests that the one who walked among us and took on human form is now our biggest advocate in times of need. The gift of God's beloved Son continues to be the source of life to all people of faith.

Mark 9:2–10   We hear the story of the Transfiguration every year on the Second Sunday of Lent, and at times, the repetition can dull our senses so that we fail to really listen to the words of the Gospel. This year, listen for Peter's spontaneous and heartfelt, "Rabbi, it is good that we are here!" The scripture says that he was so terrified that he didn't know what to say, except to admit how good it was to be present in that moment, to see the transfigured Lord with Moses and Elijah. He was terrified, but that didn't stop him from saying, "Let us make three tents." Given a preview of God's kingdom, Peter wanted to prolong the experience. He wanted it to last. What good news that is for us who wait, sometimes with our own fears, for the coming of the kingdom! As the event continues, a voice from the clouds (a manifestation of God's presence) repeats the revelation heard at Jesus' baptism (1:11): "This is my beloved Son." But this time, there is an added message: "Listen to him." If we follow that command, if we listen and follow in his footsteps, we will one day see with Peter the dazzling glory of God.

---

1 Mt 3:17; 17:5.

Connections to Church Teaching and Tradition

- In the Ten Commandments, we see how we are called to respond to God with love (CCC, 2083).

- In the Resurrection of Jesus Christ, God the Father shows forth the power in his believers (CCC, 272).

- "God is preparing a new dwelling and a new earth in which righteousness dwells . . . .[1] Then death will have been conquered, the daughters and sons of God will be raised in Christ and what was sown in weakness and dishonor will become incorruptible[2]" (GS, 39).

Exodus 20:1–17 or 20:1–3, 7–8, 12–17   If you call a meeting and tell the group that you have a set of rules to give them, it is highly unlikely that the announcement will be received as good news. That, however, is not the case in this Exodus reading. God convenes the Hebrew people and gives them a set of rules, and in doing so, he draws them more deeply into relationship with him. He addresses them with the familiar second person pronoun ("I am . . . your God . . ."), establishing an intimacy that did not exist before. He reminds them that he brought them safely out of Egypt and that he is passionate (jealous) in his commitment to them. In return he asks that they be his and his alone. This first commandment and the next two are new to the people. The remaining seven have been part of the communal wisdom that protects the common good. This time it is God, however, and not a tribal elder, who proclaims them, giving them a new authority. Though some might see the law as restrictive, God's commandments tell the people who they are—a people set aside and chosen. They provide the security of an eternal promise of faithfulness that frees them to embrace the law as a means of knowing more deeply the God who loves them with a jealous passion.

Psalm 19:8, 9, 10, 11 (John 6:68c)   The Exodus reading illustrates the power of the law to transform and define a relationship between God and his people. That said, Psalm 19 as we sing it today provides its own glorious affirmation of the gift of the law of the Lord. This psalm is a poem of praise, divided into three stanzas. The first stanza, which we do not hear today, proclaims the silent majesty of God's creation. The third stanza requests freedom from sin and merciful cleansing from unknown faults. But it is the second stanza, which we sing at today's liturgy, that magnifies this hymn of praise. With its first words, "The law of the LORD is perfect, / refreshing the soul," the psalmist begins a love song that cherishes the law of the Lord. The law of the Lord is perfect, trustworthy, right, clear, pure, and true. It enlightens the people and is the source of wisdom. It is more precious than gold. It is the law that forms God's people and draws them near. It is the law that defines this newly established covenant. In short, it is the law that gives life to the people.

1 Corinthians 1:22–25   In his life on earth, Jesus turned every expectation upside down and challenged the expectations and presumptions of nearly everyone. His death confounded some to such an extent that they were unable to see the power and hand of God in this cataclysmic event. Yet for as many Jews and Greeks who missed the point, there were others, "those who are called," who got the message. Paul makes it clear that those Jews and Greeks saw beyond the limits of human imagination and recognized that Jesus Christ is the power and wisdom of God. They didn't necessarily understand it, but they accepted that God's wisdom defied human reason. What seemed like weakness was really strength; what seemed like abject loss was the story of victory. In the view of the faithful, Christ crucified was and is not the figure of shame, but the source of new life.

John 2:13–25   John's is the only account of the Gospel that places the cleansing of the temple at the beginning rather than at the end of the narrative. We reconcile the difference in the accounts by remembering that each of the evangelists has a theological point to make and orders events accordingly. Thus, we presume that John wanted to depict the raising of Lazarus as the event that propelled Jesus from his public life toward his own suffering and death. Early on, John deems it important to describe the temple incident through a post-Resurrection lens (2:22). Not only does he make it clear that the temple is not a marketplace, but in addition, because the temple has been destroyed by the time John writes, he wants his readers to know that Jesus is the new temple, the place where humans meet the presence of God. Mindful of the invitation of Lent to grow more deeply in faith, we pray with Jesus, who leads us to the presence of God and the gift of new life.

---

1 Cf. 2 Cor 5:2; 2 Pet 3:13.
2 Cf. 1 Cor 15:42 and 53.

Connections to Church Teaching and Tradition

■ On the Third Sunday of Lent the spirit of the elect is filled with Christ the Redeemer who is the living water (RCIA 143, 150–156).

■ The water in Baptism is a sign of the Holy Spirit's active presence bringing us into divine life. The Holy Spirit is also the living water from Christ crucified which wells up in us leading us to eternal life in communion with the Trinity (CCC, 694).

Exodus 17:3–7 We may find it difficult to understand the grumblings of the people in this passage from Exodus because we live in a country where water and other resources are taken for granted. But if we have ever had to ration water supplies or travel to a country where water resources were restricted, we might have more sympathy for the nomadic Israelites. Tired and unsure of their future, they demand that Moses fix their intolerable situation. Moses himself is tremendously frustrated and minces no words with God: "What shall I do with this people? A little more and they will stone me." God answers the plea of his messenger with instructions to obtain water from the rock in Horeb.

The people demanded water, but they really wanted God to send them a sign of his presence. It is a very human story because it reveals the truth that it is easy to trust that God is in our midst when everything is going well in our lives. It is when struggle, heartache, and loss occur that we can wonder if God is present. In those difficult times, like the Israelites of old, we thirst for reassurance that God is with us.

Psalm 95:1–2, 6–7, 8–9 (8) The psalm builds on the First Reading's theme of trust in God. Considered a psalm of enthronement, Psalm 95 is sung by a people who have found the one true God. Capturing their sense of wonder and praise, the first verses (1, 2, 6, and 7) jubilantly proclaim loyalty and gratitude. The final verse, however, strikes a different theme as it recounts the desert wanderings of a people who eventually fell apart at Meribah and Massah. There, the Israelites' grumbling and complaining put God to the test. This psalm's final verse refers to that failure of faithfulness. Even though the Israelites saw God's wonderful works, they openly doubted God's presence and turned away from him with hardened hearts. The psalm's refrain calls them (and us) back, encouraging movement from our uncertainties to the freedom of trust. We are called to listen for God's voice in the people and events of each day with open hearts. For God, who is the rock of salvation, is present in joy and in struggle, and remains the Good Shepherd who will never abandon his flock.

Romans 5:1–2, 5–8 Paul's writing is complex, but his message is simple: Christ died for all humans and, in doing so, proved God's great and unconditional love for all. That supreme and generous act is the source of our hope and the reason for our trust. While God's love is beyond our imagination, we know his love through human experience. Sometimes, in the best of human circumstances, we can catch a glimpse of what it feels like to be loved by God. Married couples often say that their love for one another makes them better people. It is a statement that provides an analogy to help grasp divine love: If we truly understood what it meant to be loved by God, we would be nearly perfect people. Perfect not for the sake of perfection, but perfect because we want to respond to God's love for us. It is that selfless love that is the true source of our Christian hope.

John 4:5–42 or 4:5–15, 19b–26, 39a, 40–42 Jews were not supposed to speak to Samaritans, much less share drinking vessels with them. Jewish men were never supposed to converse with a woman, let alone a Samaritan woman. But cultural division and socially accepted discrimination didn't stop Jesus. In this Gospel, Jesus initiates a conversation with a woman of Samaria who is sitting alone at the town well in the noonday heat. She is so dumbfounded by this that she forgets her societal status and blurts, "How can you . . . ask me . . . for a drink?" Thus begins one of the longest and most fascinating conversations of the New Testament.

Jesus asks for a drink, but then reveals he is the source of water that will quench thirst for all eternity. The woman then reverses the dialogue and says, "Give me this water." At this point, the conversation shifts and the testimony of faith begins to unfold. Jesus, aware that she has been married five times, tells her to get her husband. In doing so, Jesus recites details of her life that no stranger could know. She asks Jesus if he is the Messiah. And the world is forever changed with these words: "I am he, the one speaking with you." She is the first to hear the news and share it with others. Some have said she is the first missionary to proclaim the news. What we remember is that this woman stands in a long line of witnesses who have journeyed in faith before us. Buoyed by their faith, we are called to continue that journey today.

Connections to Church Teaching and Tradition

- God loves us in spite of our sins. "By going so far as to give up his own Son for us, God reveals that he is 'rich in mercy'[1]" (CCC, 211).

- "We have come to believe in God's love: in these words the Christian can express the fundamental decision of his life. Being Christian is . . . the result of . . . an encounter with an event, a person . . . . Saint John's Gospel describes that event in these words: 'God so loved the world that he gave his only Son, that whoever believes in him should . . . have eternal life'[2]" (DCE, 1).

- "The Word of God, through whom all things were made, became man and dwelt among us[3]. . . . He reveals to us that 'God is love'[4]" (GS, 38).

- "In Jesus Christ the visible world which God created for man[5]—the world that, when sin entered, 'was subjected to futility'[6]—recovers again its original link with the divine source of Wisdom and Love. Indeed, 'God so loved the world that he gave his only Son'[7]" (RH, 8).

---

1 Eph 2:4.
2 Jn 3:16.
3 Cf. 2 Cor 6:10.
4 1 Jn 4:8.
5 Cf. Gen 1:26–30.
6 Rom 8:20; cf. 8:19–22; GS 2, 13: AAS 58 (1966) 1026, 1034–1035.
7 Jn 3:16.

2 Chronicles 36:14–16, 19–23 Margaret Wise Brown's popular children's book *The Runaway Bunny* tells the story of a little bunny who never misses a chance to run away from his mother. His mother, however, never gives up on him and eventually brings him home. For children and adults alike, it is a story of unconditional love. So, too, the First Reading today is a story of unconditional love. The book of Chronicles is a historical text that provides an account of the Hebrew people from the reign of Saul to the end of the Babylonian exile. But it is a history told with a purpose: to reveal the presence of God in the lives of the people. Through thick and thin, God never abandons his people even though they run from his love and often presume they can take care of themselves. As the reading for today unfolds, the people refuse to turn away from their sinful ways, and they ignore God's messengers until "the anger of the LORD against his people . . . [had] no remedy." Then the people are overcome by their enemies and taken to Babylon as slaves. But God does not forget them or his promises to them. In seventy years' time, Cyrus, King of Persia frees those who belong "to any part of [God's] people" and they return to the holy city, Jerusalem. God has not abandoned them as they feared, but he has brought them safely home. As we journey through this Lenten season and take stock of our own spiritual lives, it is an important lesson to remember. For though we may at times walk away from the Lord God and ignore his love, he does not give up on us. He is patient and loving and will always take us back.

Psalm 137:1–2, 3, 4–5, 6 (6ab) This psalm is a perfect response to the Chronicles reading that precedes it at today's liturgy. Banished to Babylon, the people remembered their homeland and "sat and wept." The psalm laments the great loss that the exile imposed and confirms that the people have learned a painful lesson. With a promise to repent and return to the Lord, the haunting refrain establishes a firm amendment of purpose: "Let my tongue be silenced, if ever I forget you!" This is no less true today, and we sing the words of the psalm, mindful of our own tendencies to forsake and turn from the Lord. We are reminded that the Lord, who is ever faithful, will never turn from us.

Ephesians 2:4–10 The letter to the Ephesians is a letter to the nascent Church that tells a story of God's abundant and saving love. The excerpt from this letter that we hear today begins with an acknowledgment that God, because of his great love, has brought us to new life with Christ. The letter then establishes that it is God who raised Christ, and it is God who loves so deeply that salvation is now ours. The letter further entertains a commentary on salvation. Is it earned with good works? Do we deserve it? The answer to both questions is no. This gift is not of human making, nor can it be earned. "By grace you have been saved through faith, and this is not from you; it is the gift of God." So "no one may boast." Salvation is the gift of God's divine mercy that indeed will never give up on us. In response, it is our responsibility to live as reflections and vessels of the "immeasurable riches of his grace." This Lenten season affords the opportunity to practice that embrace of grace.

John 3:14–21 John's account of the Gospel continues to make clear that salvation has come into the world with the gift of God's own Son. This passage, John 3:16, is perhaps the most commonly recognized scriptural reference in our times. That recognition factor is a curse as much as a blessing because of the manner in which we have come to know it, posted on homemade signs and held aloft amid gathered crowds at sporting events. This Sunday provides an opportunity to restore a sense of reverence and understanding to these words. They tell us that just as Moses lifted up the serpent and saved his people (Numbers 21:8–9), Jesus will be lifted up so that all who believe will have eternal life. God has so much love for the world that he gave his only Son to redeem it. The gift of salvation is not an act of condemnation. It is an act of love given by a generous God, who knows human flaws and sinfulness, yet deems the world and humankind worthy. It is the gift of a loving God who never gives up on his people.

Fourth Sunday of Lent, Year A
Light Produces Goodness and Truth

March 18, 2012

Connections to Church Teaching and Tradition

■ "Healing the wounds of sin, the Holy Spirit renews us interiorly through a spiritual transformation[1]" (CCC, 1695).

■ "When we have spread on earth . . . human dignity, sisterly and brotherly communion, and freedom—according to the command of the Lord and his Spirit, we will find them once again . . . when Christ presents to his Father an eternal and universal kingdom . . ."[2] (GS, 39).

1 Samuel 16:1b, 6–7, 10–13a   This passage introduces the great King David to posterity. We first find David in the fields tending his sheep, not in royal surroundings. It is a reminder that God's ways often challenge human presumptions. God has sent Samuel to Bethlehem to anoint one of Jesse's sons. Jesse presents seven sons, and Samuel thinks Eliab is the one. But the Lord reminds Samuel that lofty stature is not God's measure of success, for "the Lord looks into the heart," rather than at the exterior appearance.

When none of the seven proves to be the chosen one, Samuel asks, "Are these all the sons you have?" Sure enough, there is one more. David, the youngest, is tending the sheep. When David appears, the Lord pronounces, "this is the one." Samuel anoints David in the presence of his family to establish that David is filled with the Lord. From now on all would know that David's power and authority came from God.

Psalm 23:1–3a, 3b–4, 5, 6 (1)   It is no accident that this psalm is paired with the Samuel reading, for it continues the shepherd theme, inviting us to reflect on the image of God as our shepherd. In our times, shepherds are not a fixture of daily life as they once were. In the time of David, shepherds were guardians and caretakers for sheep, who were dependent on them. The shepherd fed them and protected them. If they were lost, they could not find their way home without the shepherd. The message to us is that the Lord is our shepherd who will walk with us through every dark valley. When we feel lost, he will lead us to safety. When we feel trapped, he will give us courage. When we feel alone, he will lead us to his table of plenty. No wonder this is a beloved psalm, for indeed, it reminds us that the Lord will always lead us home.

Ephesians 5:8–14   The letter to the Ephesians is written from a post-Resurrection understanding that Christ Jesus destroyed the power of darkness with his victory over death. The passage for the Fourth Sunday of Lent is part of a section of Ephesians (4:25—6:20) that outlines ethical guidelines for Jesus' followers. Though addressed to the people of Ephesus, this letter has significance for the entire body of Christ, the Church. This particular excerpt advises all to "live as children of light, for light produces every kind of goodness and righteousness and truth" (Ephesians 5:8–9). But what would define a life of light that is "pleasing to the Lord" (Ephesians 5:10)? The beginning of the chapter holds the key: "live in love, as Christ loved us" (Ephesians 5:2). Those who follow Christ the Light will learn that love of each other in the Lord identifies us as Christian.

John 9:1–41 or 9:1, 6–9, 13–17, 34–38   For people blessed with eyesight, it can be very difficult to understand what it must have been like to be the blind man in this Gospel passage. Think about a man who has been blamed all of his life for his own blindness. Think about his willingness to trust Jesus. Imagine him feeling the mud on his eyes and his walk to Siloam to wash. Consider his feeling of vulnerability as his parents left him on his own to explain this miracle. And think of his courage in response to the Pharisees' questions.

He called Jesus a prophet whose power clearly came from God. When asked a second time, his pointed response, "I told you already and you did not listen" (John 9:27), placed him among Jesus' disciples. In his final encounter with Jesus, the former blind man makes a tremendous assent to faith with the words, "I do believe, Lord" (John 9:38).

John wanted to address a community dispute between disciples of Moses and Jesus. One group thought Jesus was a sinner; the other, that he was from God. When asked to take a side, the blind man at first ignored the theological dispute: "One thing I do know is that I was blind and now I see" (John 9:25). Pushed further, he said, "we know that God does not listen to sinners" (John 9:31). It's a statement of courage that puts the blind man at odds with the authorities of his faith community. Now he sees. His trust in Jesus filled him with courage to speak the truth. Will we have this same courage?

---

1 Cf. Eph 4:23.
2 Preface for the Feast of Christ the King.

Connections to Church Teaching and Tradition

■ "To suffer with the other and for others; to suffer for the sake of truth and justice; to suffer out of love and in order to become a person who truly loves—these are fundamental elements of humanity. . . . . [The] Christian faith that had the particular merit of bringing forth within man a new and deeper capacity for these kinds of suffering . . . . The Christian faith has shown us that . . . God—Truth and Love in person—desired to suffer for us and with us" (SS, 39).

■ Christ's death has transformed human death, so while it is the end of earthly life, it is the beginning of life everlasting. "The obedience of Jesus has transformed the curse of death into a blessing[1]" (CCC, 1009).

■ "As the redeemer of all humanity, [Jesus] delivered himself up to death for the sake of all: 'No one has greater love than this, to lay down one's life for one's friends.'[2] . . . by the gift of his Spirit he established, after his death and resurrection, a new communion of sisters and brothers among all who received him in faith and love; this is . . . the church" (GS, 32).

Jeremiah 31:31–34   Some would suggest that the prophet Jeremiah had more power in death than he had in life. In life, he opposed the idolatry of the people and warned them of their errant ways, but they ignored him. The tradition holds that he suffered prison and death at the hands of his own people. But in the time of the exile, the people remembered Jeremiah and his warnings. The passage proclaimed today makes it clear that when the people finally paid attention, they knew that Jeremiah's message redefined their relationship with the Lord. They had broken the Old Covenant with their worship of many gods. But this New Covenant (the only mention of New Covenant in the Hebrew Scriptures) would be written upon their hearts, not on stone. The people would "know the LORD," and in every action and deed, God would be with them. Unlike its predecessor, this would be a lasting covenant. Something died during those years of exile, but the seeds of new life were planted.

Psalm 51:3–4, 12–13, 14–15 (12a)   Psalm 51 is considered one of the most beautiful penitential psalms of the scriptures. As we pray it this day, it is appropriate to join our own need for divine forgiveness and compassion with the needs of our ancestors in faith. With the psalmist, the Hebrew people beg the Lord for the gift of forgiveness. They yearn for a clean slate, forgiveness of sins, and a new beginning. Remembering the promise of the New Covenant, they ask for clean hearts. They know they need a fresh start and they know they need the Spirit's daily presence to help them make that start and succeed. In return, they will teach sinners the way of the Lord. As Lent's end draws near and we look to what lies ahead, we remember that this prayer can be our own. Lent provides a time to take stock and renew our efforts to live faithfully, but the renewal does not last a mere 40 days. We are in this life of faith for the long haul. Thus, today we ask for clean hearts that will sustain us over time. It is our hope and desire that our lives, in ways large and small, will bear witness to the presence of the Spirit.

Hebrews 5:7–9   This reading is rich in consolation for those who suffer the loss of health, the ravages of medical treatments, the diminished capacities of body and mind, the fear of anxiety, or the burden of depression. This is the reading that speaks to all who suffer pain of any kind, for it tells us that our Lord himself, while in human form, cried out to God with tears of pain and pleas for help. Even though he was God's own Son, he suffered with "loud cries and tears." The mystery of suffering will perhaps never be fully understood on this side of life, but we do know that God, who placed his law of love within human hearts, will fill all who suffer with strength and grace. The suffering and death of the Son remains our model. It does not mean that we have to enjoy suffering; the Lord himself did not. It means that the Lord is near, sharing our agony and heartache, and walking with us every step of the way. In the midst of pain, the gift of the Paschal Mystery may seem to elude us, but if we ask the Lord for the grace to endure, he will give us what we need until we can see the promised new life.

John 12:20–33   Those who travel on mission trips to El Salvador often find themselves at the site where the bodies of the four murdered American church women were found in 1980. Standing in the shade of an enormous nearby tree, it is not unusual for groups to recall the words of today's Gospel: "Unless a grain of wheat falls to the ground and dies, it remains just a grain . . . but if it dies, it produces much fruit." Before their deaths, the world had not heard of Ita Ford, Maura Clark, Jean Donovan, or Dorothy Kazel, but the people they served knew them to be disciples of Christ. In death, the cause of justice these women served was embraced by thousands more. They absolutely embodied the scriptures, "whoever serves me must follow me." All four left their homeland to preach the Word of God to the poor and oppressed, making it clear that God's love did not belong to only the few. These women understood that they were risking their lives. Each of them wrote letters home that as much as admitted that the "hour" was at hand, but they could not turn away. And their deaths indeed gave glory to the God of their hearts and lives. Now it is ours to imitate, to know that the deaths we experience, be they large or small, can be used by God to bring life.

---

1 Cf. Rom 5:19–21.
2 Jn 15:13.

Connections to Church Teaching and Tradition

- "The prophetic texts that directly concern the sending of the Holy Spirit are oracles by which God speaks to the heart of his people . . . According to these promises, at the 'end of time' the Lord's Spirit will renew the hearts of men, engraving a new law in them" (CCC, 715).

- "For theirs [the followers of Christ] is a community of people united in Christ and guided by the Holy Spirit in their pilgrimage towards the Father's kingdom, bearers of a message of salvation for all of humanity" (GS, 1).

- There are two prayers offered by Jesus in the accounts of the Gospel. The first is the Lord's Prayer. The second prayer occurs in the Gospel according to John just before the raising of Lazarus. Jesus' prayers teach us how to pray (CCC, 2603–2604).

Ezekiel 37:12–14 Ezekiel served on God's behalf during the time of the Judean exile in Babylon in 593 BC. Like prophets before and since, Ezekiel was both a taskmaster and cheerleader, demanding that the people turn from wayward lives and encouraging them to place their hope in the Lord. This reading conveys a message of hope as it interprets Ezekiel's famous vision of dried bones scattered throughout the plains (37:2–10). The Lord has told Ezekiel to "prophesy over these bones, and say to them: Dry bones, hear the word of the LORD! . . . I will bring spirit into you, that you may come to life" (Ezekiel 37:4–5). Even though the people live in exile like dead bones on the plain, God has not forgotten them. He promises that he will raise them from their graves of hopelessness and bring them "back to the land of Israel" (Ezekiel 37:12). He will breathe his spirit into them and give them new life. It is not a story intended as a direct commentary on the resurrection from the dead. It is instead a message of God's faithfulness to the people of Israel. Though bound in exile, they must know and remember that God will set them free.

Psalm 130:1–2, 3–4, 5–6, 7–8 (7) "With the Lord there is mercy, and fullness of redemption" (Psalm 130:7). The psalm's refrain holds the promise of redemption and new life for the people of Israel. But this psalm, considered one of seven penitential psalms, begins with the haunting lament: "Out of the depths I cry to you, O LORD; / LORD, hear my voice!" (Psalm 130:1). In the midst of this plaintive cry, the psalmist expresses a spirit of confident trust in the Lord's forgiveness. Vigilant and alert, the psalmist waits on the Lord, trusting that the Lord's generous mercy will bring redemption to his people. It is a statement of faith that we can make our own. No matter what chains restrict us, what illness or worry consumes us, or what bondage we endure, we can trust in the Lord to walk with us. We can trust the Lord to support and free us.

Romans 8:8–11 In this passage, Paul wants us to know that, through Christ's death and Resurrection, we now belong to God in a very special way. God has sent his Spirit to remain with us and help us. Paul begins by saying that the goal of human life is to please God. He cautions that self-absorption (living in the flesh) presents a big trap that drags us away from God. But Paul also reminds his readers that the Spirit dwelling within all believers is the source and strength for living faithful lives. When distracted by things of the world, God's Spirit will help the faithful focus on what matters most. When tempted to place trust in the things of this world, Christ will help the faithful remain fixed on grace. When selfishness threatens love, the Spirit of God will help the faithful to live for others. Paul promises that, with the Spirit, believers can live righteously and thus participate in divine life.

John 11:1–45 or 11:3–7, 17, 20–27, 33b–45 Can you imagine receiving a phone call with the news that your best friend who lives nearby is dying and thinking to yourself, "I'll just wait four days and see what happens"? Of course not. That is our clue that John's narrative about Jesus' friend Lazarus speaks not of the bonds of human friendship, but rather of the power of Jesus.

It helps to think of this Gospel passage as six acts of a dramatic tableau. The first act establishes the purpose of the drama: "This illness is . . . for the glory of God" (John 11:4). The second recounts Jesus' decision to return to Lazarus's hometown even though it is dangerous to do so. The third act puts Jesus and the disciples in Bethany, where they learn that Lazarus has been dead for four days, enough time for the rabbinic scholars to believe Lazarus's soul had left his body. The fourth act introduces Martha, who first chastises Jesus and then professes her belief that his power comes from God. Martha sends for Mary as the scene changes once more, and Mary goes to meet Jesus, with the crowd of mourners accompanying her. These are the people who will return to Jerusalem with news of this miracle, fueling the call to condemn Jesus of Nazareth.

The climax of the drama begins with Martha's final assertion of Lazarus's death (there will be a stench). Jesus calls on the Father ("that they may believe that you sent me," John 11:42) and then calls for Lazarus. As Lazarus emerges from the tomb, Jesus gives a final instruction: "Untie him and let him go" (John 11:45).

Connections to Church Teaching and Tradition

- " . . . Christ enjoyed in his human knowledge the fullness of understanding of the eternal plans he had come to reveal.[1] What he admitted to not knowing in this area, he elsewhere declared himself not sent to reveal[2]" (CCC, 474).

- " . . . the only Son of the Father . . . became incarnate; without losing his divine nature he has assumed human nature" (CCC, 479).

- "The Sixth Sunday [of Lent], on which Holy Week begins, is called 'Palm Sunday of the Passion of the Lord.' Holy Week is ordered to the commemoration of Christ's Passion, beginning with his Messianic entrance into Jerusalem" (UN, 30–31).

On no other Sunday of the year does Mass begin outside the nave, but on every Palm Sunday, parish priests and liturgists do their best to convince the Sunday assembly to form "a crowd" outside in order to create (and imitate) a procession with palms. It is difficult to break routine, and it is our Sunday Catholic routine to find a seat in the church and wait for Mass to begin. So consider the happy group who is prevented from taking their usual place and add to that the challenge of actually hearing the Word as it is proclaimed in an outdoor setting. The end result is that the import of the proclamation of the processional Gospel is often lost on the assembly. Nonetheless, or precisely because of this, we provide a word or two on these Gospel readings. In Year A of the Lectionary cycle, the Procession Gospel is from Matthew. In Year C, it is from Luke. In this year, Year B, either Mark or John's account of the Gospel may be proclaimed.

Mark 11:1-10   In Mark, as in the other Synoptic Gospels, the story begins in an exchange between Jesus and two of his disciples. He sends them into Jerusalem to find a colt in a particular place and bring it back to him. It is unclear if these instructions reflect Jesus' supernatural power or if they reflect arrangements he had made in advance, but the disciples do as they are told and find the colt in exactly the way Jesus predicted. They bring it to him and spread their cloaks, and Jesus sits atop the colt. The procession begins as people put branches from the fields along the road and Jesus rides among them, their thunderous greeting resounding: "Hosanna! / Blessed is he who comes in the name of the Lord." The blessing that springs from their lips is a prayer of the Hebrew tradition (Psalm 118:26) and would have been familiar to Jesus, as well. Describing this scene through the lens of the Resurrection, Mark notes that the prophecy begins to unfold in this moment: "Shout for joy . . . Jerusalem! / . . . See, your king shall come to you; / a just savior is he, . . . / riding on . . . a colt . . ." (Zechariah 9:9).

John 12:12–16   As is often the case, John's writing differs from the Synoptic accounts, and his version of this event has its own particular perspective. Unlike the other three accounts of the Gospel, there is no set of instructions to disciples sent in pursuit of a colt. Rather, the scene begins with a statement that a crowd has gathered because they heard Jesus was coming to town. The previous passage identifies this crowd as the group that had come to see this Jesus who had raised Lazarus from the dead. For John, it is the Lazarus miracle that sealed Jesus' fate among the chief priests. As a result, they wanted both Jesus and Lazarus dead. So the very adulation of the crowds on that first Palm Sunday (only John's account identifies the branches as palms) had the opposite effect on the authorities who feared his power and the loss of their own. Certainly not oblivious, but obedient to his mission, Jesus secures his own colt and enters the city. In contrast to the crowd's enthusiasm, one wonders what Jesus was thinking and feeling as he rode into the city. Was he overcome with dread? Did he realize that this was the beginning of the journey toward the Crucifixion? Did he feel alone in the midst of that great crowd of admirers? It is the stuff of prayerful reflection to ponder such questions. What we do know is that John also wrote with post-Resurrection intent, a benefit that the disciples did not have in the moment. It is John's intent to make clear that Jesus is the fulfillment of the prophecies of old (Zechariah 9:9; Zephaniah 3:16). For both evangelists, it is a very compelling moment in the Jesus story. It is the moment the prophecy begins to unfold.

---

1 Cf. Mk 8:31; 9:31; 10:33–34; 14:18–20, 26–30.
2 Cf. Mk 13:32; Acts 1:7.

Connections to Church Teaching and Tradition

- In Christ, we see a "new Adam," who, rather than refusing to obey God, remains obedient to God even to the point of his own death on the cross. Thus, Christ "makes amends superabundantly for the disobedience of Adam[1]" (CCC, 411).

- "[The Servant Songs of Isaiah] . . . show how [Jesus] will pour out the Holy Spirit to give life to the many: not as an outsider, but by embracing our 'form as slave'[2]" (CCC, 713).

- "In reality it is only in the mystery of the Word made flesh that the mystery of humanity truly becomes clear. For Adam . . . was a type of him who was to come,[3] Christ the Lord. Christ the new Adam, in the very revelation of the mystery of the Father and of his love, fully reveals humanity to itself and brings to light its very high calling" (GS, 22).

1 Cf. 1 Cor 15:21–22, 45; Phil 2:8; Rom 5:19–20.
2 Phil 2:7.
3 Cf. Rom 5:14; cf. Tertullian, *De carnis resurrectione*, 6: "For in all the form which was molded in the clay, Christ was in his thoughts as the man who was to be": PL 2, 802 (848); CSEL, 47, p. 33, lines 12–13.

Isaiah 50:4–7   We all have seen or perhaps joined the small groups of activists who stand silently at our roadsides or in front of local buildings, placards in hand, come rain or shine. They may go ignored, they may suffer abuse, but they do not waver. This is the kind of endurance that we hear of in this Sunday's First Reading. The single-minded persistence of prophets does not make them popular figures, and their speaking out often seems a lonely effort. Yet, compelled to speak the truth they know, they carry on. Today's Isaiah reading makes that clear: "The Lord God has given me / a well-trained tongue . . . / Morning after morning / he opens my ear . . . / I gave my back to those who beat me." This third servant song of Isaiah exhibits a kind of resignation and acceptance of his fate that will be echoed in today's Passion proclamation. Whether the prophet is describing his own lot in life or, as some scholars suggest, that of the community of Israel, the message is clear: adversity and difficulty do not deter a true disciple.

Psalm 22:8–9, 17–18, 19–20, 23–24 (2a)   It is difficult to hear the words of this psalm refrain and not associate them with the crucified Lord who speaks them in Mark's Gospel as we hear today (14:34) and in Matthew (27:46). But here the words belong to the psalmist whose cry of lament is filled with complaint and self pity. He is mocked, scoffed at, and insulted by those around him, who say, "He relied on the Lord; let him deliver him." Yet he cannot give up on the Lord. So complain he does (22:17–18, 19), but then reminds the Lord to ". . . be not far from me; / O my help, hasten to aid me" (22:19). These words speak of a familiar relationship that allows him to trust in the midst of great human misery. Fearful, angry, and in great need, the psalmist turns to the Lord, whose name he will ever praise and proclaim. So, too, we are encouraged to turn to the Lord in times of trouble, to speak our hearts, to complain, and to cry out with fear and loneliness. It is thus that the relationship between human and divine grows richer and deeper so that we can pray with the psalmist, ". . . hasten to aid me."

Philippians 2:6–11   Many would say that the Christ of this passage is the antitype of Adam, whose desire for power severely impaired his judgment and led him to disobedience. In contrast, Paul writes of Christ, who "though he was in the form of God," emptied himself and freely took on the form of a powerless slave. He who was immortal paradoxically took on human form, facing inevitable death. He was, in the words of this famous statement, obedient to the point of death. One can get lost in the poetry of the reading, but savoring each line makes it clear that the powerlessness and death of Christ reversed all human expectations. God, who named Jesus Christ as Lord, exalted the crucified Christ. And all of this happened to give glory to God. Paul's letter to the people of Philippi, intended to persuade them to imitate Christ's humility, is a model for us as well. In weakness, we find strength; in loneliness, we encounter God's grace. And in acceptance of all, we give glory to God.

Mark 14:1—15:47 or 15:1–39   Where does one begin to unpack the richness of Mark's account of the Passion? It is all this and more: an account of preparations for Jesus' death, his instructions to friends at a final meal, a betrayal in Gethsemane, a trial that cannot find cause to condemn him, and finally, a crucifixion that ultimately leads to life. One could focus on those who betrayed Jesus: Peter, Judas, James, and John, those passing by, the bystanders at the cross, and the revolutionaries crucified with him. Or one could reflect on those who stood with him: Simon the leper, the woman who anointed him with costly oil, Simon of Cyrene, Mary of Magdala, Salome, Mary the mother of the younger James and Joses, and the women who watched from a distance. Finally, one could preach an entire homily on the two who seem to have had a conversion of heart: the centurion who announced at Jesus' death, "Truly this man was the Son of God," and Joseph of Arimathea, a "distinguished member of the council" that had just condemned Jesus, who came forward to claim his broken body for burial. We wonder if we would have stood among the faithful women, spoken out bravely like the centurion, or condemned him out of fear like the bystanders. As this Holy Week begins, gratitude runs deep for those who remind us that hearts can be changed and action can be taken to make amends.

Triduum

Overview of Triduum

We begin the Triduum celebration with the Holy Thursday Eucharist. The scripture accounts we hear of the Last Supper address the heart of our faith. We believe the Eucharist is the body and blood of Christ, and that Jesus told us this and commanded us to eat and drink in remembrance of him. We are also called to engage in service to our neighbor, following Jesus' example of washing the disciples' feet.

On Good Friday, we journey with the Lord, the innocent servant of God, who has taken our sins upon himself as he walks the path to Calvary. At the end, Jesus says, "It is finished." It doesn't mean, "It is over." It means, "It is accomplished," or "It is perfected." He has completed the task he was given. He hands over his spirit.

We end on that most sacred night when we gather at the Easter Vigil to rejoice in the Good News of Christ's Resurrection. All of Lent has led to this pivotal night of the entire liturgical year; even Advent and Christmas prepared us for this night. Everything we celebrate for the next 50 days until Pentecost results from our belief that Jesus is risen from the dead.

First Readings

On Holy Thursday, the First Reading from Exodus is the remembrance of the Passover meal preceding the Exodus, and on Good Friday, the First Reading is from another one of the servant songs in Isaiah. At the Easter Vigil, there are seven Old Testament readings. Their proclamation makes the saving works of God throughout history present and real to us.

Responsorial Psalms

The psalms of Triduum are suitable to each of the three days. On Holy Thursday, the refrain used with Psalm 110, which comes from the New Testament's first letter of Paul to the Corinthians, speaks of the blessing cup as participation in the blood of Christ. Good Friday's Responsorial Psalm each year is Psalm 22, and its refrain contains the words of the Gospel according to Luke spoken by Jesus as he hangs on the cross: "Father, into your hands I commend my spirit" (23:46). The seven Responsorial Psalms of the Easter Vigil, which correspond to the seven Old Testament readings, abound with themes of the glorious nature of the earth and the Lord himself, the Lord's faithfulness to his people, the salvation the Lord offers, and the joyful nourishment that comes from following the Lord and his word.

Second Readings

On Holy Thursday, the Second Reading from Paul's first letter to the Corinthians gives the oldest written account of the Eucharist and reminds us of what we celebrate each time we gather to pray the eucharistic liturgy. On Good Friday, the Second Reading is from the letter to the Hebrews. This letter speaks of the high priesthood of Jesus Christ. In particular, Good Friday's passage emphasizes the sacrifice of the High Priest's own life as an offering for sin.

Gospel Readings

During the three days of Triduum, the Gospel readings present Jesus' example in his washing of the feet of his disciples on Holy Thursday, John's account of the Passion which emphasizes Jesus as Isaiah's servant of the Lord who is the one High Priest on Good Friday, and Mark's account of the women at the empty tomb and their conversation with the angel on the Easter Vigil.

Connections to Church Teaching and Tradition

- "At the last supper, on the night he was betrayed, our Savior instituted the eucharistic sacrifice of his body and blood" (SC, 47).

- "Moreover, the wondrous mystery of the Lord under the Eucharistic species . . . is proclaimed in the celebration of the Mass" (GIRM, 3).

- *"In order to make society more human, more worthy of the human person, love in social life—political, economic, and cultural—must be given renewed value, becoming the constant and highest norm for all activity"* (CSDC, 582).

- "In all of his life, Jesus presents himself as *our model*. He is 'the perfect man,'[1] who invites us to become his disciples and follow him" (CCC, 520).

Exodus 12:1–8, 11–14   In this reading, God commands Moses and Aaron to institute the feast that would be known as Passover. At the time, the community of Israel suffered bondage in Egypt. This passage comes in the midst of the description of the ten plagues through which the Pharaoh became convinced to free the people of Israel from their captivity.

Passover came to mean the meal and the date fixed on the Jewish calendar. For the first observance, a family slaughtered a lamb or a goat, eating the meat, but sprinkling the blood on the two door posts of each home. The blood became a sign for the angel responsible for the tenth plague to "pass over" the homes and spare the life of the firstborn. Ever since this event, the Jewish community has celebrated Passover each year.

Psalm 116:12–13, 15–16bc, 17–18 (see 1 Corinthians 10:16)   Several verses from a psalm of thanksgiving supply the Responsorial Psalm. The overall purpose of this psalm is to give thanks to God, but the Lectionary designates these verses because they especially fit the themes of Holy Thursday. The psalmist gives thanks by taking up "the cup of salvation" (116:13). The psalm proclaims, "Precious in the eyes of the LORD / is the death of his faithful ones" (116:15). These verses foreshadow the eucharistic cup that Jesus shared at the Last Supper, as well as his own death looming on Good Friday.

The refrain is lifted from the same epistle that gives us the Second Reading; it is not a verse from the psalm. As Christians experiencing anew the last days of Jesus, rooted in the meal traditions of our ancestors, we sing, "Our blessing-cup is a communion with the Blood of Christ." Normally, the Responsorial Psalm echoes a theme from the First Reading or the Gospel. This is a rare instance when it pertains to the Second Reading, which has not yet been proclaimed.

1 Corinthians 11:23–26   Saint Paul tells how Jesus instituted the Eucharist. With minor variations, this account also appears in Gospel accounts of Matthew, Mark, and Luke. Scholars tell us, however, that Paul wrote these epistles before the evangelists wrote their Gospel narratives. Therefore, this is the oldest account of what happened at the Last Supper, the version that lies closest to the years of Jesus' life.

At this point in his letter, Paul is probably responding to some specific questions from the Corinthians. Apparently, they had asked about the proper way to celebrate the Eucharist. Paul hands on to them what others had told him. Paul says that the supper took place on the night before Jesus was betrayed, that Jesus took bread, gave thanks, said, "This is my body that is for you," and commanded his followers to "do this in remembrance of me" (11:24). Jesus repeated this command upon taking up the cup, which he called "the new covenant in my blood" (11:25). Paul says we proclaim the death of the Lord until he comes whenever we "eat this bread and drink the cup" (11:26).

These words address the heart of Catholic faith. We believe that our Eucharist is the body and blood of Christ, that Jesus told us this, and that he commanded us to eat and drink in remembrance of him. This passage is the key that unlocks the meaning of Holy Thursday.

John 13:1–15   Jesus gives his followers a model of discipleship when he washes their feet. In John's account of the Gospel, at the Last Supper, when the reader expects to find the institution of the Eucharist that appears in Matthew, Mark, and Luke (the synoptic accounts of the Gospel), and even in Paul's First Letter to the Corinthians, it is not there. Instead, John gives a mystical interpretation of the Eucharist in the washing of the feet. Just as Paul's letter unlocks the meaning of Holy Thursday, John's narrative of the Gospel unlocks its implications. As Jesus stoops to wash feet, Simon Peter resists until Jesus warns him, "Unless I wash you, you will have no inheritance with me" (13:8). His statement probably alludes to Baptism, which became an initiation rite for all the followers of Jesus. Importantly, Jesus advises the disciples, "If I, therefore, the master and teacher, have washed your feet, you ought to wash one another's feet" (13:14). Whenever we engage in selfless, humble service of our neighbor, we follow the model that Jesus gave.

---

1 GS 38; cf. *Rom* 15:5; *Phil* 2:5.

Connections to Church Teaching and Tradition

- "This sacrifice of Christ is unique; it completes and surpasses all other sacrifices.[1] First, it is a gift from God the Father himself . . . . At the same time it is the offering of the Son of God made man, who in freedom and love offered his life to his Father through the Holy Spirit in reparation for our disobedience[2]" (CCC, 614).

- "The crucified Jesus has overcome divisions, re-establishing peace and reconciliation, precisely through the cross, 'thereby bringing the hostility to an end'[3] and bringing salvation of the Resurrection to mankind" (CSDC, 493).

- "Christ's stay in the tomb constitutes a real link between his passible state before Easter and his glorious and risen state today" (CCC, 625).

Isaiah 52:13—53:12 The Lectionary subtitles this passage the fourth oracle of the Servant of the Lord, but it is often called the fourth song of the Suffering Servant. Near the end of the book of the prophet Isaiah, we meet a figure called God's servant, who represents God but suffers greatly for the sins of others. The figure may have been a historical person at the time of Isaiah or a representation of the people of Israel. Christians read these four passages with a very specific insight: they prophesy Jesus, the servant of the Father, who suffered for our salvation.

The passage opens with a startling description of this servant. He was "spurned and avoided by people, / a man of suffering, accustomed to infirmity" (Isaiah 53:3). In the most moving verses, read with a lump in our throats, we realize that the servant's suffering should have been ours: "Yet it was our infirmities that he bore, / our sufferings that he endured . . . / We had all gone astray like sheep . . . / but the LORD laid upon him / the guilt of us all" (Isaiah 53:4, 6). On Good Friday, these verses come to fulfillment in the crucified Jesus.

Psalm 31:2, 6, 12–13, 15–16, 17, 25 (Luke 23:46) Psalm 31 appeals to God for rescue. The psalmist is desperate, "an object of reproach, / a laughingstock to my neighbors, and a dread to my friends" (Psalm 31:6). But the psalm does not dwell in despair. It trusts that God will redeem the one in distress. This singer is so convinced of salvation that the psalm concludes with an exhortation to the hearer: "Take courage and be stouthearted, / all you who hope in the LORD" (Psalm 31:25). The refrain for the psalm comes from the Gospel according to Luke. It was spoken by Jesus on the cross. Jesus, who must have known its words by heart, quotes Psalm 31 when he makes his appeal for rescue: "Father, into your hands I commend my spirit" (Luke 23:46).

Hebrews 4:14–16; 5:7–9 The sufferings of Jesus enabled him to sympathize with our weakness, making him a powerful mediator of mercy and grace. The Letter to the Hebrews explains the role of Jesus as the greatest of all high priests. This passage describes the events of Jesus' Passion: "In the days when Christ was in the flesh, he offered prayers and supplications with loud cries and tears to the one who was able to save him from death" (Hebrews 5:7). These words resemble the Gospel accounts of Jesus suffering his agony in the garden of Gethsemane. But the passage does not linger on Jesus' suffering. "[H]e was heard" (Hebrews 5:7). The Father, who could save Jesus from death, did, through his death and Resurrection.

John 18:1—19:42 This passage in the Gospel according to John is one of the most sublime testimonies to the glory of God. The narrative moves through several scenes, but it constantly teaches the meaning of Jesus' life, death, and Resurrection. We hear it each year on Good Friday.

Early on, John presents "Jesus, knowing everything that was going to happen to him" (John 18:4). Jesus is no innocent bystander. He is the omniscient God in control of the events that follow. Three times in the opening confrontation he says, "I AM," boldly claiming the name that God revealed to Moses in the burning bush. His enemies end up proclaiming the truth about Jesus in spite of themselves. Caiaphas had told the Jews that, "it was better that one man should die rather than the people" (John 18:14), fulfilling Isaiah's fourth oracle. Pilate, unable to get a straight answer from Jesus about his identity, asks, "What is truth?" (John 18:38). But it is Pilate who has an inscription made for the cross that calls Jesus, in three languages, the King of the Jews. The soldiers plait a crown from thorns and wrap Jesus' aching body in purple cloth, intending to mock, but handing over the signs of his kingship.

While the enemies of Jesus unintentionally speak the truth, his friend Peter intentionally denies Jesus three times. From the cross, Jesus takes matters into his own hands, entrusting his mother and the disciple whom he loved to each other. From these faithful disciples the Church will be born.

Before he dies, Jesus says, "It is finished" (John 19:30). That doesn't mean, "It's over." It means, "It is accomplished," or "It is perfected." He has completed the task he was given. He hands himself over to God. John has Jesus dying on the cross on preparation day, the day before Passover, so that we will see in the slaughtering of the Passover lambs a contemporaneous symbol of the one who gave his life that others might live.

---

1 Cf. *Heb* 10:10.
2 Cf. *Jn* 10:17–18; 15:13; *Heb* 9:14; 1 *Jn* 4:10.
3 *Eph* 2:16.

Connections to Church Teaching and Tradition

- "Creation is the foundation of 'all God's saving plans,' the 'beginning of the history of salvation'[1] that culminates in Christ" (CCC, 280).

- The revelation of creation is united with the revelation of the covenant. The truth of creation is expressed in the words of the prophets and the prayers and liturgy of the Church (CCC, 288).

- "A correct understanding of the environment prevents the utilitarian reduction of nature to a mere object to be manipulated and exploited" (CSDC, 463).

- "Christian hope . . . has its origin and model in the *hope of Abraham* . . . " (CCC, 1819).

Genesis 1:1—2:2 or 1:1, 26–31a *God created the heavens and the earth.* The entire Bible opens with an account of how and why all things came to be. The heavens and the earth exist by the will of God. At the time these verses were written, science had not advanced beyond a rudimentary understanding of biology and zoology. The Catholic Church does not expect members to believe in the literal words of this story. Genesis, however, defends a vital belief that we recite at the beginning of our weekly profession of faith: God is the Creator of heaven and earth.

The Easter Vigil is the pivotal night of the entire liturgical year. Lent has led up to this night; even Advent and Christmas have been preparing for this night. Everything we celebrate for the next 50 days results from our belief that Jesus is risen from the dead. Christ's Resurrection from the dead makes our own resurrection possible. As faithful followers, we believe that God created us, and that God will re-create us at the end of time. Our destiny is prefigured in the Baptisms we celebrate in Catholic churches throughout the world on this night. To reaffirm the foundation of our belief in a new creation, the Easter Vigil offers us the story of the first creation. Since God created everything out of nothing, it is not so hard to believe that God can re-create everything out of something.

Psalm 104:1–2, 5–6, 10, 12, 13–14, 24, 35 (30) *God created all things and wondrously renews what he has made.* Psalm 104 is a psalm of praise to God for the wonders of creation. It imagines the earth fixed upon a foundation, covered with the waters of the oceans, surmounted by waters enclosed in the sky, high above the tops of the mountains. Water, birds, cattle, and grain all supply the needs of humanity, the crown of God's creation.

It would be enough if this psalm praised God for the wonders of nature, but it does something more. It praises God for the way nature is renewed each year and from one generation to the next. The verse we use for the refrain calls upon God to send the Spirit to renew the face of the earth. This quality of creation, its inherent ability to renew, makes this psalm a perfect choice for the Easter Vigil. On this night, we praise God for the Resurrection of Christ, for the new life bestowed upon the newly baptized, and for the promise of eternal life revealed throughout God's word.

Psalm 33:4–5, 6–7, 12–13, 20, 22 (5b) *God is praised for the wonders of nature.* As an alternative to Psalm 104, a different psalm of creation may follow the First Reading: Psalm 33. It, too, praises God for the wonders of nature. This psalm envisions that the waters of the ocean are contained as in a flask, confined as though in cellars in the deep. Notably, Psalm 33 includes morality among God's creations. God's word is "upright," all God's works are "trustworthy," God loves "justice and right," and the earth is full of God's "kindness." Here is echoed the belief from the First Reading that what God made is "good." We praise God not just for the things that are, but for the goodness of things that are.

Christians interpret one of the verses of this psalm as a prophecy for our belief in the Holy Trinity: "By the word of the LORD the heavens were made; / by the breath of his mouth all their host." In one verse we find references to the Lord, the word, and the breath, images of the Triune God, preexisting all that is.

Genesis 22:1–18 or 22:1–2, 9a, 10–13, 15–18 *God puts Abraham to the test by asking him to sacrifice his son Isaac.* This is one of the most difficult passages in the entire Bible, and it is hard to hear it without feeling squeamish about the God who would make this request, Abraham who would fulfill it, and Isaac who would be the innocent victim. There is a happy ending, but not before the story turns our stomachs. Adding to the grim nature of God's request is that Abraham had no son until he was over one hundred years old. God had promised that Abraham's progeny would be as numberless as the sands on the shore of the sea, but the patriarch was not yet a father of one. Now, at incredibly advanced ages, Abraham and Sarah had become first-time parents, and this was the son God wanted him to sacrifice.

The story is retold at the Easter Vigil because it foreshadows the life of Jesus. He was an only child, as was Isaac. He was innocent, yet walked up a hill carrying on his shoulders the wood of his sacrifice. But there, the similarities end. Isaac was saved from death; Jesus was saved through death.

---

1 GCD 51.

Connections to Church Teaching and Tradition

■ "But because of the union which the person of the Son retained with his body, his was not a mortal corpse like others. . . . [This statement] can be said of Christ: . . . 'For you will not abandon my soul to Hades, nor let your Holy One see corruption'[1]" (CCC, 627).

■ "As proclaimed in the prayers for the blessing of the water, baptism is a cleansing water of rebirth[2] that makes us God's children born from on high" (RCIA, *Christian Initiation*, General Introduction, 5).

■ The words of the prophet Isaiah: "For the mountains may depart and the hills be removed, but my steadfast love shall not depart from you"[3] show the everlasting nature of God's love (CCC, 220).

■ "When she delves into her own mystery, the Church . . . discovers her link with the Jewish People,[4] 'the first to hear the Word of God'[5]" (CCC, 839).

Psalm 16:5, 8, 9–10, 11 (1) *God will reveal the path of life.* Those in the most difficult circumstances yearn for the confident trust of Psalm 16. When things go wrong, we turn to God for assistance. Sometimes we demand help; often we hope against hope for it. But Psalm 16 airs an aroma of confidence: "with [the Lord] at my right hand I shall not be disturbed." This psalm flows naturally from the story of Abraham and Isaac. Abraham, too, possessed the charism of confidence. He believed that, even in the most difficult circumstances, God would be faithful to the covenant. Psalm 16 fits the Easter Vigil because of its references to death and life. This psalm appears each week in Thursday's night prayer from the Liturgy of the Hours. Before going to bed, Christians pray these words, confident that wakefulness will follow sleep, and life will follow death.

Exodus 14:15—15:1 *God frees Israel from slavery through the waters of the Red Sea.* This paradigmatic reading from the Old Testament must be proclaimed in every celebration of the Easter Vigil. The liturgy encourages the use of all the Old Testament readings at the Vigil, but permits a smaller number for exceptional circumstances. This reading is never omitted because it roots our understanding of Baptism and resurrection.

In the story, Egypt has enslaved the Israelites, and God has appointed Moses to lead them from the clutch of the pharaoh into freedom. Their only route traverses the Red Sea, which parts for their passage, but returns to swallow up the pursuing forces of the pharaoh, his chariots, and his charioteers. On the other side of the waters, Israel is poised to enter the Promised Land.

The Exsultet and the blessing of baptismal water, which are both heard in the Vigil, point out the significance of this passage, and hence of this night. God freed Israel from its foes through water, and God will free the catechumens from the clutches of Satan and sin through the waters of Baptism. Set free from the Pharaoh, Israel entered the Promised Land. Set free from sin, the neophytes enter the life of grace as members of the Body of Christ. At the center of all this imagery is Jesus Christ, who was set free from death to life through the mercy of the Father.

Exodus 15:1–2, 3–4, 5–6, 17–18 (1b) *The people of Israel sing praise to God for granting them freedom.* The Responsory that follows this reading from Exodus also comes from Exodus. It is the very song that Israel sings upon reaching the dry shores beyond the Red Sea. It retells the events of this Passover night: the loss of the pharaoh's chariots in the Red Sea and the redemption of God's chosen people when God "planted them on the mountain" (Exodus 15:17). Throughout the song, the people give praise to God. It is the Lord who has covered himself in glory. Yes, they have experienced freedom from slavery, but they do not rejoice in their own accomplishment. They praise God.

Isaiah 54:5–14 *God reestablishes the covenant with Israel. The Maker of Israel becomes the Spouse of Israel.* This passage from the prophecy of Isaiah meets Israel at a very different moment in history. Many years have passed since the dramatic rescue of the Chosen People from the hand of Pharaoh. The people have dwelled in the Promised Land and have enjoyed too much prosperity. They have been lured away by other beliefs.

But God did not relinquish the covenant. Isaiah uses a startling image: "The LORD calls you back, / like a wife forsaken and grieved in spirit" (Isaiah 54:6). God says through Isaiah, "For a brief moment I abandoned you, / but with great tenderness I will take you back" (Isaiah 54:7). God compares this event to the days of Noah, when God swore never again to cover the earth with the waters of wrath. God is not angry with the Chosen People. God takes them home.

God still takes pity on us in our sin. Even those who have not yet been baptized are God's children. God is yearning to receive them with great tenderness as they enter the waters of Baptism. Catholics who have spent this Lenten season in repentance can hear these consoling words and take heart that their penance has been noticed, their prayers have been heard, and that God is anxious to renew with them the everlasting covenant of mercy.

---

1 *Acts* 2:26–27; cf. *Ps* 16:9–10.
2 Cf. *Titus* 3:5.
3 *Isa* 54:10; cf. 54:8.
4 Cf. NA 4.
5 *Roman Missal*, Good Friday 13: General Intercessions, VI.

Connections to Church Teaching and Tradition

- Jesus accepted his suffering and death freely. "The obedience of Jesus has transformed the curse of death into a blessing[1]" (CCC, 1009).

- "By its very nature water cannot be treated as just another commodity among many, and it must be used rationally and in solidarity with others" (CSDC, 485).

- "All evangelizing activity is understood as promoting communion with Jesus Christ. Starting with the 'initial'[2] conversion of a person to the Lord, moved by the Holy Spirit through the primary proclamation of the Gospel, catechesis seeks to solidify and mature this first adherence" (GDC, 80).

Psalm 30:2, 4, 5–6, 11–12, 13 (2a) *In thanksgiving, we sing praise to God.* We thank God for release from a serious threat, not for just any unexpected gift. The writer of Psalm 30 experienced death threats from enemies. Death seemed near, but somehow God rescued the singer "from among those going down into the pit" (Psalm 30:4). At the time, it seemed as though there was no way out, but in retrospect, it seems as though God's anger lasted "but a moment" and his good will lasts "a lifetime" (Psalm 30:6). This psalm takes up the main theme of the Easter Vigil: the triumphant Passion of our Lord Jesus Christ. He could have sung this psalm himself: "O LORD, you brought me up from the netherworld . . . / At nightfall, weeping enters in, / but with the dawn, rejoicing" (Psalm 30:4, 6). All the participants in the Easter Vigil can sing this along with Christ. Those to be baptized are to be lifted from their former way of life to membership in the body of Christ. Those who have already been baptized have expressed sorrow for their sins and experienced the joy of God's mercy. With Christ, we are all brought up from the netherworld on this night that shines more brightly than the dawn.

Isaiah 55:1–11 *God invites us to life-giving water, renews the covenant, and shows the power of his word.* Isaiah offers a second prophecy for our reflection. It extends again to a people who had drifted from the covenant, but who discover that God's mercies are without end. The prophecy opens with an invitation to drink water, a symbol that will occupy center stage at the Easter Vigil in the next part of the ceremony. We cannot live without water, and our relationship with God slakes our spiritual thirst. The Lord is near, and Isaiah urges us to call upon him, forsaking the ways of sin. The risen Christ is very near to all who seek him. Catechumens have left the desert of life-without-Christ, and the faithful have abandoned their sins through the penance of Lent. The waters of the covenant will renew us. Strengthening the image of water, God speaks through Isaiah about the effectiveness of rain and snow. They come down from the heavens and do not return there "till they have watered the earth, / making it fertile and fruitful." God's word does that in our lives. It comes to us like living water, and it produces the effect for which it was sent.

Isaiah 12:2–3, 4, 5–6 (3) *With joy, we draw water at the fountain of salvation. We sing praise to God.* Isaiah supplies not just the two previous readings, but also the Responsory for the second one. Like the passage from Exodus that follows the Third Reading, this canticle resembles the structure and content of a psalm, but it exists in another book of the Bible. The Lectionary offers us this passage to follow the previous reading because of the similarity in the way it applies the image of water, and because it comes from the same biblical book.

The canticle rings forth with praise of God. The singer proclaims, "I am confident and unafraid" (Isaiah 12:2). God is the source of salvation, just as a fountain is the source of life-giving water. On this Easter night, preparing for the celebration of Baptism, we are reminded of all that God promises, and how confidently we stand in faith.

Baruch 3:9–15, 32—4:4 *To know wisdom is to know God.* Changing the tone of the evening, the prophet Baruch chides Israel for forsaking the fountain of wisdom. He ascribes the troubles of Israel to the people's infidelity to the covenant. The solution? "Learn where prudence is, / where strength, where understanding" (Baruch 3:14). To know wisdom is to know God. Just as creation unveils the wisdom of God, so to know the wisdom of God is to draw near to our Maker. On this wondrous night, we grasp the wisdom of God's plan. The plan existed from the beginning of creation, but it was revealed to human beings slowly, through history. At the time of Baruch's prophecy, people still did not fully comprehend that Jesus would reveal the resurrection. Yet even without complete knowledge, people were able to perceive the wisdom of God in imperfect ways.

Hearing this reading, and standing on the other historical shore from the Passion of Christ, we praise God for the gift of revelation made plain to us. Those who are approaching the waters of Baptism have come to the same insight. They put their faith in the Resurrection of Christ, and they participate in his life because of the interior wisdom they have received.

---

1 Cf. *Rom* 5:19–21.
2 AG 13b.

Connections to Church Teaching and Tradition

- "He who makes the profession of faith takes on responsibilities that not infrequently provoke persecution" (GDC, 83).

- "Baptism is, therefore, above all, the sacrament of that faith by which, enlightened by the grace of the Holy Spirit, we respond to the Gospel of Christ" (RCIA, *Christian Initiation*, General Introduction, 3).

- "Baptism, the cleansing with water by the power of the living word,[1] washes away every stain of sin, original and personal, makes us sharers in God's own life[2] and his adopted children"[3] (RCIA, *Christian Initiation*, General Introduction, 5).

- "It is desirable that the liturgy of Lent and Paschal time should be restored in such a way that it will serve to prepare the hearts of the catechumens for the celebration of the Paschal Mystery, at whose solemn ceremonies they are reborn to Christ in baptism" (AG, 14).

1 Cf. *Eph* 5:26.
2 Cf. *2 Pet* 1:4.
3 Cf. *Rom* 8:15; *Gal* 4:5.

Psalm 19:8, 9, 10, 11 (John 6:68c)   *The Lord has the words of everlasting life.* Psalm 19 has two parts, and these verses come from the section that revels in the beauty of God's word. It resembles the longest psalm in the Bible, 119, which meditates line by line on the word of God through a variety of synonyms and attributes. These verses of Psalm 19 praise the "law," "decree," "precepts," "command," and "ordinances" of the Lord, which rejoice the heart and enlighten the eye. This psalm builds upon the theme of wisdom from the previous reading. We come to know God through meditation on his decrees. God revealed these to us in the covenant, so they detail the wisdom that exudes from the very being of God. For Christians, Jesus Christ is the perfect expression of God's wisdom. He is God's wisdom. He is the Word made flesh. For this reason, the Lectionary gives us a refrain taken from the Gospel according to John, not from the psalm itself. The verse is spoken by Peter after Jesus has given the discourse on the bread of life. The teaching revealed the very reason Jesus came, to offer us eternal life through the eating of his body and drinking of his blood. Many of those who heard him speak these words, however, turned away. Jesus looked fearfully at his closest followers and asked if they, too, were going to leave him now. Peter said no, "Lord, you have the words of everlasting life" (John 6:68c). That statement of faith becomes the refrain we sing to a psalm that praises the wisdom of God. It also foreshadows the initiation of those who will share Holy Communion for the first time at this Mass.

Ezekiel 36:16–17a, 18–28   *God sprinkles clean water upon the chosen people and gives them a new heart.* The prophet Ezekiel addresses a people who had experienced exile from their homeland because of their infidelity, but learned now that God had not abandoned them. As a sign of renewing the eternal covenant, God offered the people cleansing and renewal through the gift of a new spirit. Israel's sin was not covered up, but it was forgiven, and the people grew stronger in faith.

On a night when the waters of Baptism contain the symbolism of new life, this passage prophesies all that Christianity has to offer. Those who have failed to love God as they should are cleansed from all sin. Some are baptized and others will renew their baptismal covenant through promises and holy water. All will experience the gift of the new spirit that God places in the heart of believers. God never goes back on the covenant; it is eternal. Even though we sometimes fail to keep the covenant, God always gives us the opportunity to renew it.

Psalm 42:3, 5; 43:3, 4 (42:2)   *Our souls thirst for God like a deer that longs for running streams.* The Lectionary offers three possible Responsories to the Seventh Reading. The first, from Psalm 42, is sung whenever Baptism will be celebrated at the Vigil.

The psalm asks God for the gift of God's light and fidelity, so that those who receive it may approach the dwelling place of God, and specifically the altar of God. These verses eloquently prophesy the journey of the catechumens, who thirst for the waters of Baptism, and attain it through the light and fidelity that God extends to new believers through the covenant. Having been refreshed by the waters of Baptism, the neophytes come to the altar of God, where they participate in Holy Communion, the intimate union that makes them fully the body of Christ, a dwelling place for God most high.

Isaiah 12:2–3, 4bcd, 5–6 (3)   *In joy we draw water from the springs of salvation.* In this song of praise, we thank God for all that he has accomplished. This is exactly the Responsory that follows the Fifth Reading of the Easter Vigil. It is offered again as one of the alternatives following the Seventh Reading. In practice, it could logically be sung here whenever the seven readings are abbreviated and the Fifth Reading has been eliminated. But the Responsory may be used twice on the same night.

Here, the English Lectionary recommends it as one of the options if Baptism is not celebrated during the Vigil. This may seem puzzling because the image of water is so strong at the beginning of these verses. In fact, the liturgical books are not consistent on this point. The *Ordo Lectionum Missae* actually recommends this psalm, not the previous one, when Baptism is to be celebrated.

Jesus Is Risen from the Dead

Connections to Church Teaching and Tradition

- Through the liturgy of the Easter Vigil, the Church hears and relives the events of salvation history. "But this also demands that catechesis help the faithful to open themselves to this spiritual understanding of the economy of salvation as the Church's liturgy reveals it and enables us to live it" (CCC, 1095).

- "To accomplish so great a work Christ is always present in his church, especially in liturgical celebrations. . . . He is present in his word since it is he himself who speaks when the holy scriptures are read in church" (SC, 7).

- "The Resurrection of Jesus is the crowning truth of our faith in Christ . . ." (CCC, 638).

Psalm 51:12–13, 14–15, 18–19 (12a)   *We ask God to create within us a clean heart.* Tradition calls 7 of the 150 psalms penitential. This one is perhaps the greatest of them. It expresses the remorse we feel after sinning and our cries for forgiveness. These particular verses, coming at the end of the psalm, focus on renewal. Although we have sung this text often during Lent, we may complete its sentiments at the Vigil, when we put our sinful ways behind us and seek a clean heart. These verses work well after the passage from Ezekiel, which employs a similar image—a new heart. In reestablishing the covenant with us, God remakes us. We reenter the covenant not as the same people, but as those who have known sin, repented of it, received forgiveness, and resolved not to sin again. This psalm is recommended for an Easter Vigil that does not include Baptism. It more nearly suits the faithful Christians coming for renewal after observing a rigorous Lent.

Romans 6:3–11   *Christ has been raised from the dead.* Through Baptism, we enter the mystery of his death and Resurrection. After hearing and singing up to fourteen passages from the Old Testament (seven readings and seven responsories), the New Testament makes its bright appearance. We hear Paul say, "We know that Christ, raised from the dead, dies no more; death no longer has power over him" (Romans 6:9). This is the first scriptural proclamation from tonight that Jesus is risen. Paul compares the Resurrection of Christ and Baptism. This passage underscores our liturgical practice of celebrating Baptism at the Easter Vigil. It also affirms our preference for baptizing infants on any Sunday, our weekly observance of the Resurrection.

Psalm 118:1–2, 16–17, 22–23   *We give thanks to God, whose mercy endures forever.* This psalm gives many reasons for thanksgiving. It opens with the simple assertion that the Lord is good, and that "his mercy endures forever" (Psalm 118:1). It then announces the power and deeds of God's right hand. Two of the verses prophesy the meaning of this Easter night. You can imagine Jesus singing this psalm: "I shall not die, but live, / and declare the works of the LORD" (Psalm 118:17). Christians can affirm, "The stone which the builders rejected / has become the cornerstone" (Psalm 118:22). His enemies thought they had put Jesus to death, but he has become the cornerstone of life.

The refrain for this psalm is a triple alleluia. It doubles as the Gospel acclamation. No words can fully express the joy of this night, so we resort to a Hebrew acclamation that needs no translation: Alleluia! Throughout Lent, we have abstained from singing that word. We have introduced the Gospel with a different acclamation of praise. But now, the word returns. Our "fasting" from the alleluia is over. We rejoice that Christ is risen.

Mark 16:1–7   *Jesus is risen from the dead.* All four accounts of the Gospel message reach a climax to sound this chorus. Christ is risen! Mark opens his report of the Resurrection with a rather pedestrian statement: the women had gone shopping. The stores would have been closed for the Sabbath, but on the next day, the women bought the spices they needed to anoint Jesus. This detail reveals that they had no clue what awaited them at the tomb. To report the rising of Jesus, Mark carefully notes the rising of the sun. To help interpret the newness of the Resurrection, he says that it is the first day of the week.

The ordinariness of the story returns. The women see a large stone and wonder who will roll it back for them. Then the women are amazed to see a young man clothed in white. They hear the most important news that has ever been spoken: "[Jesus] has been raised; he is not here." They see the empty tomb. They receive the commission to report this good news. The young man instructs them to tell the disciples—and Peter. Apparently, Peter was going to need a special message because of his misbehavior and his doubts, but also because of his leadership among those who would hear the word. Each of us needs that from time to time. We always rely on the message of those who have received a deeper insight into their faith.

Easter

Overview of Easter

Outside of Ordinary Time, Easter is the longest season in the liturgical year. The 50 days from Easter Sunday until Pentecost Sunday are designated as weeks *of,* not *after,* Easter. Appropriately, all of the Lectionary readings come from the New Testament, with emphasis on the Acts of the Apostles and the Gospel according to John. The First Letter of John provides the Second Reading for each of these Sundays.

The prefaces to the Eucharistic Prayer offer special insight into the emphases of the season, just as they do in other seasons. During Easter we are reminded that Christ's Resurrection is ours as well, that a new age has dawned, and that the joy of this season renews the whole world. On Pentecost Sunday, the preface proclaims that in sending the Spirit, God has brought the Paschal Mystery to completion. No other season brims with such life and promise.

First Readings

The First Readings offer select scenes from the Acts of the Apostles for our Easter reflection. We begin on Easter Sunday with Peter summarizing the mission, death, and Resurrection of Jesus. Next, on the Second Sunday of Easter, we hear about the unity of the community formed in Jesus' name. Then, Peter preaches conversion on the Third Sunday, and on the Fourth Sunday he explains that a miracle he worked was performed in Jesus' name. On the Fifth Sunday we hear of Paul's entrance into the community, and then on the Sixth Sunday we learn of Peter's acceptance of the Gentiles. After the solemnity of the Ascension of the Lord, we hear the account of the Pentecost event. In sum, the readings outline the growth of the early Church under the influence of the Spirit.

Responsorial Psalms

An optional communal response to every psalm of this season is "Alleluia," which could also summarize the message and mood of these psalms. Three times we pray from Psalm 118 (Easter Sunday, Second Sunday of Easter, Fourth Sunday of Easter), repeating its paschal acclamation: "The stone which the builders rejected / has become the cornerstone" (118:22). Three additional themes dominate the Easter psalms: the plea for God's light and spirit, the proclamation that God's power has been shown to the nations, and joy in Christ's ascension to the heavenly throne. They all offer variations on the theme expressed in the response to the Easter psalm: "Give thanks to the LORD, for he is good, / for his mercy endures forever" (118:1).

Second Readings

The majority of the Second Readings come from the First Letter of John. Taken all together, there are, as in the psalms, some extended themes. True to John, the most often repeated theme is love: the love of God for humanity, the love we should show to one another, and, most spectacular of all, the effect of God's love, as we become children of God who will be like Christ in glory. Paul takes up that latter theme, teaching that we who have the firstfruits of the Spirit can live by the Spirit and will appear with Christ in glory. Together, the readings promise unimaginable union with God.

Gospel Readings

The readings for the Easter season draw heavily on the Gospel according to John. On Easter Sunday, we journey once again with Mary and then Peter and the disciple to the inexplicably empty tomb, reminding us that even for those of us who know how the events progressed, Easter calls us to contemplate mystery. The Gospel reading on the Second Sunday of Easter depicts the risen Lord with his gift of peace and mission of

FOUNDATIONS FOR PREACHING AND TEACHING © 2011 Liturgy Training Publications.

reconciliation. On the Third Sunday of Easter, we hear another account of Christ's appearance to the disciples. This time, he eats with them and reminds them of the mission to preach forgiveness to all the world.

The rest of the readings from the Gospel according to John portray Christ's love for his people. He is the Good Shepherd who lays down his life for them, the true vine that gives life to all who remain with him. He is the one who chose them and wants them to inhabit his love. These weeks celebrate not only Christ's Resurrection, but its historical consequences, especially the human vocation to become like him in union with God.

Good News Cannot Be Contained!

Connections to Church Teaching and Tradition

■ "As he had been sent by the Father, the Son himself sent the apostles,[1] saying, 'Go therefore and make disciples of all nations, baptizing them in the name of the Father, and of the Son, and of the holy Spirit. . .'[2]" (LG, 17).

■ "Jesus invests the evangelization which he enjoins on the apostles with a universality which knows no frontiers: 'Go into all the world and preach the gospel to the whole creation.'[3] The twelve apostles and the first generations of Christians . . . developed from it a program of action" (EN, 49).

■ The Church is called to proclaim the Paschal Mystery of Christ's death and Resurrection to the whole world (CCC, 571).

Acts 10:34a, 37–43 On this Easter morning, we are invited to place ourselves among the people of the household of Cornelius as they gathered to hear Simon Peter talk about the ministry of Jesus. Both of these men—Peter and Cornelius—received a divinely inspired vision that led them to one another. They must have recognized the gift of that grace because it was extremely unlikely that a Jew (Peter) would be a guest in a Gentile home. What they heard remains ours today as we hear the First Reading: Jesus of Nazareth, anointed by God with the Holy Spirit, healed many people. He was put to death but was raised by God. We have seen him and have eaten with him. He has sent us to preach this Good News. And this is the truth we speak to you today: "Everyone who believes in him will receive forgiveness of sins through his name." Peter took a very bold step that day to broaden the mission of the followers of Jesus. Because of the vision he received, Peter had come to believe that all people were to be included in the great work of preaching the story of Jesus Christ. The Good News could not and should not be contained, for it is meant for all people for all time.

Psalm 118:1–2, 16–17, 22–23 (24) This psalm of thanksgiving was the accompaniment for a procession to the temple to celebrate a victory. The psalmist gives voice to the great joy of the people, expressing their overwhelming gratitude for the faithfulness of the Lord. That joy spills out in their song. The psalmist might well have been rejoicing because a once-defeated king later rose to power. But the early Christian community heard in these words vindication that relieved the sting of Jesus' rejection and execution. For those who have been rejected for living as Jesus did—for feeding the hungry, living simply, championing the marginalized, loving unconditionally, and pursuing the cause of peace—the words help stay the course. For one day all will come to know that those rejected in God's name are the cornerstones of faith. On that day, all people will sing with the psalmist: "This is the day the Lord has made; / let us rejoice and be glad."

Colossians 3:1–4 The Colossians reading urges us to die to self in order to focus on the Lord, for having been baptized in Christ, the concerns of the world should diminish in meaning. For those who are caught up in the things of this world, however, this reading is an invitation to re-order our lives. On the day of glory, the worldly things that can consume human hearts will have no significance.

1 Corinthians 5:6b–8 Some have called this Corinthians reading the first Easter sermon. Leading up to this passage, Paul has chastised the people for their wicked behavior. Now he makes it clear that to honor the Paschal sacrifice and live as the new life demands, Christians have a responsibility to one another to live with sincerity and truth.

Sequence: *Victimae Paschali Laudes* This Sunday, the Church sings a sequence—an ancient, poetic song that precedes the singing of the Gospel acclamation. The Easter Sequence, *Victimae paschali laudes*, is a song of praise to the Paschal Victim that also reflects the Gospel account of Mary's encounter with the risen Lord.

John 20:1–9 Mary Magdalene is the first person at the tomb in all four Gospel accounts. In the Synoptic accounts, she brings oil to anoint the body of the Lord. In John's account of the Gospel, the anointing has already taken place, but Mary is still the first person on record to go to the tomb. She is the messenger who then brings Peter and the Beloved Disciple to see that the stone has been moved. There are no angels in this Gospel to suggest that a body has inexplicably been raised. There are only cloths that lay on the ground, the head cloth arranged in a separate place, all to indicate that this is not the scene of a robbery. In those first moments, it is not clear what it all means, and only the Beloved Disciple "sees and believes." Time and future appearances of the Lord will add believers to the community. As we gather on this Easter day, we remember and celebrate that Jesus is indeed risen and walks among us still. Yet, it is only with eyes of faith that we recognize him—in the breaking of bread, in the preaching of his Word, and in the presence of his people gathered in his name.

---

1 Cf. Jn 20:21.
2 Mt 28:19–20.
3 Mk 16, 15.

Come to Believe

Connections to Church Teaching and Tradition

- "According to the Christian message, therefore, our relationship to our neighbor is bound up with our relationship to God; our response to the love of God, saving us through Christ, is shown to be effective in his love and service of people. Christian love of neighbor and justice cannot be separated. . . . Because every person is truly a visible image of the invisible God and a sibling of Christ, the Christian finds in every person God himself and God's absolute demand for justice and love" (JM, 34).

- The apostles had faith in the Resurrection because of their direct interactions with the resurrected Christ (CCC, 644).

- "'Everything the true Christian has is to be regarded as a good possessed in common with everyone else,'[1] . . . A Christian is a steward of the Lord's goods[2]" (CCC, 952).

Acts 4:32–35   "The community of believers was of one mind and heart . . . . they had everything in common." These scriptures describe the Christian community of two thousand years ago. We can also see it replicated in recent times in groups such as the Jesuit Volunteer Corps communities. Living on minuscule monthly stipends, these mostly young adults share all things in common, including prayer. House duties are divided. Decisions about the house budget are made together. When the grocery bill exceeds that budget, they decide as a group what must be sacrificed. All food is held in common; they cook and eat together. They are communities in their most basic, difficult, and joyous sense. They are by no means perfect, as perhaps the first one wasn't perfect, either. But groups like these share in the work of that early community who "bore witness to the resurrection of the Lord Jesus." They are present day witnesses who call us to believe more deeply by their commitment in faith to one another and to the greater good.

Psalm 118:2–4, 13–15, 22–24 (1)   Some verses from Easter Sunday's Psalm 118 are repeated in today's liturgy, including the proverb, "The stone which the builder rejected . . . ." But this week, we hear the reason for this psalm's expressed gratitude: "I was hard pressed and was falling, / but the LORD helped me" (118:13). For most of us when we fall, our enemies are the temptations of our hearts, not neighboring nations. Hard pressed by life's complex challenges, we fail to resist temptations, hold our tongues, manage our egos, or seek the greater common good. Yet if we steadfastly ask for God's help and try and try again to imitate God's mercy, we learn that God is there when we fall. His strength will sustain us, giving us courage when afraid, strength when weary of our own sinfulness, and persistence to start anew each day.

1 John 5:1–6   We often forget that the early Church was a work in progress. It didn't just pop up one day with doctrine intact. But with the help of the Spirit, belief gradually developed about the divinity of Jesus the Christ, his death and Resurrection, and the promise of eternal life. This second reading provides a glimpse of this unfolding process in the early Johannine community. Countering various challenges to faith, John establishes that Jesus is indeed begotten of the father. Faith demands acceptance of Jesus as the Son of God, and those who come to believe must live accordingly. "For the love of God is this, that we keep his commandments." The complexity of the passage diminishes when the preceding verses (4:20–21) identify the commandment: "This is the commandment we have from him: whoever loves God must also love his brother." Here is what it means to live accordingly. Here is the familiar truth of faith. Here is the means of eternal life, the blueprint for victory that is meant to conquer the world. Love God and love one another.

John 20:19–31   John makes a wonderful statement with the last sentence this Sunday's Gospel. It states the purpose for his entire account: "These are written that you may come to believe" (20:31). Although it is not clear that the author was an eyewitness, it is clear that whoever wrote it possessed an earnest desire to keep a record of Jesus' appearances for generations to come. This is a Jewish author who writes that the disciples hid in fear of those Jews who had killed Jesus. Locked in a room, huddled together, they recognize Jesus in their midst and hear his greeting of peace. It is peace that forgives all things and commissions them to continue his work. He breathes on them and says, "Receive the Holy Spirit." It is a scene reminiscent of the Genesis account of God's breath giving Adam new life. Now, Jesus is the source of new life for all people. Thomas misses this appearance and makes it clear that he doesn't believe any of it. This gives the evangelist the opportunity to write of a second appearance and provide more evidence for posterity. Jesus returns a week later and shows Thomas his wounds, proving he is the crucified one.

We are the recipients of the legacy of that long-ago evangelist who insisted that "these are written that you may come to believe." His divinely inspired testimony, echoing through the years, calls us here today. It calls us to believe more deeply and live more faithfully. Thus, may we be signs of God's mercy as we continue to tell the story with the witness of our lives.

---

1 *Roman Catechism* I, 10, 27.
2 Cf. Lk 16:1, 3.

Connections to Church Teaching and Tradition

- "Peace is not merely the absence of war . . . .Peace is the work of justice and the effect of charity[1]" (CCC, 2304).

- "Earthly peace is the image and fruit of the peace of Christ, the messianic 'Prince of Peace'[2]" (CCC, 2305).

- "The church, in preaching the Gospel to everyone and dispensing the treasures of grace in accordance with its divine mission, makes a contribution to the consolidation of peace over the whole world and helps to strengthen the foundations of communion among people and nations" (GS, 89).

Acts 3:13–15, 17–19   It is fitting that we listen to this sermon of Peter just after we have celebrated Christ's Resurrection. Here, Peter is preaching a strong sermon in which he reviews with his listeners how the people freed Barabbas, a murderer, and had Jesus put to death. This injustice was done even though the God of Abraham, Isaac, and Jacob had glorified Jesus. The audience to whom he is preaching includes both some who participated and some people from the general population. Peter declares that the people "denied the Holy and Righteous One" (3:14) but God raised him from the dead. Peter's accusations in this sermon are strong, but true. Jesus suffered because of ungodly elements such as human ignorance, ruthlessness, selfishness, and sinfulness. Peter does, however, agree that they did this terrible deed out of ignorance. Yet his goal here is to call everyone to repentance and conversion. Nothing is too great to be forgiven. God will forgive, he proclaims, if you reform your lives and turn to God.

Psalm 4:2, 4, 7–8, 9 (7a)   Psalm 4 is linked closely to Psalm 3, as an individual lament with the theme of trust in the Lord. This psalm paints a picture of a wonderful God—a God who listens to us, hears our cries, and relieves our distress. Our God is a God who smiles with love on us even though we continue to need to be called to repentance. How fitting and comforting it is to be reminded of this gracious and protecting God just after the strong accusations we just heard from Peter. We can rejoice knowing that this is how God relates to us today, too. The Lord will heal us and will answer us when we call.

1 John 2:1–5a   The same message continues in this passage from 1 John. The original context of these particular verses seems to have been initiation into the Christian community. During the initiation ceremony, each person was to make a public confession of his or her sinfulness. Following that, they were reminded that Christ, whose death and Resurrection were expiation for all sins, is our advocate. In this context, as elsewhere, the community is reminded that "to know [God] is to keep his commandments" (2:3). What a timeless message! It was true for the early Christians and is true for us today: One's behavior must reflect his or her knowledge of God. To know Christ is to be obedient to his commands. Knowledge of God cannot be separated from ethical conduct. This is the price of the privilege of being called a follower of Christ.

Luke 24:35–48   The first words out of Jesus' mouth when he appears to the disciples are "Peace be with you." This *shalom* is the greeting Jesus had taught the disciples to say whenever they entered a house. These are words that he had spoken over and over during his public life, as peace is at the heart of his message. This greeting epitomizes what all the followers of Christ are to live by. Gathered as they were, listening to the report of the disciples on the way to Emmaus, the disciples were startled and indeed terrified when Jesus suddenly appeared in their midst. Once he showed them proof that it was he, the disciples' terror turned to incredulous joy. In this apparition, Jesus does three things that are integral to his life: he greeted them with peace, he once again shared a meal, and he taught them. He asked for food and ate it in front of them, we are told. Eating together was significant throughout Jesus' life on earth, and he shared meals many times, including at the Last Supper. Here, again, he is showing us the importance of shared meals. Then he begins to teach. He uses the Law of Moses to emphasize that he is the Messiah. He points out specifically how what the prophets and psalms taught had now been fulfilled in him. The apostles were able to understand because they opened their hearts and minds to his message. Everything about this Gospel makes his message so clear. Christ came to fulfill the law, and now that he has risen, those who follow him are to continue preaching his message, especially his message of peace.

---

1 Cf. Isa 32:17; cf. GS 78 §§ 1–2.
2 Isa 9:5.

Connections to Church Teaching and Tradition

- "[God] has placed in man a longing for truth and goodness that only he can satisfy" (CCC, 2002).

- "Everyone is obliged to follow this law, which makes itself heard in conscience and is fulfilled in the love of God and of neighbor. Living a moral life bears witness to the dignity of the person" (CCC, 1706).

- "Finally, the laity should visualize their lives with charity and, to the extent of each person's capability, give concrete expression to it in works" (AA, 16).

Acts 4:8–12   Peter and John were preaching to the people and proclaiming that in Jesus there is resurrection of the dead. This claim disturbed the authorities, who then had Peter and John arrested and taken into custody. Since it was evening, however, they waited until the next day to meet and interrogate them. The following day, Peter and John were made to stand in the midst of the leaders and defend their words. This event was the beginning of formal opposition to their profession that Jesus was the one for whom they had all been waiting. This opposition ultimately led them to proclaim the Good News to the Gentiles as well. While the Jewish leaders were questioning them, Peter was so filled with the Holy Spirit that he didn't hesitate to name Jesus as the one in whose name the healing had taken place. Furthermore, he quotes Psalm 17 when he tells them that the stone they rejected (Jesus) has become the cornerstone. This accusation no doubt further alienated the Jewish leaders.

Psalm 118:1, 8–9, 21–23, 26, 28, 29 (22)   The cornerstone image is continued here in this thanksgiving song. The response, "The stone rejected by the builders has become the cornerstone," refers to an ancient proverb. It held that a piece of stone which the builders thought was too poor to be put in a prominent place in the structure is not thrown away. In fact, it is actually given the most prominent and significant place as the cornerstone of the entire structure. Here, the community reminds itself that trust in the Lord is more important than trust in men, even princes. Because the Lord is good and is merciful, whoever comes in the Lord's name is blessed.

1 John 3:1–2   In this brief section from 1 John, we can almost feel the writer's wonder and enthusiasm. "See what love the Father has bestowed on us," he writes (3:1). Believers are worthy of being called children of God, and even more is going to be revealed to them. They shall actually become like him when the time of revelation comes. They will see God as he truly is. Our faith tells us that this promise is made to all believers. We, too, are the children—the sons and daughters—of God.

John 10:11–18   This Sunday's Gospel, the story of the Good Shepherd, is one that is quite familiar. It is rich with meaning and, like all scripture readings, is both comforting and challenging. In this context, good means noble or ideal, and not just good at being a shepherd. It refers to the bond, the connection that is so strong that, unlike bad shepherds who steal or even eat some of the sheep, Jesus the Good Shepherd actually dies for his sheep. This image of Jesus dying for his sheep was a common and often-used theme in the early Church. The shepherd knows his sheep, and Jesus knows his followers. They are recognizable because they try to imitate the qualities of the good shepherd. They watch out for each other, care for those in need, protect the vulnerable, and sometimes even offer their lives for others. They are noble. They strive for the ideal of living a good Christian life. They, like the good shepherd, do these things of their own will.

The reference to other sheep that do not belong to this fold can refer to future generations of disciples. In fact, by the time John finished recording his Gospel account, the community knew that other Christian communities also existed. These communities traced their origin to Peter, who had the title of shepherd. Thus, the reference could be about those communities.

Jesus went even further in this analogy and preached how the Father loved him because he freely offered his life. Jesus predicted his own Resurrection in laying down his life and taking it up again. By being obedient to the Father because of the great love between them, Jesus is reversing the disobedience of Adam. The Good Shepherd does not lead out of fear or obedience. The Good Shepherd does what is best for others out of love, no matter how great the sacrifice.

We Are Connected as Parts of the Vine

Connections to Church Teaching and Tradition

- "Today, there is an inescapable duty to make ourselves the neighbor of every individual, without exception, and to take positive steps to help a neighbor whom we encounter" (GS, 27).

- "In his preaching he clearly described an obligation on the part of the daughters and sons of God to treat each other as sisters and brothers. In his prayer he asked that all his followers should be one" (GS, 32).

- "Your word is a lamp to my feet, / a light for my path" (Psalm 119:105).

- "Christ the Lord . . . commanded the apostles to preach [the Gospel] to everyone as the source of all saving truth and moral law, communicating God's gift to them[1]" (DV, 7).

Acts 9:26–31   In this reading from Acts, we have dramatic examples of change and growth in unity. Paul, formerly a persecutor and rabid member of the Pharisee sect, has undergone a remarkable change in his conversion to Christianity. As for the members of the mother Church in Jerusalem, they did not trust his conversion and were afraid of Paul when he returned to Jerusalem. It had been a few years since Paul had become a follower of Christ and, although he changed in his belief, his theological style was still forceful and argumentative. Barnabas intervened and brought about change in the community so that they came to accept Paul. Barnabas was trusted. He was kind and forgiving, and explained that Paul had a dramatic conversion and was now preaching the Good News. In fact, Barnabas became somewhat of a mentor and helped launch Paul on his extraordinary ministry (Acts 15:36–39). Unity was not easy for the early Church, which was often faced with controversy. Yet, it remained one body and, as the reading tells us, grew in numbers. Paul returned to Jerusalem six times and became equal to the other apostles. While he retained controversial views on some matters, such as Gentile converts needing to be circumcised and obey dietary laws, Paul never thought of founding his own church. He was strongly attached to the Church, which in turn, adopted his letters as part of the Bible.

Psalm 22:26–27, 28, 30, 31–32 (26a)   The response in this psalm, "I will praise you, Lord, in the assembly of your people," is in keeping with the other readings today. We are reminded that, on an individual level, we are expected to praise the Lord through our words and habitual actions. We are also to remain part of the assembly of God's people, praising and living the Gospel precepts as a community.

1 John 3:18–24   The opening sentence of this reading summarizes so well what is expected of each follower of Christ. We are not just to give lip service to what we believe, we are to live it out in deed. It is not enough to say that we love one another. We must take it to the next level, so to speak, and show it in our actions. God knows what is in our hearts, we are told. God's commandment is that we believe in his Son, Jesus Christ. And furthermore, we are to do what he commanded. That is, we are to love one another. It is in living out the love we profess that we stay connected to Christ. We know this through the Holy Spirit.

John exhorts us to have confidence in the Lord because God is the source of forgiveness. No matter what negative thoughts we may have about ourselves or our actions, God does not condemn us and will always hear our prayers. This whole reading is the closing section of a part of John's letter (3:1–24). Here, as in an earlier section, he encourages confidence because of God's love for believers who strive to live out their faith.

John 15:1-8   This Gospel about the vine and branches is rich with meaning and levels of analogy. At the heart of it, John shows the cost of Church unity and the intimacy and interconnectedness of her members. Jesus is the vine that provides life and sustenance. Apart from the vine we can do nothing. If we stay connected, however, we will produce abundant fruit. We will be part of the source of life because we share the same lifeblood that flows through the interconnected veins and arteries. Jesus is the heart and gives us life and strength. We are warned, however, that those who become separated will wither and die. Like rejected branches, they are thrown into the fire.

Just as vines need to be pruned in order to remain as fruitful as possible, so does the Church. It may be that a self-centered member needs to be cast off. Pruning is important for the health of the vine, but it is not enough. A vine must be nurtured, fed, and watered. Jesus teaches that it is his word that nourishes all those connected to the vine: the Church. At the beginning of the reading he reassures the disciples that they are not in danger of pruning because they are already pruned due to hearing the word.

At the end of the reading he makes the connection between following his teachings and glorifying the Father. If you do what he teaches, you can ask in confidence for what you need. If you follow him, you will bear much fruit. As members of the vine, we are called to put aside our own wants and look to the needs of the larger community.

---

1 See Mt 28:19–20 and Mk 16:5. Council of Trent, *Degree On the Canonical Scriptures*: Denz. 783 (1501).

FOUNDATIONS FOR PREACHING AND TEACHING © 2011 Liturgy Training Publications.

Connections to Church Teaching and Tradition

- "This love is not something reserved for important matters, but must be exercised above all in the ordinary circumstances of daily life" (GS, 38).

- "Charity is love received and given. . . . Its source is the wellspring of the Father's love for the Son, in the Holy Spirit. Love comes down from the Son. It is creative love, through which we have our being; it is redemptive love, through which we are recreated. Love is revealed and made present by Christ[1] and 'poured into our hearts through the Holy Spirit.'[2] As the objects of God's love, men and women become subjects of charity, they are called to make themselves instruments of grace, so as to pour forth God's charity and to weave networks of charity" (CIV, 5).

- "God, who has a parent's care for all of us, desired that all men and women should form one family and deal with each other as brothers and sisters" (GS, 24).

Acts 10:25–26, 34–35, 44–48   In an amazing sequence of events, the doors of the Chosen People are opened to Gentiles as well as Jews. Two messengers came to Peter as he was preaching and invited him to go with them to the house of Cornelius. This was very significant, since Cornelius was a Roman soldier, not a Jew. Cornelius was a good man, however, and his whole household was God-fearing. When Peter entered the house, Cornelius knelt before him in reverence. Peter, however, insisted that Cornelius stand, saying that he himself was also human, not a god.

In what transpired, Peter saw that God accepts not only Jews but all nations who act uprightly or lead good lives as God-fearing people. Not only did Peter sense this, but the Holy Spirit made it perfectly clear. While Peter was preaching, the Holy Spirit came upon everyone there, uncircumcised Gentiles included. It must have been quite a joyous sight as the whole household praised God and spoke in tongues. Peter immediately ordered that these Gentiles could be baptized, since God clearly showed that all were welcome in the name of Jesus Christ.

Psalm 98:1, 2–3, 3–4 (see 2b)   This psalm continues the theme of God's love for all peoples. God's saving power is revealed to all nations. A new song can be sung, for the Lord has revealed his salvation. He has come to the house of Israel; however, "all the ends of the earth have seen / the salvation by our God" (98:3). Surely, this universal gift is worthy of the song of praise we offer. Surely this is a wonderful thing for us to sing about.

1 John 4:7–10   The message from John in this brief pericope couldn't be clearer or more direct. God is love. Everything flows from him. The focus is on the second part of the double commandment. We are to love God and we are to love our neighbor. We are to love one another because of God's love. If we do not love one another, John tells us, we do not know God. In fact, love is what distinguishes those who know God from those who don't. We are reminded of just how great God's love for us is, as he sent his only Son. Love is clearly God's initiative, and while God's love is revealed to Christians in Jesus, the Christian community, which now has life through that love, also reveals God's love (John 5:26; 6:57).

John 15:9–17   Having just taught his disciples that they are connected to him and to each other as branches on the vine, Jesus now deepens the relationship. He preaches the importance of love, the centrality of love, and the interconnectedness that comes about as a result of love. He has proved his love by his death, and his love provides not just the example, but also the very foundation for love among his followers. In verse 9, he reminds them of the Father's love for his Son, which is the model of his love for his disciples: "As the Father loves me, so I also love you." We remain in his love by keeping his commandments, just as Jesus keeps his Father's commands.

The doctrine in this reading is, of course, the same as in the second. Christian love is traced to the Father as its source. It is expressed in the redemption of Jesus and then in the mission of all his followers who are to love one another as God loves us. This passage also points to the upward direction of obedience. Jesus' response to the love of the Father is lived out in his obedience to the Father's commands. Likewise, Jesus' followers are to respond to his love through obedience to his commands. To make the point dramatically clear, to teach unmistakably what it means to love, Jesus reminds them of the ultimate sign of love: "No one has greater love than this, to lay down one's life for one's friends" (15:13). Thus, love is more than a feeling. Love is action. Jesus' standard of perfection makes that perfectly clear.

In John 8:31–33, Jesus has taught the disciples about the transition from being a slave to being free. Slaves do not belong to the family permanently; they will be set free by the truth that he brings. Thus, he will no longer call his disciples slaves. He has taught them what the father taught him. Unlike slaves, they know what the master is doing. They are now friends, rather than slaves. This reading ends with the same straightforward imperative that the previous reading begins, "Love one another" (15:17).

---

1 Cf. Jn 13:1.
2 Rom 5:5.

Connections to Church Teaching and Tradition

- "The church on earth is by its very nature missionary since, according to the plan of the Father, it has its origin in the mission of the Son and the Holy Spirit[1]" (AG, 2).

- "We are coming to see that any local church has no choice but to reach out to others with the gospel . . . . To say 'Church' is to say 'mission'" (TEE, 16).

- "We do not know the moment of the consummation of the earth and of humanity[2] nor the way the universe will be transformed. The form of this world, distorted by sin, is passing away[3] and we are taught that God is preparing a new dwelling and a new earth in which righteousness dwells,[4] whose happiness will fill and surpass all the desires of peace arising in human hearts[5]" (GS, 39).

Acts 1:1–11   These opening verses of the Acts of the Apostles form the bridge from Luke's account of the Gospel to the second volume of his account of the ministry of Jesus and his disciples. Although it is not mentioned in any of the Gospel accounts, in Acts, Luke refers to a period of 40 days during which Jesus appeared to the disciples, instructing them "through the Holy Spirit." It is interesting to note that 40 days was the amount of time Jesus passed in his desert temptations, the amount of time Moses spent on the mountain of God (Exodus 34:28), and the amount of time Elijah spent walking through the desert to Mount Horeb, the "mountain of God" (1 Kings 19:8).

At the end of the 40 days, the disciples acted much like they did before Jesus' death and Resurrection, as they asked for privileged information about the future they envisioned for the kingdom of God. Like Jesus did when he taught his followers to pray for everything they wanted (Luke 11:9–13), he indicated that the Holy Spirit would give them all that they needed to do their part to witness to him throughout all the earth.

Psalm 47:2–3, 6–7, 8–9 (6)   This psalm, so appropriate for the solemnity of the Ascension, depicts the Lord taking a throne. While the psalm does not indicate the location of the lofty throne, other citations depict the divine throne "in heaven" (Psalm 123:1), "above the flood" (Psalm 29:10), or high above the temple (Isaiah 6:1). The image of taking a seat on the heavenly throne complements the image we have from Acts of Jesus being taken up. His taking the throne symbolizes that a new reign has begun.

In the first strophe, we hear the unbounded acclaim God's kingship elicits. The reception we give to the most famous and beloved celebrities seems paltry in comparison to all peoples of the earth clapping and shouting praise. This is a veritable pep rally for the Lord!

The second and third strophes point out that we enter into such joyous celebration precisely because God is King—the reign of God has begun. As Jesus returns to the Father, a new phase of history begins because, as Paul says in 1 Corinthians 15:25, "he must reign until he has put all his enemies under his feet."

Ephesians 4:1–13 or 4:1–7, 11–13   The connection of this reading from Ephesians with today's feast is clearly Paul's citation of Psalm 68:18–19: "God's chariots were myriad, thousands upon thousands; / from Sinai the Lord entered the holy place. / You went up to its lofty height, / you took captives . . . ." Paul has reworked the image of that psalm, adjusting it to his own purpose. Interpreted in the light of the rest of the reading, it becomes clear that Paul wants the community to remain acutely aware of the gift they have received from the Lord. It is the Lord who descended to earth and finally ascended who has given them grace so that he might fill all things until they attain the full stature of Christ, whose body they are. Behind Paul's words lies the sense found in John 16:7, that the departure of the Lord was necessary for the coming of the Spirit, the one who bestows the gifts.

Mark 16:15–20   Most scholars agree that the Gospel written by Mark ends with verse 8 of chapter 16, the dreadfully disappointing statement that the women disciples "fled from the tomb . . . [and] said nothing to anyone, for they were afraid." As a later addition to Mark, today's reading seems to be a summary of the Resurrection accounts found in other accounts of the Gospel. Knowing who wrote this addition to the Gospel is less important than accepting it as part of the inspired word of God, which we know came through many authors.

The focus of this reading is the disciples' mission, just as Jesus' message to them before the Ascension was. Verse 15 reflects Matthew 28:19, but adds a note that reminds us of John 3:18, emphasizing the connection between belief in Christ and salvation. The special powers Jesus promises the disciples here were mentioned in Matthew 10:1 and Luke 10:19.

Finally, without much ado and no details whatsoever, the text explains that Jesus was taken up and took his seat at God's right hand. In keeping with the theme of the day, the last words of the Gospel return our focus to the mission and announce its success.

---

1 Cf. LG, 1.
2 Cf. Acts 1:7.
3 Cf. 1 Cor 7:31; St. Irenaeus *Adversus Haereses* V, 36, 1:PG 7, 1222.
4 Cf. 2 Cor 5:2; 2 Pet 3:13.
5 Cf. 1 Cor 2:9; Apoc 21:4–5.

God's Spirit Brings Our Love to Perfection

Connections to Church Teaching and Tradition

- "As the firstborn of many, and by the gift of his Spirit, [Christ] established . . . a new communion of sisters and brothers . . . in which all as members one of the other would render mutual service. . . . This solidarity must be constantly increased until that day on which it will be brought to perfection" (GS, 32).

- "The order which prevails in human society . . . must be brought into effect by justice. It needs to be animated and perfected by men's love for one another. . . . But such an order . . . finds its source in the true, personal, and transcendent God . . . the deepest source from which human society, if it is to be properly constituted, creative, and worthy of man's dignity, draws its genuine vitality[1]" (PT, 37–38).

- "Dialogue is not advanced by [technological] progress, . . . but takes place at a deeper level in a community of persons which calls for mutual respect for each one's full spiritual dignity" (GS, 23).

Acts 1:15–17, 20a, 20c–26   The scene we visit today takes place immediately after the Ascension of the Lord. The Christian community has returned to Jerusalem and is waiting in prayer. The decision and process of choosing a successor to Judas is literally the first act of the apostles after Jesus' Ascension.

Why was that necessary? If we look at the rest of Acts, we find little mention of the Twelve. While the bishops are the successors of the apostles, being an apostle never became a formal role or function in the Church. When the apostles eventually died, no one received that title. But at this point of Luke's account, they will play an important symbolic role representing the patriarchs of the 12 tribes of Israel to whom they first direct their mission.

Peter sets out what is required: the one chosen must be a man who was with them through Jesus' ministry and who could witness to the Resurrection. In the end, by deciding to draw lots, the group left the decision up to the Lord, who is the knower of hearts. Matthias, who will not be mentioned again, was the one chosen to fill out the Twelve who will address the Jews of different tongues and nations on the day of Pentecost.

The idea that there was only one definition of apostleship is refuted by Paul's use of the word. Interestingly, Paul, who would defend his right to be called an apostle, did not meet the requirement of having followed Jesus in his lifetime. Paul also called his "relatives" Andronicus and Junia apostles (Romans 16:7).

Psalm 103:1–2, 11–12, 19–20 (19a)   "Bless the Lord!" That phrase doesn't mean that we literally bless or give gladness to God; rather, it is an exuberant expression of praise. Blessing God acknowledges the divine power and glory. It is often an expression of thanksgiving. This psalm is especially appropriate to today's celebration because, following the solemnity of the Ascension, we sing that the Lord has set up his throne in heaven.

The second and third strophe of the psalm could make it sound as if the divine majesty puts a great distance between God and earthly creatures. That feeling is tempered not only by the mention of God's kindness, but also by the explanation that God uses the distance to separate us from our sin.

1 John 4:11–16   This selection of 1 John offers a guide to union with God and neighbor. There is an intimation here that we can't love God directly because no one has ever seen God. Nevertheless, we are told that if we love God's beloved people, the circle can be complete; we can love those whom God loves because God remains in us. When we remain in God, the Spirit keeps us mindful of the truth about God's love expressed in Jesus.

This helps to explain what the author meant in saying that God's love is brought to perfection in us. The implication is that our love of God can be ever-growing, in a constant process of becoming deeper, broader, and ever more complete. As if moving through a spiral, we continually experience the stages of love of neighbor, love of God, the presence of the Spirit, and faith in Jesus. Each of these builds on the other, bringing God's love to perfection in us.

John 17:11b–19   In this selection from Jesus' last discourse, we hear him pray for his followers, asking that they be consecrated in his word. The word *consecrate* or *sanctify* indicates that something is separated from its surroundings and made holy, or wholly dedicated to God. When Jesus asked that his disciples be consecrated, he prayed that they would become God's own: people so graced that they would be able to be fully dedicated to the mission they were to receive from him.

In a movement of thought typical of John, Jesus identifies the disciples with himself and himself with the Father. Just as the Father sent him, so he sends them. Then, bringing the idea full circle, he says, "I consecrate myself for them, so that they also may be consecrated in truth" (17:19). Jesus' death and Resurrection are his freely accepted consecration. They are also the revelation of the truth in which the disciples will be consecrated.

---

1 Cf. Pius XII's broadcast message, Christmas 1942, AAS 35 (1943) 14.

Your Sons and Daughters Shall Prophesy

Connections to Church Teaching and Tradition

- "'[T]he apostle of the Apostles,' Mary Magdalene was the first eyewitness of the Risen Christ. . . . This event, in a sense, crowns all that has been said previously about Christ entrusting divine truths to women as well as men" (MD, 16).

- "[The laity] by Baptism are incorporated into Christ . . . [they are] sharers in their own way in the priestly, prophetic, and kingly office of Christ and play their part in carrying out the mission of the whole Christian people in the church and in the world" (LG, 31).

- "The Church . . . must experience itself as a Church without borders . . . attentive to the growing phenomenon of human mobility in its diverse sectors . . . it is crucial to develop a mind-set and spirituality for the pastoral service of brothers and sisters on the move . . . to facilitate the encounter between the foreigner and the welcoming particular church. Bishops Conferences and dioceses must prophetically assume this specific ministry" (*Aparecida*, 412).

Genesis 11:1–9   One wonders what God saw as wrong with the tower that Noah's descendants were building. One response is that the people had been commanded to fill the earth, but they decided to stay in one place. Another possibility mentioned in *midrash* (Jewish interpretation) was that as the tower grew, it took a full year to get bricks from the base to the top. Preserving bricks became more important than safety, and they were valued more than human life. Underneath it all, the story of Babel is an explanation of how humanity came to be so diverse. Interestingly, the commands of Genesis 1:28 and 9:1 indicate that God willed the diversity that marks creation.

Exodus 19:3–8a   God's twofold message to Moses reminds him that his history gives him reason to believe in the promise for the future. In the second section of the reading, God visits the people with amazing signs of power, culminating in fire accompanied by trumpet blasts. This theophany is a precursor to Pentecost, when the Spirit will appear like tongues of fire.

Ezekiel 37:1–14   In this vision, Ezekiel watches God reverse the ravages of death, culminating with the divine breath (spirit) to bring people back to life. This reading focuses on the life-giving Spirit, freely given to God's people. "I will put my spirit in you that you may live."

Joel 3:1–5   In the Old Testament, God's gift of the Spirit generally implied the empowerment of the receiver to live a vocation. Here, the gift of the Spirit brings the people into direct communication with God, allowing them to prophesy, dream, and see visions. The Spirit comes not only to prophets, but to young and old, women and men, master and servant.

Psalm 104:1–2, 24, 35, 27–28, 29, 30 (see 30)   This and last week's psalm (103) are the only psalms that pronounce the invitation "Bless the Lord, O my soul," and it is done twice in each psalm (103:1, 22; 104:1, 35). Our verses acclaim the marvels of the Creator in the diversity of creation. Even more, they sing gratefully of our dependence on God. Our antiphon begs God to send the Spirit, whose presence, as proclaimed in many of the Old Testament readings, transforms all of creation.

Romans 8:22–27   As Paul explains to the Romans, we enjoy the first fruits of the Spirit, which means we are already enjoying the life of the new creation, but only in an initial or anticipatory way. Paul indicates that it is not just humanity enjoying the first fruits, but that all of creation is straining toward fulfillment of God's promise. This statement is unparalleled in Paul's letters. Here, Paul not only refers to the future "redemption of our bodies" or bodily resurrection, but to the transformation of all of creation. Like the revivification of Ezekiel's dry bones, creation itself will be restored to the harmony God intended. All of this is foreshadowed in our having received the first fruits of the Spirit. We cannot imagine what will happen as we enjoy the fullness of the Spirit, but for now, we can trust that the Spirit aids us in our weakness and teaches us to pray with unfathomable longing for God.

John 7:37–39   This incident takes place on the last day of the Feast of Tabernacles, when priests processed solemnly and drew water to take to the temple. The water ceremony expressed thanksgiving and was often associated with Isaiah 12:3. The Feast of Tabernacles celebrated the "day of the Lord," or God's triumph: the day when God pours out a spirit of compassion and supplication (see Zechariah 9–14). It was also a time to pray for rain. When Jesus described himself as a font of living water, the life-giving water is the revelation he gives. The last verse of this reading might seem to imply that the Spirit did not exist, but that is not the author's intent. The presence of the Spirit in the Gospel according to John is first mentioned when the Spirit descends on Jesus at the beginning of his ministry. Jesus then speaks of the Spirit and promises the Spirit to the disciples, as we will hear in the Gospel for the solemnity of Pentecost. As he dies, Jesus hands over his spirit, and when he appears to the disciples, Jesus gives them the Spirit. The remark in John 7:39 indicates that Jesus' Spirit was not yet available to believers in the way that it would be.

Connections to Church Teaching and Tradition

- "In all her members, the Church is sent to . . . make present, and spread the mystery of the communion of the Holy Trinity" (CCC, 738).

- "The human community that we build by ourselves can never, purely by its own strength, be a fully fraternal community, nor can it overcome every division and become a truly universal community. The unity of the human race, a fraternal communion transcending every barrier, is called into being by the word of God-who-is-Love" (CIV, 34).

- "All Christians by the example of their lives and the witness of the word . . . have an obligation . . . to reveal the power of the holy Spirit by whom they were strengthened at confirmation, so that others, seeing their good works, might glorify the Father[1] and more perfectly perceive the true meaning of human life and the universal solidarity of humankind" (AG, 11).

Acts 2:1–11   In Luke's account of the event of Pentecost, the only account we have in our scriptures, we hear more about the response of the people who witnessed the event than about the event itself. Earlier, the disciples had chosen Matthias to fill out the number of 12 symbolic patriarchs who represented people of Israel. On the day of Pentecost, we hear that there were Jews from "every nation under heaven," in other words, people representing the ends of the earth.

If the account of the advent of the Spirit is spare, it is also laden with symbolism. Luke indicates that the 120 people mentioned earlier (1:15) were gathered as a community. The imagery of the wind and the fire remind us of Exodus 19:18 when God came in fire, and Ezekiel 37:9 where the spirit came from the four winds (see also 2 Samuel 22:8–16). In recording the detail that "tongues as of fire" rested on the gathered disciples, Luke is emphasizing the fact that the Spirit came to each individual in the community.

In the Old Testament, being filled with the Spirit of God indicated that an individual was called to prophecy. In this experience it was an entire community who received the Spirit and began to speak the prophetic word so that all could understand it.

Psalm 104:1, 24, 29–30, 31, 34 (see 30)   Today we sing part of the same psalm that we prayed in yesterday's vigil Mass. Again, we praise God for the diversity of creation and recognize the dependence of every creature on God. Today we do not repeat that wonderful refrain, "Bless the Lord, O my soul." Instead, in our last stanza we praise God's glory and ask that the Lord be glad with all of creation, especially with our song of praise. Most of all, we repeatedly cry out, "Lord, send out your Spirit!"

Galatians 5:16–25   We need to take care not to allow a dualistic mind-set fashion our interpretation of Paul's message to the Galatians. In Paul's day, there were two particular words that could refer to the physical dimension of people and animals. One of them, here translated as "flesh," could emphasize human frailty and ego-driven desire. The other, usually translated as "body," had a range of meanings, but the word was consistently used for the flesh that is redeemed and will undergo resurrection. Paul is not opposing body and spirit, but warning of the dangers of a lifestyle of self-indulgence.

When we read the list of fruits of the Spirit, we note that, with the possible exception of self-control, all of them are social virtues; they are practiced only in relationship to others. No more than he is promoting body-rejecting asceticism, is he speaking to individuals. Paul is instructing the community about how to be a community living under the influence of the Spirit.

Sequence: *Veni, Sancte Spiritus*   This Sunday, the Church sings one of four sequences—ancient, poetic songs that precede the singing of the Gospel acclamation. In the Pentecost Sequence, *Veni, Sancte Spiritus,* the Church prays for the Holy Spirit to come. Using beautifully poetic titles, the sequence calls on the Father of the Poor, the Comforter, Divine Light, Sweet Rest, and Healer, emphasizing that if the Holy Spirit is absent, we have nothing. When the Holy Spirit is present, we have the salvation of the Lord.

John 15:26–27; 16:12–15   There are two key ideas in this selection from Jesus' farewell discourse. The first is that Jesus will send the Advocate, the Spirit of truth, to testify through the disciples. Earlier in the discourse, John indicated that the role of the Advocate would be to judge the world (16:8), to help the disciples remember all that Jesus taught (14:26), and to dwell in the disciples (14:17).

The second key teaching of this reading is that the Spirit of truth will continue to impart the revelation Jesus has given. The truth that the Spirit teaches is more than intellectual; it also implies the grace needed to put Jesus' teaching into daily communal practice. All of this points to the idea that as time moves on, the Spirit will continue to guide the Christian community into knowing how to live the truth that Jesus revealed: how to live as disciples, and how to give witness to Christ's message in each era.

1 Cf. Mt 5:16.

Ordinary Time in Summer and Fall

Overview of Ordinary Time in Summer and Fall

For the next six months we will celebrate Ordinary Time, the longest season of our liturgical year. These Sundays, beginning with the solemnity of the Most Holy Trinity and the Most Holy Body and Blood of Christ, are punctuated by the solemnities of the Assumption and All Saints, as well as the solemnity of the Nativity of Saint John the Baptist. The season of Ordinary Time ends with the solemnity of Our Lord Jesus Christ, King of the Universe, the last Sunday of the liturgical year.

As we in the northern hemisphere enjoy summer and fall, Mark and John will present us with Jesus the teacher, the healer, and the one who will willingly suffer. Between these great festive seasons, Ordinary Time invites us to immerse ourselves in word and sacrament in order to hear anew Christ's invitation to a closer and deeper discipleship. The Virgin Mary, John, and all the saints offer us examples of how to do that.

First Readings

The First Readings of this season complement the Gospel readings and familiarize us with Old Testament history and theology. Seven of the readings come from the Pentateuch, the first five books of the Old Testament. The rest are from the prophets, historical books, and wisdom literature.

A number of these readings focus on the covenant; others, on God's providence in nourishing and healing. Three focus on vocation and suffering as the fate of God's servant. Genesis reminds us of God's plan for humanity, and Daniel predicts the travails of the end times. All of them remind us of our shared roots with the Jewish people.

Responsorial Psalms

The psalms we sing and pray this season complement the Sunday theme and still convey a message of their own. If we meditate on them as a group, their overwhelming message is God's compassionate care for us. At the center of the season, on the Nineteenth Sunday in Ordinary Time, we hear the invitation, "Taste and see the goodness of the Lord" (34:9). While we read that as a sacramental invitation, it also reminds us that our awareness of God's kindness is experiential as well as spiritual and theological. When we prepare to taste and see, we set out on the path of thanksgiving and ever greater consciousness of God's providence.

Second Readings

We find three major strands of thought in our Second Readings. The first, from 2 Corinthians and Ephesians, could be called Christocentric, inviting us to imitate Christ, remembering that we were chosen by God in Christ and should imitate Christ by sharing, by creating peace, and by submitting to one another out of love.

The second major theme is James's insistence that faith demonstrates itself in action, most especially in care for the poor. The third emphasis of these readings is the uniqueness of Christ, the Alpha and Omega, the true high priest after whom no other will be necessary.

Gospel Readings

The Gospel readings for this season are drawn from three of our four evangelists. We begin with Matthew's "great commission" to baptize in the name of the Trinity, and then Mark's Last Supper. We then return to Jesus' ministry, shared with the disciples. On the Seventeenth Sunday in Ordinary Time, we begin five weeks of pondering the Bread of Life discourse, John's portrayal of Jesus as the Word made flesh and of union of Christ as the fulfillment of all God's historical promises.

FOUNDATIONS FOR PREACHING AND TEACHING © 2011 Liturgy Training Publications.

On the Twenty-second Sunday in Ordinary Time, we return to Mark's account of the Gospel. A few basic themes will make the rest of the season, with the dominant theme being discipleship and its implications. We will hear that disciples must accept Jesus' own self-giving and imitate it by giving all for God and neighbor. Watching a widow, Jesus teaches how disciples' eyes should perceive reality, and he reveals himself as the one who gives sight and hearing. The last Sundays of the season bring themes of the end of the world and of Christ, whose kingdom is in, but not of, this world.

Connections to Church Teaching and Tradition

- "The Church has an obligation to proclaim the faith and salvation which comes from Christ. . . . Since this mission continues . . . in the course of history . . . the church . . . must walk the road Christ himself walked, a way of poverty and obedience, of service and self-sacrifice even to death" (AG, 5).

- "The church is called to a deep and profound rethinking of its mission. . . . What is required is confirming, renewing, and revitalizing the newness of the Gospel rooted in our history" (*Aparecida*, 11).

- "We must do all we can to overcome suffering, but to banish it from the world altogether is not in our power. . . . Only God is able to do this: only a God who personally enters history by making himself man and suffering within history. We know that this God exists, and hence that this power to 'take away the sin of the world'[1] is present in the world. Through faith . . . hope for the world's healing has emerged in history" (SS, 36).

Deuteronomy 4:32–34, 39–40 This reading comes from a sermon of Moses and can be considered a summary of the whole book of Deuteronomy. Here we meet Moses as a preacher who wants to both instruct and persuade his people. His homily begins with the invitation to look at everything that has happened since the creation. He asks his people what has ever happened that could possibly compare with what their God has done for them.

Moses reminds them that God has spoken directly to them. Beyond that, they have been formed as a nation that belongs to God and God alone. God has rescued them from their enemies. All of this is proof to them that this God who enters their history is the one true God in heaven and on earth. The only fitting response to this is to keep the commandments and to enjoy the benefits of belonging to such a God.

Psalm 33:4–5, 6, 9, 18–19, 20, 22 (12b) In response to Moses' teaching, we cry out, "Blessed the people the Lord has chosen to be his own." As we pray the psalm, we begin with praise of God's dependability, fairness, and kindness. We then marvel at the power of God's word and works: the visible extensions of God's very being. Finally, recalling what it means to be God's own people, we sing in joy for the "watcher-over," the God who takes note of our hope and preserves our life. We promise to wait for the Lord and discern the everyday signs of God's kindness.

Romans 8:14–17 In this selection from Romans, Paul adds to what Moses proclaimed to the Israelites in the desert. Moses recalled God's historical activity; Paul reminds his listeners of God's activity within them. All that the people can do in response is allow themselves to be led by that Spirit who makes them heirs, not of a land or a tradition, but of God, the Father of Jesus. Here we may well be reminded of Jesus' prayer, "And I have given them the glory you gave me, so that they may be one, as we are one, I in them and you in me, that they may be brought to perfection as one . . ." (John 17:22–23). Finally, unlike Moses who promised the security of a "long life on the land," Paul reminds his fellow believers that if they are led by the Spirit of God, they will share in Jesus' fate.

Matthew 28:16–20 These last four verses of Matthew's account of the Gospel are filled with symbolic meaning. They summarize the entire Gospel in the moment when Jesus definitively hands over his mission to the disciples. The fact that Jesus meets the disciples on a mountain recalls other mountain events, including Jesus' third temptation, the Sermon on the Mount, the Transfiguration, and Jesus' arrest. As it was in the Old Testament, the mountain was an important meeting spot between God and humanity.

Earlier in the Gospel when Jesus had sent out the disciples, they were to go only to the people of Israel (10:5). Now, they are being sent throughout the whole world. This implies a new understanding of Jesus. As they accompanied him through the ministry, the disciples struggled to understand him as Israel's promised Messiah, even though his vision and realization of salvation was different from their hopes and expectations. Now, they are called to understand him as universal; they are to proclaim his message to the Gentiles as well as the Jews.

Matthew's description of baptism in the name of the Father, Son, and Spirit is unique in the New Testament. Doing something "in the name of" another implies solidarity, or identity with the one named. In calling for a Trinitarian baptism as the expression of discipleship, Matthew summarizes his teaching about Jesus as the Son of the Father and the one through whom God's Spirit was at work. Finally, that baptism is a sign of commitment to "do everything I have commanded you," implying that belief is not an intellectual assertion, but an entire way of life. Taken together, these readings remind us of God's ongoing presence to us and our responsibility to proclaim the Gospel by the way we allow the Spirit to lead us in action.

1 Jn 1:29.

Solemnity of the Most Holy Body and Blood of Christ   June 10, 2012
A *New—and Eternal—Covenant*

Connections to Church Teaching and Tradition

- "In Israel, God is called 'Father' . . . because of the covenant and the gift of the law to Israel 'his first-born son'[1] " (CCC, 238).

- "We bless God for the dignity of the human person. . . . We bless Him for the gift of faith that enables us to live in covenant with Him until we share eternal life. We bless him for making us his daughters and sons in Christ, for having redeemed us with the price of his blood and for the permanent relationship that he establishes with us" (*Aparecida*, 104).

- "By its union with Christ, the People of the New Covenant, far from closing in upon itself, becomes a 'sacrament' for humanity,[2] a sign and instrument of the salvation achieved by Christ . . . for the redemption of all.[3] The Church's mission stands in continuity with the mission of Christ: 'As the Father has sent me, even so I send you'[4] " (EDE, 22).

Exodus 24:3–8   In this scene in the Sinai desert the people already have a significant history with God. They knew their God as the one who had heard their cries (Exodus 3:7), who led them out of Egypt, and who gave them bread and water in the desert. They understood themselves as a people special to the Lord. As this scene begins, they had already promised obedience to God's word (19:8). They had seen the effects of God's presence (20:18) and had received the law. Now as they repeat their acceptance of God's law, Moses formalizes the covenant with a sacrifice.

Scholars say that the Hebrew verb for *covenant* means "to bond" or "to eat bread with." In this case, Moses symbolizes that bonding by sprinkling blood, first on the altar of the Divine Presence, and then, after reading the law, on the people. Because blood was a symbol of life, the sprinkling expressed a profound sharing of life. This was a precursor of temple sacrifices, especially the ritual for the annual Day of Atonement.

Psalm 116:12–13, 15–16, 17–18 (13)   This hymn of thanksgiving is sung by someone who God rescued from the danger of death. When the psalmist calls the death of God's faithful ones "precious," the phrase intends to explain that the death of the faithful costs a great deal to the God of life. The "cup of salvation," which may have originally been part of a sacrifice (Exodus 29:40), leads us to meditate on our communion with the blood of Christ. Praying this psalm helps us share in the experience of Israel in the desert, giving thanks for deliverance, and promising to be faithful and to give witness.

Hebrews 9:11–15   The epistle to the Hebrews is not so much a letter as it is a homily about the significance of Christ. Reflecting on Israel's sacrificial liturgies, the author presents Jesus as the definitive high priest whose sacrifice accomplishes deliverance from transgressions. In the liturgy for the Day of Atonement, the high priest passed into the Holy of Holies with the blood of a goat. He would sprinkle that blood on the mercy seat, which represented the divine presence. When he came back out, he came as a representative of God to sprinkle the people and bring atonement or the righting of all that had gone wrong in creation. According to the author of Hebrews, Jesus accomplished the final sacrifice by offering himself through the Spirit to God. He is the priest who established a New Covenant (Jeremiah 31:31–34) that will never end.

Sequence: *Lauda Sion*   This Sunday, the Church sings one of four sequences—ancient, poetic songs that precede the singing of the Gospel Acclamation. The sequence for the Most Holy Body and Blood of Christ, *Lauda Sion*, is ascribed to Saint Thomas Aquinas. The sixth stanza of the sequence reminds us of the history of the eucharistic feast.

Mark 14:12–16, 22–26   The details of Mark's account of the Last Supper communicate some surprising things. First of all, the disciples asked Jesus where they should prepare the Passover "for you." He sent them off to ask their mysterious host where to find the room where Jesus would eat *with his disciples*. Because this meal is going to summarize the life of Jesus and the meaning of discipleship, Mark makes it a point to show that the disciples who have resisted understanding Jesus' impending suffering (8:31; 9:32, 10:32) still resist the idea of participating in his Passover.

Mark explains that Jesus took the bread and blessed it and broke it. The blessing Jesus pronounced would have included prayers thanking God for key events in the course of salvation history. Jesus' identification of his body with the bread made a tremendous and potentially shocking theological statement; he was inserting his life into the traditional history of salvific events.

Finally, he gave them the cup and interpreted it as the sacrifice of his own blood in a New Covenant. But as Mark tells it, Jesus invited them to take the cup, they all drank, and only then did he explain what it meant. Just as he had asked them earlier if they could drink his cup (10:38), now he shared it with them both as gift and call to communion with his self-giving. All that he had done with them led to what this moment symbolized: as ignorant as they were willing, they were being ushered into the New Covenant.

1 Ex 4:22.
2 Cf. AG 5.
3 Cf. LG 9.
4 Jn 20:21.

Eleventh Sunday in Ordinary Time
Bear the Fruits of the Kingdom of God

Connections to Church Teaching and Tradition

- "The kingdom belongs *to the poor and lowly* . . . . those who have accepted it with humble hearts. Jesus is sent to 'preach good news to the poor'[1]" (CCC, 544).

- "Jesus, Son of God, was sent by the Father to restore the harmony between himself and humanity that had been disrupted by sin. He came to teach and show us love. . . . He proclaimed the coming of God's Kingdom by his words and deeds in obedience to the will of his Father" (USCCA, 91–92).

- "[Jesus] poured out on his disciples the Spirit promised by the Father.[2] From this source the Church . . . receives the mission of proclaiming and establishing among all peoples the kingdom of Christ and of God, and is, on earth, the seed and the beginning of that kingdom" (LG, 5).

Ezekiel 17:22–24 Believers often tell the story of faith in hindsight. In painful times it may be difficult to see the hand of God. This is true in the story from Ezekiel the prophet. When the Israelites experienced many of their people being taken off into exile by the Babylonians, they were desolate and turned to Egypt rather than to God to be saved. They experienced another destruction of their land and people by Babylonia and finally began to realize that it was their unfaithfulness that caused their suffering and loss. The prophet reminded them that God promised never to abandon them. Using the image of a cedar tree, he told them God would save a remnant of the exiles, placing a tender shoot high on the mountain to dwell in majesty. Their God is so powerful that even a withered, lowly, almost dead branch will prosper and bloom.

Ezekiel told the Israelites to practice faithfulness, trust God, and fulfill their part of the covenant. A new twig will sprout, connecting to the coming Messiah from the sprout of David's tree, or lineage. The new king will practice the true virtues of a king: humility, faithfulness to the covenant, and concern for the least for whom God cares.

Psalm 92:2–3, 13–14, 15–16 (see 2a) Birthday greetings often wish people many more years of life. The Responsorial Psalm conveys that image of anticipating the promise of long life like palms and cedars. The symbolic connection of these trees to royalty is found in Ezekiel, 1 Kings, and Isaiah. They convey longevity, loyalty, and strength. The psalm says those who practice justice will bear fruit like these trees, even in old age.

Echoing the tree metaphor of the First Reading, the psalm invites us to join our voices in thanksgiving to God for all he has done. The righteous and just are like trees planted in royal courts, giving witness to the king's splendor. Yet the king is called to serve God's people with the righteousness and justice that the Lord bestows. The steadfast compassion that God so freely gives must be rooted in the king's actions. We, too, are called to bear these same fruits as witness to the justice and peace of God's kingdom on earth in how we act toward the children of God, our brothers and sisters.

2 Corinthians 5:6–10 The images in Paul's writings are not always clear, both due to the shifting in translation and because of long phrases and sentences. His image of being at home in the body and away from the Lord conveys his acknowledgment that we are not with Christ at the moment; we are separated. Only death will bring us to that union and ability to be at home with the Lord. In their earthly time, believers are to walk in faith. Paul uses that often-quoted phrase (and sung hymn): "We walk by faith, not by sight" (2 Corinthians 5:7). Faith acknowledges our belief here and now even though we do not see. Faith allows us, like the Israelites, to stay rooted in our belief in God and the covenant as fulfilled in his Son, Jesus Christ. Paul says all will be judged according to the good or evil they have done. Followers of Christ are urged to live their lives well, with courage and confidence, so they will live with Christ for eternity.

Mark 4:26–34 Jesus often used common experiences to help people understand his teachings, and he used images for God and his kingdom. In the first parable we do not understand how a seed grows and produces; but that is how the reign of God manifests itself. In the second, the kingdom of God is like the smallest of seeds but becomes so large that birds build nests in the shades of its branches.

Sometimes the term "kingdom of God" causes us to imagine a place, perhaps associated with heaven, and we all aspire to that kingdom. Scripture scholars also translate kingdom as reign, which may convey a broader image than a specific place. Jesus speaks about the kingdom of God as a way of being or following God's way: if we believe and practice a way of life, then God's reign would look like this. The image helps us understand our role in this. Our work is to proclaim this kingdom of God by demonstrating through our actions toward God and one another that we are true followers. Like the palm and cedar trees, like the mustard seed and the seed upon the ground, we show the fruits of our belief here on earth in our treatment of one another, in the way we practice justice and peace, and in the way we right our relationships with our sisters and brothers.

---

1 Lk 4:18; cf. 7:22.
2 Cf. Acts 2:23.

FOUNDATIONS FOR PREACHING AND TEACHING © 2011 Liturgy Training Publications.

Solemnity of the Nativity of St. John the Baptist (Vigil) June 23, 2012
I Place My Words in Your Mouth

Connections to Church Teaching and Tradition

- "Jesus came to set this fire upon the earth, until all is ablaze in the love of God. We pray this fire will come upon us as disciples as we, led by the Spirit, carry out Christ's great commission to go and make disciples of all the nations" (GMD, 69).

- "Of her very nature, the Church is missionary. This means her members are called by God to bring the Gospel by word and deed to all peoples and to every situation of work, education, culture, and communal life in which human beings find themselves" (USCCA, 501).

- "In [John the Baptist], the Holy Spirit concludes his speaking through the prophets. John completes the cycle of prophets begun by Elijah[1]" (CCC, 719).

Jeremiah 1:4–10 Prophets knew they faced rejection and scorn, and suffering for their warnings. Jeremiah might be excused for his reluctance; he knew what hostility might face him if he carried the word and instruction of God to a people often stubborn and unwilling to change their ways. The promise of God to Jeremiah is that he would give him the necessary words. He simply had to be willing to be an instrument. God touches Jeremiah's mouth, giving him the words to preach and prophesize. God goes on to tell Jeremiah that, as a result of this action of giving him the words, he will be able to root up, destroy, tear down, and destroy—powerful actions signifying not Jeremiah's ability but God's power and might. Jeremiah's story tells of a faithful prophet, one in a long line of those sent by God to remind his people of their covenant. In the Gospel today we hear of another great prophet, John, the last one before Jesus himself. John, we are told by Luke, "will turn many of the children of Israel to the Lord their God" (Luke 1:17). This is the role of a prophet: to bring God's people home to God by preaching the words of his justice wherever God commands.

Psalm 71:1–2, 3–4a, 5–6ab, 15ab, 17 (6) The use of Psalm 71 for the feast of the vigil of John the Baptist's birth seems appropriate to commemorate his mission and dedication to the Messiah who was to come after him. This psalm of lament is full of strong images for God: stronghold, refuge, rock, and fortress. From the very beginning in the womb, the psalmist is confident that God is worthy of this trust and hope; God is a shelter worthy of this dependence. In the First Reading we hear a similar image of being formed by God before birth in response to Jeremiah's protest that he is too young to preach God's message. Who wants to go to hostile and unwelcoming nations to offer a message of God's promise? But Jeremiah's can trust that this is his task, for it is God who does the sending. It seems an appropriate psalm to link with this feast of John the Baptist, who also experienced God in his mother Elizabeth's womb when she was greeted by Mary carrying the Son of God. John has been blessed before birth to carry the message entrusted by God. He can be certain that God will give him strength for the journey.

1 Peter 1:8–12 The opening lines of the First Letter of Peter address the Gentile converts of Asia Minor. These sojourners scattered far from home are told they are a chosen race sanctified by God's grace. The spirit of Christ was preached to them by the prophets who told them of this grace of salvation. This passage seems a fitting one to celebrate John the Baptist, one of the greatest prophets the world has ever seen.

Luke 1:5–17 The promised birth of a baby after waiting for a long time is a cause of great joy; Elizabeth and Zechariah have long waited for a child, trusting in God. There are several Old Testament stories of women who have longingly awaited a birth of a child: Sarah (Genesis 15:3; 16:1); Rebekah (Genesis 25:21); Rachel (Genesis 29:31; 30:1); the mother of Samson (Judges 13:2–3); and Hannah (1 Samuel 1:2). With this image, Luke connects the story of John the Baptist to a long heritage of Old Testament figures who have played a role in Israel's history. This child, Zechariah is told, is no ordinary child, for he will not only be a source of joy to them but "will be filled with the Holy Spirit even from his mother's womb, and he will turn many of the children of Israel to the Lord their God" (Luke 1:15–17). He will be a prophet, the last before the coming Messiah, who will prepare the people for the coming of the Lord. In Luke's account of the Gospel, John the Baptist prepares himself in the desert until he comes forward to announce the coming of the Lord. But as Luke recounts in chapter 3 of his Gospel account, John constantly points the way to the coming Messiah. John baptizes, urging repentance and a change of heart to prepare for the Messiah, who will baptize with the Holy Spirit and fire. John fulfills the promise of his birth by preaching to the people what God commands as he prepares the way for the Lord.

---

1 Cf. Mt 11:13–14.

Connections to Church Teaching and Tradition

- "The Acts of the Apostles shows how the Holy Spirit transformed the Apostles from being fearful disciples, huddling behind closed doors, into courageous witnesses for Christ. . . . Beginning with the gift of the Spirit at Pentecost, the disciples became dynamic missionaries. He filled those disciples with the gift of courage so that nothing stopped them from proclaiming the love of Christ for all people" (USCCA, 103).

- "God's people . . . share in Christ's role as prophet. This means both teaching and witnessing God's Word to the world. A real prophet, by teaching and good example, leads others to faith. . . . While witness is essential, we should be always aware of opportunities to share our faith verbally with each other and with all those who do not yet profess it" (USCCA, 117–118).

- "Those who practice charity in the Church's name will never seek to impose the Church's faith upon others. They realize that a pure and generous love is the best witness to the God in whom we believe and by whom we are driven to love" (DCE, 20).

Isaiah 49:1–6   The First Reading is the second "servant song" from Second Isaiah. Some scripture scholars suggest the image refers to Israel and how she is called to act in response to her covenant. Others suggest that they refer to an individual, such as an ideal king who is anointed by God and acts as God would to the poor and lowly. Prophets, too, were alluded to as servants of God. The images are also referenced as a prediction of the Messiah who would be the true one to witness in God's name. In any case, the reading suggests that the servant is called by name even before birth to act in God's name. This servant will trust in God completely, despite difficulty or even death, for "my reward is with the LORD, / my recompense is with my God" (Isaiah 49:4). In placing this reading on the feast of John the Baptist, the Church recognizes both John's legacy of calling people to return to God and also his willingness to point toward the coming Messiah who would fulfill all the hope of Israel for a king who would act with righteousness and justice. Both Elizabeth and Zechariah announce John's name in the Gospel. But as a servant of God, John's name was known by God long before his birth.

Psalm 139:1b–3, 13–14ab, 14c–15 (14)   The psalm used for today's celebration of the birth of John the Baptist speaks of God's intimate knowledge from the time we were made in our mother's womb. The psalmist says that God so lovingly and tenderly probes, knows, and understands us, that it is as if our very being was formed by God, knit together and wonderfully made. The final verses of the psalm, which we do not hear on this feast, speak of how fiercely we must be willing to do what God requires. "Do I not hate, LORD, those who hate you? / Those who rise against you, do I not loathe? / With fierce hatred I hate them, / enemies I count as my own" (Psalm 139:21–22). Our response to being so lovingly made is to defend our God with all the power we have within us. John the Baptist did just that with his preaching, witness, and eventual death at the hands of the enemies of God's word and God's Son.

Acts 13:22–26   John is mentioned in the reading from Acts as the prophet who heralded the coming Messiah and who in humility declared his own unworthiness to fasten the sandals of Jesus. John had been called by name from birth by God and he was aware of his identity as a servant of the Lord, but not as the Messiah. He knew that the one coming after him was the true Messiah who would be the salvation of the world. John is the precursor, the preparer, the herald, the servant of the Lord. He points the way. We, too, are called by name to do the same by living lives of witness and proclamation to the coming reign of God. We are called to serve God as faithfully as John did.

Luke 1:57–66, 80   Though this Gospel story from Luke is all about the wonders and miracles at the birth and naming of John the Baptist, it leads directly to the action of God. "All who heard these things took them to heart, saying, 'What, then, will this child be?' For surely the hand of the Lord was with him" (Luke 1:66). John the Baptist was certainly of God. The readings on this solemnity emphasize how a servant of God is formed in the womb and called by God. Despite hardship or suffering, a servant is confident in God's presence and clear about his mission. John was clear. He was to call attention to the one who was to come after him. In the First Reading, the passage from Isaiah says this about the suffering servant: "I will make you a light to the nations, / that my salvation may reach to the ends of the earth" (Isaiah 49:6). John knows this truth, and his proclamation about the coming Messiah is a message to the entire world that the light that has come is the Christ. John's eventual martyrdom happens because he chose to continue in his role, announcing the coming of Christ and to point to the Lord as the salvation of the world. God called John before he was born and sent him on a mission to proclaim the coming of the Lord. John is a faithful witness to present-day disciples who are also called to testify to the light of the world now. John's testimony was strong and clear, as ours must be as well.

FOUNDATIONS FOR PREACHING AND TEACHING © 2011 Liturgy Training Publications.

Connections to Church Teaching and Tradition

- "Prayer *to Jesus* is answered by him already during his ministry, through signs that anticipate the power of his death and Resurrection" (CCC, 2616).

- "While Jesus sometimes simply spoke some words to accomplish a healing, he often touched the afflicted person to bring about the cure. In the Church's Sacrament of the Anointing of the Sick, through the ministry of the priest, it is Jesus who touches the sick to heal them from sin— and sometimes even from physical ailment" (USCCA, 251).

- "It is Jesus himself who . . . will raise up those who have believed in him . . . . Already now in this present life he gives a sign and a pledge of this by restoring some of the dead to life[1]" (CCC, 994).

Wisdom 1:13–15; 2:23–24   Even though the book of Wisdom is not part of Protestant Bible translations, the teaching of today's reading is something that all Christians can accept and believe. Written approximately one hundred years before the birth of Jesus, this may well have been the last Old Testament book written. This passage combines insights from both Jewish and Greek thought, affirming that all humans are created for immortality because we are all created in the image and likeness of God. By reinterpreting Genesis 3, the author asserts that God created us for eternal life. Death entered the world through the serpent, who is equated with Satan. Those who cooperate and live the way God created us will never die, despite the ravages of physical death. Those who do not live in this manner will not experience eternal life. The author, in the tradition of Wisdom literature, is presenting us with a choice: eternal life or everlasting death. We trust in God and pray that God helps us to choose rightly.

Psalm 30:2, 4, 5–6, 11, 12, 13 (2a)   Psalm 30 is a song of praise and thanksgiving to God, who has rescued the psalmist from some horrendous fate, a fate comparable to those who go down to the netherworld or the pit of death. God is a God of life who desires not death but life. Calling upon and trusting in the Lord results in reliable deliverance by God. Having experienced God's deliverance, the psalmist invites the whole community to praise and thank God because God's good will lasts a lifetime. God acts on our behalf to change our weeping into rejoicing and our mourning into dancing. God is ever gracious and reliable, ready to answer whenever we call. Praise and thanksgiving to God are always appropriate and fitting.

2 Corinthians 8:7, 9, 13–15   Paul encourages his Corinthian community to share with others their material abundance. He praises them for excelling in following Christ, and for the many gifts they have received through the Spirit. Other communities are in need, and Paul asks the Corinthians to share so that all may have life's necessities. Paul exhorts the Corinthians to imitate Jesus, who, as God, was rich beyond all measure yet chose to become poor, to become human, for their sake. So, too, they are to share their riches with others in need, thus being true imitators of Jesus. Those helped would, in return, be motivated to share whatever riches they possess. In this fashion all would experience the graciousness of God, richly expressed in Christ Jesus.

Mark 5:21–43 or 5:21–24, 35b–43   This passage speaks of faith in God, which enables us to cross boundaries and reach out to one another. In doing this, we become living witness to God's compassion and healing touch. Mark's Jesus confronts the powers of evil, sickness, and death, while affirming life. In sandwiching one healing event within another, Jesus highlights the essence of discipleship. The request by Jairus, a synagogue official, that Jesus come to heal his daughter surrounds the healing of the hemorrhaging woman. The woman, long afflicted with hemorrhages, dares to reach out and touch Jesus in public, without his knowledge or consent. In so doing, she violates both social customs and religious purity laws. Yet, her trust in God and in Jesus' healing powers emboldens her to act. Jesus, deeply touched by her faith, restores her to community life by calling her "daughter" and sends her on her way both healed and at peace. As Jesus continues on to Jairus's home, news of the daughter's death reaches them. Jesus counsels Jairus not to fear, but to have faith. In the midst of the crowd's ridicule and doubt, Jesus approaches the dead girl and touches her, calling her to rise. Like the hemorrhaging woman, Jesus breaks both social customs and ritual purity laws by touching the dead body of a woman he does not know. This daughter of God is brought to life by Jesus, and he encourages her parents to give her something to eat. Both incidents address issues of what discipleship entails. Jairus and the hemorrhaging woman call us to have faith in God's life-giving touch. Like Jesus, disciples are called to cross boundaries so that God's healing touch and compassion can be experienced and activated. Both stories focus on Jesus' mission to lead people from isolation, sickness, and the powers of evil, to God and the life-giving support of family and community.

1 Cf. Mk 5:21–42; Lk 7:11–17; Jn 11.

Connections to Church Teaching and Tradition

- "The eyes of faith permit us to see Jesus Christ. . . . The essential thing is that we keep our eyes fixed on the Lord. Is it really worth it, you ask? Yes, as long as we place our total faith and trust in Jesus, and let him take over" (SWJCB, 345).

- *"Jesus Christ is the son of God made man in whom and thanks to whom the world and man attain their authentic and full truth.* The mystery of God's being infinitely close to man—brought about in the Incarnation of Jesus Christ . . . shows that *the more that human realities are seen in the light of God's plan and lived in communion with God, the more they are empowered and liberated in their distinctive identity and in the freedom that is proper to them"* (CSDC, 45).

Ezekiel 2:2–5   Through the power of God's spirit, Ezekiel is called to speak on God's behalf to a people characterized as "hard of face and obstinate of heart." Ezekiel already knows that his prophetic ministry and message will be rejected. Despite the anticipated negative response, Ezekiel still feels empowered by God's Spirit to speak in God's name. Whether people "heed or resist," the prophetic word of God will be proclaimed, and people will "know that a prophet has been among them." To speak God's word in the face of opposition and rejection takes great courage and phenomenal trust in God. A prophet makes people uncomfortable by contrasting their limited knowledge of things with God's unlimited wisdom and understanding. In order to be faithful to their call, prophets have to keep their eyes fixed on the Lord, ever deepening their relationship to God, and always attuning themselves to God's ways. No matter what the response, they are assured that they have been faithful to God's call and to their mission.

Psalm 123:1–2, 2, 3–4 (2cd)   This psalm of lament expresses the feelings of both individuals and communities at experiencing the "mockery of the arrogant, / . . . the contempt of the proud." Such experiences lead them to a deeper trust in God, who alone can help them. As they praise and acknowledge the majesty and power of God "enthroned in heaven," they fix their eyes on the Lord and wait upon God's provident help and mercy. Such trust and confidence in God enables the community to carry on despite tribulations. The contempt of others, no matter how debilitating, does not overwhelm them. In humility and confidence, they plead with God and wait on the Lord to act on their behalf. Ezekiel's awareness of certain rejection in the First Reading would have easily led him to pray this psalm as he went about his prophetic ministry.

2 Corinthians 12:7–10   Some who opposed Paul's mission were undermining his person and message to the Corinthian community by claiming that Paul was a false prophet who fancied his visions and spiritual experiences above his message. Paul responds that even though he has much to boast concerning his visions and spiritual insights, preaching Christ Jesus was his exclusive focus. Paul views the hardships, insults, and persecutions (the "thorn in the flesh" that he experiences in his ministry) as a healthy antidote from the Lord that readily curbs his temptation to "being too elated" in himself. Through persistent prayer, Paul discerns that his "thorn in the flesh" is the Lord's way of keeping him balanced. Paul trusts God's care and support in the midst of trial and weakness, so that success in ministry becomes God's work, not his. He argues that he is "content" with weakness, for then he can truly experience the support and strength of God working through him. Paul's focus on the Paschal Mystery, on new life and meaning coming only through suffering and death, continually motivates his message and ministry.

Mark 6:1–6a   Today's theme of eyes fixed on the Lord in the midst of rejection, misunderstanding, and opposition continues in Mark's narrative of Jesus' return to Nazareth. News of Jesus' mighty deeds against the forces of evil through healings and exorcisms has reached Nazareth. Jesus' return sparks misunderstanding and rejection from those who think they know him best. By preaching and teaching in the synagogue, Jesus arouses jealousy and resentment. Who does he think he is, putting on such airs in our midst! We know exactly who he is, who his family and relatives are, and what the status of his humble origins is. In so thinking, the residents of his hometown reject anything Jesus says, refusing to believe or accept him. Like Ezekiel and Paul, Jesus must have felt the pain that rejection and misunderstanding generates. For Mark's Jesus, this rejection, along with others, prefigure the ultimate rejection that will culminate in the Crucifixion. Yet, despite such rejection, Jesus is aware of God's presence in his life and trusts in God's help and support.

Jesus is in the long line of prophets who are called to proclaim God's word. Such a call and commitment demand a focus on God's word and message and not on how people will receive it. Consequently, following Jesus will bring about misunderstanding and rejection. A disciple is one who keeps eyes fixed on the Lord, trusting in God's care and support no matter what happens.

FOUNDATIONS FOR PREACHING AND TEACHING © 2011 Liturgy Training Publications.

Connections to Church Teaching and Tradition

- "The Lord Jesus endowed his community with a structure. . . . Before all else there is the choice of the Twelve with Peter as their head[1]. . . . The Twelve and the other disciples share in Christ's mission and his power, but also in his lot[2]" (CCC, 765).

- "God graciously arranged that what he had once revealed for the salvation of all people should last for ever in its entirety and be transmitted to all generations. Therefore, Christ the Lord . . . commanded the apostles to preach it to everyone . . . . In order that the full and living Gospel might always be preserved in the church the apostles left bishops as their successors. They gave them 'their own position of teaching and authority.'[3] . . . Thus, the apostolic preaching . . . was to be preserved in a continuous line of succession until the end of time" (DV, 7–8).

- "It is the special vocation of the laity to seek the kingdom of God by engaging in temporal affairs and directing them according to God's will" (LG, 31).

1 Cf. Mk 13:14–15.
2 Cf. Mk 6:7; Lk 10:1–2; Mt 10:25; Jn 15:20.
3 See Leo XIII Encyclical *Providentissimus Deus*: EB 114; Benedict EV, Encyclical *Spiritus Paraclitus*: EB 483.

Amos 7:12–15   Around the year 750 BC, Amos, a herdsman from Judah who also tended sycamore trees, hears God calling him to prophesy to the northern kingdom at the royal sanctuary in Bethel. Amos travels to Bethel to proclaim God's judgment on the prosperous north for its failure to act with justice toward the poor. Amaziah, priest of Bethel, banishes him because he has dared to call into question the king's and the people's fidelity to God's covenant in their dealing with the poor and needy. In an attempt to undermine his words of judgment, Amos is accused of profiting from his prophetic vocation. Amos responds by letting Amaziah know that this prophetic task was not his choice but God's. He is not a prophet that can be bought by priests or kings to make religiously or politically correct pronouncements. Rather, Amos' only loyalty is to God who called him and to the words that God commissioned him to speak. No one persuaded Amos to be a prophet. God chose him and sent him to announce God's word to an unjust and oppressive people. Amos can only be faithful to God, trusting that God knows better than we do.

Psalm 85:9–10, 11–12, 13–14 (8)   Psalm 85 expresses the longing of a suffering and deprived community for restoration, justice, and peace among people and throughout the land. Such longing is linked to God's covenant love and fidelity, which the community recalls and activates. God is the only one who can help them, and they turn to God's covenant promises for assurance and fulfillment. God's covenant qualities—loving kindness, truth, justice, and peace—are personified to act on behalf of the people and the land, restoring both economic prosperity and communal well-being. Renewed attentiveness to covenant promises focuses the community's hope and anticipates restoration. God will activate those covenant qualities and send them forth to restore the people. The community trusts that God will be faithful and will respond to their call for help.

Ephesians 1:3–14 or 1:3–10   This powerful message to the Ephesians begins with a blessing of God, and then goes on to stress the Trinitarian nature of God, who chose us in Christ "before the foundation of the world." In Christ, we were chosen for adoption, for filial relationship with God, "to be holy and without blemish before him." God's endless choice and love were manifested through Christ, in whose blood we are redeemed. That filial relationship, made possible through Christ, makes us privy to God's eternal plan of salvation for all humanity. The promised Holy Spirit, given to all at Baptism, is the "first installment of our inheritance" as children of God. All this calls forth from us is blessings and praise of God to be shared with all creation. In Baptism, God gifts us with the Spirit, choosing us to be children and heirs, and empowers us to be living witnesses of Christ. All are chosen by God for love and intimacy. Knowing this, we are called to share that knowledge with others so that all may become aware of God's deep mysterious love and enter deeply into it.

Mark 6:7–13   Mark's account of Jesus sending forth the Twelve two by two emphasizes Jesus' desire to send out his followers to continue his mission. Mark's Jesus has come to announce and activate God's reign by confronting the powers of evil in whatever way they manifest themselves. Sickness, death, and possession by demons were all manifestations of the power of evil at work. In sending out his followers, Jesus gives them "authority over unclean spirits," the same mission that he has initiated by his presence among them. In sending them off, Jesus instructs them to let go of things that could prevent them from being effective ministers. To travel light, to trust and depend on others, and to be content with what others offer are all necessary components of mission. Jesus further warns them that rejection will be a component of their ministry experience. When rejection occurs, they are to "shake the dust off [their] feet" and move on.

The Twelve go forth, successful in preaching repentance, healing, anointing, and driving out demons. They, and we, are commissioned to reconcile, heal, and drive out evil. When we are faithful to Jesus' guidance and instructions, we become instruments through which God's care and love are actualized in the world. By carrying on the work of proclaiming and activating God's reign, we become living witnesses to Jesus.

Connections to Church Teaching and Tradition

- Jesus selected the apostles and called them to share in his mission. Jesus continues to protect and guide his flock (CCC, 1575).

- "Through the signs of his presence, it is the Face of the Lord that we seek and desire; it is his Word that we want to hear and keep" (CCC, 2656).

- "The church is, accordingly, a *sheepfold*, the sole and necessary entrance to which is Christ.[1] It is also a flock, of which God . . . would himself be the shepherd,[2] and whose sheep . . . are . . . at all times led and brought to pasture by Christ himself, the Good Shepherd and prince of shepherds,[3] who gave his life for his sheep[4]" (LG, 6).

1 Cf. Jn 10:1–10.
2 Cf. Isa 40:11; Ezek 34:11.
3 Cf. Jn 10:11; 1 Pet 5:4.
4 Cf. Jn 10:11–15.

Jeremiah 23:1–6 The Hebrew word for *shepherd* shares a root with the verb *to rule*. Kings were called shepherds because their primary responsibility was to manifest care for all and to rule with justice. Jeremiah rants against kings for their failure to care for God's people, resulting in the exile which scattered God's people from their land. Jeremiah warns the kings that God will deal with them in the same fashion they dealt with the people. God will then take over the king's responsibilities, restoring the people to the land and ruling them with justice and peace.

Jeremiah then articulates poetically the hope that one day God would "raise up a righteous shoot to David." Such a king would rule wisely, justly, and do "right in the land." Peace, security, and right relationship would be so evident under this "righteous shoot" that they would name him, "the LORD, our justice." Christians believe that this "righteous shoot to David" is Jesus, who perfectly epitomizes God's justice and compassion toward all. Jesus, the Good Shepherd, knows us and cares for us. Should we not listen deeply to his voice?

Psalm 23:1–3, 3–4, 5, 6 (1) Psalm 23 is the best known psalm in the whole psalter. It presents the Lord as a shepherd who cares for the sheep. The shepherd leads the sheep to food and water that nourishes. The shepherd's rod and staff both protect the sheep from enemies and guide them into right paths. Care and concern for the sheep manifests itself in the shepherd, preparing a secure space and table in the very sight of one's enemies. All this is possible because God's covenant love, God's goodness and loving kindness, "follow" us at all times. We are thus assured of an everlasting relationship with God. Nothing could be more secure than to be with the shepherd. What is demanded is trust in God, who will provide for our every need. Listening to and being guided by the Lord, our Good Shepherd, will always lead to security, harmony, and right relationship with all. For Christians, Jesus is that Good Shepherd who models care and concern for all, and calls us to the same mission.

Ephesians 2:13–18 The author of Ephesians tackles the division that tore apart the early followers of Christ, between Jews and Gentiles who accepted Christ as their Lord and Messiah. Because of their different traditions, teachings, and rituals, Christian Jews articulated and lived out their lives differently than Christian Gentiles. This division between them led some Christian Jews to advocate that the only correct way to follow Christ was through the Jewish Torah and rituals. The letter to the Ephesians addresses and corrects this mistaken notion.

The blood of Christ has saved all humanity, restoring unity between God and humanity, as well as between all people. Christ is "our peace," who in his body "broke down the dividing wall of enmity." Those who were near, the Jews, and those who were far, the Gentile Ephesians, are united as one in the sacrifice of Christ, who destroyed death and all that divided humanity. Because of Christ, all now have "access" to God through the power of the Spirit. Jesus is our true shepherd who gathers us as one and leads us safely to God through the Spirit.

Mark 6:30–34 After their successful mission to preach and heal, Jesus instructs his apostles, those sent by him, to rest awhile in a deserted place, away from the ever-present crowd. Setting out in a boat to a deserted place, the crowds notice where they are heading. When Jesus and the apostles arrive at the deserted place, the crowd is there already. Frustrated in their attempt to seek a deserted place to rest, Jesus looks at the crowd and is moved with pity for them, for "they were like sheep without a shepherd." Jesus "began to teach them many things." Mark provides this setting to articulate some strongly held beliefs of his community. Jesus is the true shepherd who is not only attuned to the people's needs, but also is willing to sacrifice his own needs for theirs. Unlike the leadership of his day, Jesus leads by instructing the community in the ways of the Lord, as well as providing for their physical needs. This deserted place is Mark's setting for the feeding of the five thousand, another clear manifestation of the shepherd's care for the people. The hope of Jeremiah for a true shepherd is fulfilled for Christians in the person of Christ.

Connections to Church Teaching and Tradition

- "Love faces a vast field of work and the Church is eager to make her contribution with her social doctrine, which concerns the whole person and is addressed to all people. So many needy brothers and sisters are waiting for help . . . 'How can it be that today there are still people dying of hunger?'" (CSDC, 5).

- "The words of Christ . . . will then resound for all people: 'Come, O blessed of my Father, inherit the kingdom prepared for you . . . for I was hungry and you gave me food, I was thirsty and you gave me drink . . . as you did it to the least of my brethren, you did it to me'[1]" (CSDC, 57).

- "*The social teaching of the Church is also fertile soil for dialogue and collaboration in the ecumenical sphere.* This is already happening in various places . . . concerning . . . the miseries of today's world such as hunger and poverty . . . [and] the unequal distribution of the goods of the earth . . . . This . . . increases awareness that all are brothers and sisters in Christ" (CSDC, 535).

2 Kings 4:42–44 Elisha, the disciple of Elijah, is a prophet attending to the people and the Lord at the place of worship, the tent made during the Exodus. An offering of 20 barley loaves from the harvest's first fruits, the best of the crop, is offered to the Lord. The bread is to be placed before the Lord and later consumed by those who served at the Lord's tent. Instead of offering it to the Lord, Elisha commands that it be given to the people to eat. The most likely reason is the presence of famine in the land, and these hundred people need food.

The servant alerts Elisha that the loaves will not be enough for so many people. Elisha insists that the loaves be shared, and that God would make certain that there would be more than enough, with bread to spare. Elisha's words become reality when bread is left over after all have been satisfied. This event becomes the prototype for the Gospel feeding stories. Our God knows our needs and works with what is available to provide abundantly for all our needs.

Psalm 145:10–11, 15–16, 17–18 (see 16) The refrain from Psalm 145 highlights the fact that "the hand of the Lord feeds us; he answers all our needs." This praise psalm is replete with reasons for calling upon all people to praise God. Foremost among those reasons is that God is always faithful and can be relied upon whenever anyone calls. All who trust in the Lord never go away empty or unsatisfied, for the Lord feeds us and "answers all our needs." God is always openhanded in response to our needs.

The last stanza emphasizes two qualities of God that need remembering and deserve praise. The Lord is "just" in all things, attuned to right relationship with all of creation, providing all that is needed for life. The Lord is "holy," a reality that suffuses all of creation and everything that God does. This covenant love is what enables us to trust and call upon God in our need, and what enables God to draw near to all who call. Praise of God is therefore fitting, just, and proper.

Ephesians 4:1–6 Many New Testament letters contain sections known as *ethical exhortations*. Such exhortations are practical suggestions for ethical living that flow from the author's theological and doctrinal presentation. Chapters 4–6 of Ephesians provide such an ethical exhortation. Given the divisions between Jew and Gentile that plagued Jesus' early followers, Ephesians emphasizes unity and oneness. Through his life and death, Jesus broke down the barriers that divide us, calling all to be one through the power of his Spirit.

To do this well, Ephesians exhorts us to live "with all humility and gentleness, . . . bearing with one another through love." Unity is based on the "one body and one Spirit" that bonds Jesus' followers. Sharing "one hope, . . . one Lord, one faith, one baptism, one God and Father of all" should energize and activate unity and oneness. Our Trinitarian God is one, totally powerful and totally present in us and in all of creation. What better reason do we need to strive toward unity and oneness?

John 6:1–15 The Gospel passages for the next five Sundays focus on chapter 6 of John's account of the Gospel, known as the Bread of Life discourse. The miracle of feeding the multitudes is the only one that appears in all four accounts of the Gospel. The accounts are usually suffused with language that directly relates to the eucharistic action of Jesus' followers.

John's version is replete with eucharistic themes that connect back to Moses, Passover, manna, Elisha, and barley loaves. The emphasis throughout is on God's perennial desire to provide for all living things. With a large crowd following him, Jesus articulates his desire to feed them, thus activating another sign that communicates his identity and mission.

"Five barley loaves and two fish" become signs of the God's transforming power among us. Jesus takes charge by directing that people recline as he takes, gives thanks, and personally distributes the bread and the fish till all "had their fill." Twelve baskets are left over.

The sign clearly underscores Jesus' identity as the divine one, ever generous, openhanded and always ready to nourish us. To follow Jesus is to perceive his identity and to understand his mission. In John's account of the Gospel, signs are done so that all may see and believe. In so doing, we become living witnesses to God's transforming power in our lives. We make Jesus' mission our own by loving others as he loved us, and by being willing to give of ourselves so that others may be fed.

---

1 Mt 25:34–40.

Connections to Church Teaching and Tradition

■ "The other sacraments . . . are bound up with the Eucharist and are directed towards it.[1] For in the most blessed Eucharist is contained the entire spiritual wealth of the church,[2] that is, Christ himself, our Pasch and our living bread, who gives life to people through his flesh—that flesh which is given life and gives life by the holy Spirit" (PO, 5).

■ "However, no Christian community is built up which does not grow from and hinge on the celebration of the most holy Eucharist" (PO, 6).

■ "The Kingdom inaugurated by Christ perfects the original goodness of the created order and of human activity . . . . Freed from evil and being placed once more in communion with God, man is able to continue the work of Jesus, with the help of his Spirit" (CSDC, 325).

---

1 "The Eucharist is as it were the completion of the spiritual life and the summit of all the sacraments" (St. Thomas Aquinas, *Summa Theologiae* III, q. 73 a. 3 c); cf. *Summa Theologiae* III, q. 65 a. 3.

2 Cf. St. Thomas Aquinas *Summa Theologiae* III, q. 65, a. 3, ad 1; q. 79, a. 1, c. et ad 1.

Exodus 16:2–4, 12–15　Soon after crossing the Red Sea, Moses is confronted by the people's complaints for meat and bread. They grumble to Moses and God, desiring the food they had as slaves in Egypt rather than the minimal desert nourishment as free people more deeply connected to God. The people question the value of their liberation by God when food is so scarce.

Despite the grumbling and calling their liberation into question, God responds by providing nourishment in the desert with a material for bread and with quail for meat. Manna, a sweet-tasting insect residue, is a natural occurrence in the desert, while quail are easily available when they land exhausted from their European migration to Sinai. Both natural occurrences are interpreted as manifestations of God's care and covenant love. Despite their doubts about the value of freedom without food, God does not give up on the people, providing constant care and nourishment.

Psalm 78:3–4, 23–24, 25, 54 (24b)　Remembering God's "glorious deeds" and passing those stories on to future generations is the focus of Psalm 78. Both remembering and passing on are crucial if cultural identity and values are to be learned and cherished. The psalmist wants all to know "the glorious deeds" that God has wrought. Foremost among those deeds is manna, the "heavenly bread" that God rained down from heaven for nourishment in the desert.

God "commanded the skies above / and opened the doors of heaven" to show provident care for the people. God's care was bountiful and magnificent, allowing humans to partake of "the bread of angels." Such care enabled God's people to enter the "holy land" God had gifted them with and to establish Mount Zion as the Lord's holy mountain. Such "wonders" must never be forgotten, and each generation is responsible to pass those stories to the next. These memories will be recalled and refashioned by future generations in their experience of Jesus, the "heavenly bread."

Ephesians 4:17, 20–24　The Ephesians are directed to live fully in Christ and not like the Gentiles or pagans, those who do not know Christ. "Truth is in Jesus" and not in the "futility" of the mind. Since the Ephesians have been taught in Christ, they are to live the truth of Christ in all things. They are to put away their old selves, their former ways of living and thinking, characterized by deceit and futility. In Christ, they have become new creations, "renewed" in their minds and bodies, living lives in accordance with "God's way in righteousness and holiness of truth."

Righteous living demands that we live lives of justice, lives of right relationship with God, others, and all of creation. Such just lives are lived in the transparency of truth that we have learned from Christ. If "truth is in Jesus," then our whole beings are to be so transformed into Christ that we no longer think and act as before. In Christ we find the fullness of all we need to live, know, and be satisfied.

John 6:24–35　John's Bread of Life discourse continues this Sunday with Jesus' strong affirmation, "I am the bread of life." After the multiplication of the loaves and fishes, the crowd follows Jesus because they are attracted by the wonders that he can accomplish. John's use of layered meanings to the words spoken by both Jesus and the crowd are evident in this passage. While the crowd speaks of surface realities like bread, sign, and works, Jesus reworks these concerns into faith in him as the "Son of Man" on whom "the Father, God, has set his seal."

Jesus is concerned that they seek him as the wonder-worker who can provide for their material needs, but do not seek to believe in him as the one sent by God. Jesus challenges them to work for food "that endures to eternal life," which he can give to them, if only they open their minds and hearts to see his true identity. Such work, if done well, would ultimately be God's work, enabling faith to flower in those who are open to seeing and understanding Jesus more deeply.

Still the crowd demands a sign similar to the "bread from heaven" given to their ancestors in the desert. Jesus responds that God is the source of the true bread that nourishes and endures forever. Still thinking of their physical needs, the crowd asks for such bread. Jesus asserts that "I am the bread of life," which endures and always satisfies both hunger and thirst. With the crowd, we too are challenged to come to Jesus, the bread sent by God to nourish and satisfy all our needs.

Nineteenth Sunday in Ordinary Time

Jesus, Our Source of Nourishment

Connections to Church Teaching and Tradition

- "I cannot let this Holy Thursday . . . pass without halting before the 'Eucharistic face' of Christ and pointing out . . . the centrality of the Eucharist. From it the Church draws her life. From this 'living bread' she draws her nourishment. How could I not feel the need to urge everyone to experience it ever anew?" (EDE, 7).

- Jesus is the only one who can reveal God to others because he has seen him and knows him (CCC, 151).

- "'*Daily*' . . . taken literally . . . refers directly to the Bread of Life, the Body of Christ" (CCC, 2837).

1 Kings 19:4–8   This event in the Elijah narratives takes place soon after Elijah has overcome the prophets of Baal on Mount Carmel. Furious at Elijah, King Ahab and his wife Jezebel are determined to kill him. Fleeing to the desert, Elijah becomes despondent and dejected, asking God for death. The prophetic vocation is fraught with opposition, rejection, and persecution, and Elijah has had enough for one lifetime. But God has other plans. Resting under a broom tree, Elijah twice experiences an angel waking him and ordering him to eat. Elijah eats and drinks from the hearth cake and water miraculously provided. Nourished and refreshed, Elijah is again energized, walking forty days and nights to encounter the Lord at Horeb, or Mount Sinai.

Like Moses, Elijah journeys through the desert to encounter the Lord and to be reenergized for service to God and others. Like Moses and the people in their desert journey, God does not give up on Elijah, but nourishes and sustains him. Christians affirm that God nourishes us on our life's journey through Christ, the living bread that came down from heaven.

Psalm 34:2–3, 4–5, 6–7, 8–9 (9a)   For the next three Sundays, various verses from Psalm 34 will be our response to the readings, all connected with the same refrain, "Taste and see the goodness of the Lord." The refrain correlates with the Bread of Life Gospel passages from John, chapter 6. On all three Sundays, we will be invited to come to know the Lord not just with our minds, but with our whole being. To "taste and see" the Lord is to experience the Lord holistically, not superficially or intellectually.

Psalm 34 is a psalm of praise to God who has rescued the psalmist from danger, fear, and affliction. The psalmist invites all to trust and have confidence in God, who hears our pleas and responds to our calls for help. The "angel of the Lord," a euphemism for God, actually "encamps" around those who call upon the Lord and "delivers" them. The psalmist again invites all to put trust in God by playing on the image of food. Taste and you will see, or experience, the goodness of the Lord.

Ephesians 4:30—5:2   Using baptismal imagery, this passage from Ephesians exhorts the community to live in imitation of God, as exemplified in Christ. Anything that disrupts the love, unity, and harmony of the community "grieves" the Spirit of God. Rather, all bitterness, rivalry, and anger must be replaced by kindness, compassion, and forgiveness. In imitation of God who has forgiven us in Christ, we are called to forgive one another.

Christ was willing to sacrifice himself completely for our sake. Through our Baptism, we are called to give of ourselves for others. In so doing, we become living witnesses to Jesus, through the power of the Spirit. Like Jesus, we too become "a fragrant aroma" to God and to all we encounter. In the Spirit, we become more like Jesus, the source of all our growth, nourishment, and right living.

John 6:41–51   The Gospel continues Jesus' argument with an unbelieving crowd after his declaration in being the bread that came down from heaven. The crowd, in murmuring reminiscent of the lack of faith in God during the Exodus desert experience, responds that they know Jesus' parentage, so how can he claim heavenly origins. Jesus responds that to know him demands that they be open to being drawn to him by the Father, who is the true teacher in all matters of faith. If they were open to the Father's actions in their lives, they would come to know and accept Jesus, the "bread of life."

Jesus continues to instruct them by affirming that to know him is to know the Father. Since he is the "bread of life," whoever believes in him will have eternal life. The desert manna that came down from heaven did not provide eternal life. Rather, Jesus, the "living bread that came down from heaven," is true bread that provides eternal life to all who believe and partake, "whoever eats this bread will live forever."

Jesus, our true source of nourishment, goes on to specify that the bread he will give is his "flesh for the life of the world." Partaking of Jesus, the "bread of life," calls all who partake to give of themselves for the life of the world. We are nourished by Jesus so that we can nourish others both physically and spiritually. Jesus came to model how to be sources of nourishment for one another, by being willing to partake of the rich nourishment that the Father has given us in Christ.

Connections to Church Teaching and Tradition

- The assumption is the dogma recognizing that Mary was taken up body and soul into heavenly glory at the end of her earthly life (CCC, Glossary).

- Mary was full of grace from the moment of her conception. Our belief in the immaculate conception of Mary leads naturally to our belief in her assumption (CCC, 491).

- In her assumption, Mary participates in the Resurrection of Christ and anticipates the resurrection of other Christians (CCC, 966).

Revelation 11:19a; 12:1–6a, 10ab   Some statues and paintings of Mary depict her with bright garments, standing on the moon, and wearing a crown of 12 stars. The images are taken from today's passage in the book of Revelation, which the Church interprets as a prophecy concerning Mary as the Mother of God and the one for whom God prepared a special place on the occasion of her assumption. On the surface, this chapter tells of a huge red dragon waiting to devour the newborn son of a woman giving birth. The dragon apparently intends to stop the son from becoming the ruler of all the nations, but ultimately has no power to do so. References to Mary are few outside the four accounts of the Gospel, so this passage from Revelation has become a favorite one to hear at celebrations of Our Lady. The imagery affirms many things: that God has made her special, that she is a mother, that her son is a ruler, that the son will have power over enemies of all kinds, and that God will prepare a place for the child's mother. This reading is heard on the solemnity of the Assumption of Mary because it mentions that special place: "[S]he had a place prepared by God." The Catholic Church believes that Mary was assumed body and soul into heaven at the end of her earthly days. Through her immaculate conception, God had prepared her for the birth of Jesus. Through her assumption, God rewards her role in the history of salvation.

Psalm 45:10, 11, 12, 16 (10bc)   Mary's assumption into heaven can be compared to the joyful occasion when a bride enters a new home with a groom. It is a scene filled with love, excitement, comfort, and safety, promising an enduring future of happiness. Psalm 45 was probably composed for the wedding of a king. The bride in question is becoming his queen. She is instructed him to "turn your ear, / forget your people and your father's house." She makes her new home with the groom. The liturgy today reinterprets this psalm in the light of the assumption. Mary is brought to heaven, to a new home, where she will rule as queen. Although we are accustomed to thinking of Mary as God's daughter and mother, this Responsorial Psalm calls her God's bride. The greatest joy that many people can imagine—the bliss of newly married life—is but a foreshadowing of the joy that awaits God's faithful people in heaven.

1 Corinthians 15:20–27   The Resurrection of Christ triumphed over death. All suffered because of Adam's sin, but all may be brought to life because of Christ. We believe that Christ is risen, but also that his Resurrection made it possible for others to rise as well. Saint Paul calls Christ "the firstfruits of those who have fallen asleep." Others will follow. In the assumption of Mary, we affirm a similar belief. We believe that she has been taken to heaven to enjoy eternal life with Christ. We believe that the Resurrection of Christ made this possible. We hope in our own resurrection because of the assumption of Mary. After all, Jesus was the Son of God. His Resurrection was miraculous, but he was God. Mary was just like us. For her to enjoy eternal life brings the point home: God invites us into the same future.

Luke 1:39–56   When Mary visited Elizabeth, their conversation summarized many key points of our faith. Mary is "blessed . . . among women"; that is, she was made special among all others for her role in salvation history. Elizabeth calls her "the mother of my Lord," because she carries Jesus in her womb. Mary is also blessed because she believed that the Lord would fulfill the promises she heard. In her great hymn of praise, the Magnificat, Mary praises God for lifting up the lowly, and for remembering the promise to Abraham and his children forever. The accounts of the Gospel do not tell about how Mary's earthly life came to an end, nor do they explicitly tell of her assumption into heaven. The Catholic Church believes in her assumption because of other beliefs made clear in scripture passages like these. If she is truly "blessed . . . among women," then it is logical to conclude that God prepared an eternal home for the one who was made worthy to become the mother of his only Son.

FOUNDATIONS FOR PREACHING AND TEACHING © 2011 Liturgy Training Publications.

Connections to Church Teaching and Tradition

- "When for the first time Jesus spoke of this food, his listeners were astonished and bewildered, which forced the Master to emphasize the objective truth of his words: '. . . unless you eat the flesh of the Son of Man and drink his blood, you have no life within you.'[1] This is no metaphorical food: 'My flesh is food indeed, and my blood is drink indeed'[2]" (EDE, 16).

- "At the Last Supper . . . Our Lord instituted the Eucharistic Sacrifice of His Body and Blood . . . . those who participate in it through holy Communion eat the flesh of Christ and drink the blood of Christ and thus receive grace, which is the beginning of eternal life, and the 'medicine of immortality' according to Our Lord's last words: 'The man who eats my flesh and drinks my blood enjoys eternal life, and I will raise him up on the last day'[3]" (MF, 4–5).

- "The Father in heaven urges us . . . to ask for the bread of heaven. [Christ] himself is the bread who . . . furnishes the faithful each day with food from heaven"[4] (CCC, 2837).

---

1 Jn 6:53.
2 Jn 6:55.
3 Jn 6:55.
4 St. Peter Chrysologus, *Sermo* 67: PL 52, 392; cf. Jn 6:51.

Proverbs 9:1–6 Wisdom, personified as a woman, is pictured making preparations for a rich feast of meat and wine. Her home set upon seven columns indicates both lavishness and the universal appeal of her dwelling, seven being a perfect or universal number. She sends out her maidens to invite the "simple" and those who lack understanding to come and feast in her house. Those who accept her invitation will learn wisdom and live enriched lives that "forsake foolishness."

The invitation to the "simple" indicates the necessity for a childlike innocence and openness to seeing, learning, and believing. The arrogant and those who think they know all find the invitation useless. The appeal is universal, addressed to all who are open to learning. The rewards are life guided by Wisdom, something that endures no matter what life brings.

To partake in food and drink that nourishes for a lifetime is what Wisdom offers. This passage provides a backdrop to the Bread of Life discourse in chapter 6 of John's account of the Gospel. Christians believe Jesus is the wisdom of God who invites us to partake of his flesh and blood, food that nourishes for eternal life.

Psalm 34:2–3, 4–5, 6–7 (9a) Praising and thanking God for help in time of need summarizes these verses from Psalm 34, a thanksgiving psalm with strong wisdom motifs. Within the context of a liturgical setting, the psalmist invites the community to "glorify the Lord" for delivering the psalmist from "all my fears." The psalmist continues with a call to look to the Lord at all times, for the Lord hears and answers the call of the poor and lowly.

The psalm's wisdom elements come to the fore in the form of instructions on how to deal with life, especially during difficult times. Seeking the Lord and trusting in God's provident care and response is the mainstay of a life lived in the company of wisdom. Such wisdom demands a childlike attitude, openness, and dependence upon God. Immersed in this wisdom, life becomes "radiant with joy" no matter what comes.

Ephesians 5:15–20 This moral exhortation, or *parenesis*, addressed to the Ephesians is full of wisdom language and instruction. The community is admonished to live wisely, not like the foolish. They are to seize every opportunity to live wisely, for wisdom is constantly challenged by the evil and disruption around them. Living wisely demands an attunement to the "will of the Lord," leading to understanding and God-like living, in contrast to ignorance infected by the powers of evil. Drunkenness and debauchery are signs of a life lived in foolishness and ignorance.

Wisdom living is "filled with the Spirit," continually evoking each community member to give thanks to God in the name of Jesus, for all of life. *Eucharista*, the Greek word for *thanksgiving*, is to be expressed both communally and holistically "in psalms and hymns and spiritual songs, singing and playing to the Lord in your hearts." The heart of any Christian wisdom community is the offering of thanksgiving to our Trinitarian God, in all places and at all times.

John 6:51–58 For four Sundays, we have been proclaiming the Bread of Life discourse from John's account of the Gospel, chapter 6. Today's reading brings the various strands of the discourse to focus on the meaning and significance of the Christian community's eucharistic gathering. Picking up from last Sunday's reading, Jesus asserts once again that "I am the living bread that came down from heaven." Those who partake of this bread, Jesus' flesh given for the life of the world, will live forever. The crowd, thinking literally as usual, cannot comprehend Jesus' words. Jesus begins to elaborate rather clearly and repeatedly his intended meaning. Four times, in clear and direct speech, Jesus affirms that "my flesh is true food, and my blood is true drink." If we desire to have eternal life and be one with Christ, as he is one with the Father, then we are to eat his flesh and drink his blood, that same incarnate flesh and blood that was given "for the life of the world." We do not become one with Christ through our minds or hearts. We become one with him by feeding on his body and blood, thus allowing him to remain with us and allowing us to be one with him. This sacramental indwelling unites all those who partake of Jesus' flesh and blood, forming one body and one mind. To be Christian is to be deeply one with God by partaking of Jesus, our true food and true drink. Then come, eat and drink.

Connections to Church Teaching and Tradition

- "'Will you also go away?':[1] the Lord's question echoes through the ages, as a loving invitation to discover that only he has 'the words of eternal life'[2] *and that to receive in faith the gift of his Eucharist is to receive the Lord himself*" (CCC, 1336).

- "[Jesus] unveiled the authentic content of his messianic kingship . . . in the transcendent identity of the Son of Man 'who came down from heaven'[3] " (CCC, 440).

- "The Church . . . believes in the life-giving presence of Christ . . . active . . . through the Eucharist, the bread that gives eternal life" (CCC, 1509).

Joshua 24:1–2a, 15–17, 18b   After the death of Moses, Joshua is the designated leader who oversees the people's entrance into the Promised Land. With God's help, they are successful in settling the land, defeating some occupants and forming alliances with others. Chapter 24 recounts a covenant renewal ceremony at the sacred site of Shechem in which those new to the covenant and those already committed to it are asked to make a clear and public choice either for or against God.

Joshua offers three choices of gods: the god of your fathers beyond the rivers; the god of the Amorites in whose land you now dwell; or the God of the Israelites, Yahweh. As for Joshua and his household, the choice is clear: "we will serve the LORD." The tribes respond with clear awareness of all the Lord had done in liberating them from Egypt, in providing for them on their desert journey and in assisting them in settling in the land. Their choice is clear: "we also will serve the LORD." In today's Gospel, Jesus challenges his disciples to make a similar choice.

Psalm 34:2–3, 16–17, 18–19, 20–21 (9a)   For three Sundays, we have sung different verses of this praise and thanksgiving psalm with the refrain "Taste and see the goodness of the Lord." Today's verses emphasize that God "has eyes for the just / and ears for their cries," while "the LORD confronts the evildoers, / to destroy the remembrance of them." The psalm provides guidance and instruction for the wise, showing them how to live in peace and security no matter what life brings. The lowly, the just, and the brokenhearted, along with the wicked, will experience vicissitudes in life. While evildoers place their trust in other powers, the Lord is attuned to the cries of the lowly and the just, rescuing and delivering them from all distress. Their trust in God enables them to handle life's many difficulties. God even watches over all their bones so that none may be broken. God's love and care evoke praise and thanksgiving at all times.

Ephesians 5:21–32 or 5:2a, 25–32   The heavily patriarchal household codes of the times become the hinge on which the author of Ephesians hangs the Christian virtue of being "subordinate to one another out of reverence for Christ." Mutual love demands mutual subordination to one another out of love. While mutual deference between wives and husbands is implied, only the wife is told to be subordinate to the husband, who is the "head of his wife." Further, the husband is compared with Christ, whose love and willingness to die for the Church becomes the model of how the husband is to relate to his wife. The conclusion is stark for modern ears: "as the church is subordinate to Christ, so wives should be subordinate to their husbands in everything."

Mutual love and subordination is what the author intended, with the husband's self sacrificing love compared to Christ's. But the argument subordinates only the wife to the husband, and historically, the text has been used to justify a wife's inferiority. Any reflection on this passage needs to emphasize the mutual love, subordination, equality, and dignity of both husbands and wives. Serving one another in the Lord is the choice that both spouses have made.

John 6:60–69   Today concludes the Bread of Life discourse we have been proclaiming for five Sundays. Some of Jesus' own disciples "were murmuring" because they found his claim to be the living bread come down from heaven difficult to accept. Jesus responds that if this is difficult for them, how would they react if they saw him returning to where he came from? Jesus insists that the "flesh," their human way of viewing things, is of no avail. What is needed is spirit and life; namely, belief in the words that Jesus has spoken to them.

Belief in Jesus' words and claim do not come naturally. It is a gift given by the Father that enables understanding of Jesus' words and identity. Some will believe. Others will not. As many of his followers leave him, Jesus turns to the Twelve and asks, "Do you also want to leave?" Similar to his confession at Caesarea Philippi in the other accounts of the Gospel, Peter speaks for the Twelve, affirming that Jesus has the words of eternal life, and they have come to believe in him as the Holy One of God.

It appears that the Twelve have received the Father's gift of faith in Jesus and have made their choice. Believing that he has come from God, they have chosen to be one with him and to serve Christ as he serves them.

1 Jn 6:67.
2 Jn 6:68.
3 Jn 3:13.

Be Doers of the Word

Connections to Church Teaching and Tradition

■ "The joys and hopes, the grief and anguish of the people of our time, especially of those who are poor and afflicted, are the joys and hopes, the grief and anguish of the followers of Christ as well. Nothing that is genuinely human fails to find an echo in their hearts" (GS, 1).

■ ". . . the invitation we give to celebrate Peace resounds as an invitation to practice Justice: 'Justice will bring about Peace.'[1] We repeat this today in a more incisive and dynamic formula: 'If you want Peace, work for Justice'" (DOP).

■ "Action on behalf of justice and participation in the transformation of the world fully appear to us as a constitutive dimension of the preaching of the Gospel, or in other words, of the Church's mission for the redemption of the human race and its liberation from every oppressive situation" (JM, 6).

■ "[The Church] recognizes that anyone who ventures to speak to people about justice must first be just. . . . Hence we must undertake an examination of the modes of acting and of the possessions and life style found within the Church herself" (JM, 40).

Deuteronomy 4:1–2, 6–8 Before entering the Promised Land, Moses admonishes the Israelites to "hear" the Lord's statutes and decrees. The *Shema'*, or "Hear, Israel," is Deuteronomy's solemn and cultic manner of calling the people to wholehearted attention and appropriation of God's Word. Only active attentiveness to God's Word will lead to fullness of life and possession of the land God promised. Not adding to or subtracting from God's commands, a common stipulation in the laws of the ancient world, insured fidelity to what had been communicated.

Two reasons are given for attentiveness and fidelity to God's commands. Observance of God's law insures God's blessings on the land and the people. Secondly, the wisdom and intelligence of God's laws will be evident to all nations through the Israelites' manner of living. Their closeness to God and the wisdom of God's commands manifested when they live lives of justice will be admired and envied by all nations. Therefore, *Shema'*, "Hear, Israel."

Psalm 15:2–3, 3–4, 4–5 (1a) Psalm 15 has temple and ritual worship as its backdrop. Some have called it an "entrance liturgy" for pilgrims or anyone desiring to know the requirements for temple worship. The response given by the temple priests is both an instruction in living and an examination of the life path one has chosen to walk. Living in the presence of the Lord demands a life lived justly, exercising right relationship with all in thought, word, and deed.

Specific examples of right relationship are offered to the worshipper who desires temple entrance. These include doing justice, speaking truth and not slander, causing harm to no one, fearing the Lord, not charging interest on money lent (usury), and not accepting bribes. Living thusly will bring about communal harmony and peace; along with personal well-being and integrity. Choosing this path insures God's blessings, for it integrates God's commands with everyday living and enables authentic communal worship.

James 1:17–18, 21b–22, 27 For the next five Sundays, the Second Reading will proclaim selections from the letter of James. The letter is better characterized as a moral exhortation to the baptized, those given "birth by the word of truth" who are the "firstfruits" of God's creative activity. James begins by highlighting his image of God. God, the source of all goodness, showers us with abundant blessings. Since God is changeless, God can be relied upon eternally. God desires to recreate the world, with those baptized into Christ being the "firstfruits" of God's creative love.

James exhorts God's "firstfruits" to welcome God's word with humility and to become "doers of the word and not hearers only." Warning that we can easily delude ourselves, James specifies what is required to stand before God "pure and undefiled." Care and concern for all powerless and defenseless people, "orphans and widows," is foremost. "Doers of the word" are ever diligent about removing all that would prevent them from serving God and others. James exhorts all to be and do justice.

Mark 7:1–8, 14–15, 21–23 This Sunday's return to Mark's account of the Gospel has Jesus being confronted by some religious authorities who question his disciples' fidelity to religious laws, especially ritual purity. Since Mark writes primarily for a non-Jewish audience, he spells out some of the pharisaic regulations concerning ritual purity. Jesus responds to their questions by quoting from Isaiah, who criticized the people of his day for external show in worship without internal conviction, and for elevating human precepts to the level of doctrine.

Jesus challenges the Pharisees and scribes by asserting that defilement has its source not in external actions but in interior disposition. One cannot judge merely on the basis of external actions. Rather, one has to search the heart and one's interior disposition to adequately and justly judge external actions. The list of vices, a common catalogue in moral exhortations, is used as examples of actions that manifest an interior disposition averse to God and neighbor. True defilement begins in the heart.

Mark's Jesus is not saying that laws and regulations have no value. Rather, Jesus is emphasizing the necessity of establishing laws and traditions that enhance, not minimize or distort, a person's relationship to God and others. They should help all be effective "doers of the word and not hearers only."

1 Cf. Isa 32:17.

Connections to Church Teaching and Tradition

- "Love for widows and orphans, prisoners, and the sick and needy of every kind, is as essential to [the Church] as the ministry of the sacraments and preaching of the Gospel" (DCE, 22).

- "The church . . . claims charitable works as its own mission and right . . . mercy to the poor and sick, charitable works and works . . . for the alleviation of all kinds of human need, are especially esteemed in the church[1]" (AA, 8).

- "Parishes should be measured by our help for the hungry, the homeless, the troubled, and the alienated—in our own community and beyond" (CSL).

- "The Fathers . . . of the Church . . . taught that people are bound to come to the aid of the poor and to do so not merely out of their superfluous goods" (GS, 69).

Isaiah 35:4–7a   Isaiah's salvation proclamation begins with a call to "be strong, fear not." No matter what struggles surround or overwhelm us with fear, trust that God "comes" to save. God's salvation is for all, most especially for those suffering any physical infirmity that would prevent them from full participation in religious, cultural, and communal involvement. The blind, the deaf, the lame and the mute will experience God's saving power, enabling them to become full and active members of the community. Creation will also be renewed with new life and fertility as deserts teem with life from streams and rivers that overflow in abundance. Both people and nature will experience the life-giving power of God that restores and renews. Isaiah firmly asserts that God does not and will not give up on us no matter how bad things may appear. All are called to be open to the saving power of God, a power that is attuned to the weak and the powerless, the frightened and those bereft of life. Christians believe that in the person of Jesus, God's salvation has come, healing, renewing, and restoring all to newness of life.

Psalm 146:7, 8–9, 9–10 (1b)   This "Hallelujah" psalm calls the entire community to praise the Lord with all their being (soul). Such total praise is due because God "keeps faith forever," secures justice, feeds the hungry, and liberates the captives. The Lord heals and restores the blind and those bowed down. The stranger, the fatherless, and the widow—all those socially and economically powerless and marginalized—are cared for by God's empowering love. Our faithful God is attuned to all who are in need of healing, care, protection, and fullness of life. We are called to be people who imitate God in our dealings with all, most especially those in need. A life of justice challenges us to work toward establishing right relationship with all. To be open to God operating in our lives demands that we be open to all who are in need of God's healing touch and renewing love.

James 2:1–5   James counsels all followers of Christ to live lives that manifest love for all, most especially the poor and those that society easily marginalizes because of their looks, appearance, or social status. The assembly of believers is not to operate according to the standards of those who discriminate based on wealth or possessions. James refers to these people as "judges with evil designs." We have been called by God to be "brothers and sisters" in the Lord. In Christian communities, all are treated equally, with preferential option given to the poor. The poor are especially close to the Lord because they are more attuned to depending on God and trusting God above all else. The rich tend to put their trust in other objects besides God. Ultimately, James states that God chose the poor to be "rich in faith and heirs of the kingdom." We are to imitate God in love of the poor, caring for them as they challenge us by their deep trust and love of God.

Mark 7:31–37   This miracle of the deaf mute person is unique to Mark and is unique in the manner in which Jesus performs the miracle. Jesus' touching the deaf mute (inserting fingers in his ears and placing saliva on his tongue) are not Jesus' usual manner of healing. Mark communicates lessons through this narrative that are instructive for discipleship. The locale places Jesus in Gentile territory. For Mark, Jesus' mission is not exclusively for Jews, but for all people. Jesus breaks boundaries so that all might experience God's saving power. Gentiles are open to approaching Jesus, a Jew, to request healing. Jesus does not shrink from touching, going out of his way to use fingers, saliva, groaning, and a word of command—*Ephphatha*, "be opened"—to heal and restore the person to wholeness.

Made whole by becoming able to speak and hear, the healed deaf mute becomes a sign of God's reign and saving power, realized and activated through Jesus. Isaiah's salvation oracle in the First Reading is being fulfilled in the person of Jesus. The forces of evil are being defeated through Jesus' life-giving touch. Both Jew and Gentile, along with disciples then and now, are made aware that Jesus opens ears and mouths, enabling all to hear God's words and to speak God's praises. We, like the deaf mute, are made whole, in order to reach out to others and make them whole with God's help. Like the crowd, we, too, are "exceedingly astonished," for Jesus "has done all things well."

---

1 Cf. John XXIII, Encyclical *Mater et Magistra*: AAS 53 (1961) p. 402.

God Comes to the Aid of the Faithful

Connections to Church Teaching and Tradition

■ "Our experiences of evil and suffering. . . . can shake our faith. . . . It is then we must turn to the *witnesses of faith*: to Abraham . . . , to the Virgin Mary who . . . walked into the 'night of faith'[1] in sharing the darkness of her son's suffering and death" (CCC, 164–165).

■ "The Son of God 'loved me and gave Himself up for me.'[2] By suffering for us he not only gave us an example so that we might follow in his footsteps,[3] but he also opened up a way. If we follow this path, life and death are made holy and acquire a new meaning" (GS, 22).

Isaiah 50:5–9a Popular preaching often makes an association between sin and suffering, or between holiness and good fortune. Those links cannot be legitimated by using the Old Testament, much less the New Testament. Throughout scriptural history, the prophets suffer for remaining faithful to their vocation, and the psalms often depict the innocent as undergoing unjust punishments. In today's reading, Isaiah describes the servant of God as one who is willing to undergo torment.

As we ponder this reading, there is no indication of who is inflicting the suffering. The central characters are the testifying servant and God. Unlike the complaints we hear from prophets in some prophetic books (Jeremiah 20), the servant of Isaiah 50 expresses nothing but gratitude. He recognizes God as the one who opens his ears, who keeps him from disgrace and from being proven wrong. This is the song of a disciple who values a faithful relationship with God above all else.

Psalm 116:1–2, 3–4, 5–6, 8–9 (9) This psalm of thanksgiving follows the song of the servant in beautiful harmony. Whereas the servant proclaimed that God had opened his ear, we are invited to join the psalmist in singing the praise of the God who gives ear to our cries. There is no doubt that the psalmist knew mortal danger as well as near despair. But, the plea "LORD, save my life" shows that even in the midst of a living nightmare, one can both have and express faith.

The third strophe of our psalm speaks in a particular way to the theme proclaimed by the servant. As it expresses God's special concern for the little ones and those brought low, it emphasizes the fact that, although we frequently forget it, before God we are all little and lowly. The gratitude this psalm expresses reminds us that only when we recognize our own frailty can we become aware of the immense privilege of walking in the sight of God in the land of the living.

James 2:14–18 Our selection from James fits well with today's other readings. It responds to the question, What does it mean to have faith? James insists that genuine faith in Christ is more than intellectual. Real faith is demonstrated through Christ-like actions, such as caring for the needy. The teaching in this reading from James leads us into our Gospel reading, where Peter is told that authentic faith in Jesus as Messiah implies a readiness to accept and share his cross.

Mark 8:27–35 This incident takes place during Jesus' final journey with the disciples (Mark 8:27—10:45). They are entering into a long period in which Jesus tries to teach them who he is and what it means to be his follower. Today's Gospel provides a summary statement of each of those points.

Jesus asks, "Who do you say that I am?" This question touches the central theme of Mark's account of the Gospel. While Peter's response, "You are the Christ," sounded very good, his understanding of what that implied had little in common with Jesus' own understanding of himself and his mission. That is why Jesus ordered the disciples not to tell anyone about him: they didn't know what they were talking about!

Faced with their lack of understanding, Jesus had to shatter their expectations. Mark tells us that "he began" to teach them. That "beginning" would last through the rest of the Gospel. It was beyond their imagination that a Messiah would be rejected and killed. The job of a warrior Messiah was to route Israel's enemies, not suffer at their hands. The job of a priestly Messiah was to rebuild or renew the temple, not be rejected by all the religious leaders.

Jesus' retort to Peter's rebuke underlined the problem they had to deal with. Peter had pulled Jesus aside to plead against the fate he predicted. When Jesus called Peter "Satan," the effect was not to say he was a devil, but rather a tempter. The phrase "get behind me," pointed out that Jesus, not Peter, was the teacher. The place for a disciple was following the master's lead, not vice versa.

Jesus had discerned God's plan. He knew that his confrontation with evil would lead evil to lash out at him. Peter's perspective focused on safety and triumph. Jesus knew that his prophetic ministry would bring him suffering, but he also trusted that God would see him through. That was and still is a hard message to communicate.

---

1 LG 58; RM 18.
2 Gal 2:20.
3 Cf. 1 Pet 2:21; Mt 16:24; Lk 14:27.

Connections to Church Teaching and Tradition

- "Only the great certitude of hope that my own life and history in general, despite all failures, are held firm by the indestructible power of Love, and that this gives them their meaning and importance, only this kind of hope can then give the courage to act and to persevere" (SS 35).

- "The way of perfection passes by way of the Cross. There is no holiness without renunciation and spiritual battle[1]" (CCC, 2015).

- "St. Paul often asks the faithful to pray for him so that he might proclaim the Gospel with confidence and conviction. Prayer needs to be accompanied by sacrifice. The redemptive value of suffering, accepted and offered to God with love, derives from the sacrifice of Christ himself, who calls the members of his Mystical Body to share in his sufferings, to complete them in their own flesh[2]" (RMI, 78).

Wisdom 2:12, 17–20   The book of Wisdom, also called "The Wisdom of Solomon," confronts the problem of evil. The book opens up with an exhortation to justice (1:1–15) and then moves into reflections on wickedness (1:16–2:24). The wicked are characterized as believing that life is short, that we were born by chance and we will soon be no more. Therefore, life is always ripe for revelry as we use our strength against the weak. Because of this, the wicked are characterized as friends of death (cf. 1:16). The first rationale the wicked use for besetting the just one is that he opposes their actions. Second, the just one proclaims faith in God, a faith that is an affront to their way of life. Their decision to condemn the just one becomes a test of their whole thesis. If they are correct, the just one will die as meaninglessly as they live. But the response of Wisdom goes on to say that "they erred / . . . . For God formed man to be imperishable / . . . the souls of the just are in the hand of God" (2:21—3:1).

Psalm 54:3–4, 5, 6–8 (6b)   This psalm comprises only eight verses, including the instruction to the music leader. The psalmist begins asking God, "by your name save me." Appeal to the name of God implied an appeal to God's strength and faithfulness: the essence of the divine character. It was a way of asking God to become visibly active in the petitioner's life. The whole of the psalm, like the Responsorial itself, proclaims faith that God will care for the unjustly oppressed one.

James 3:16—4:3   At the beginning of this letter, James described doubters at prayer as similar to the tossing waves of the sea, people of two minds, at war within themselves (1:6–8). In today's passage, he returns to the topic of division, this time both within the individual and in the community. What is the cause of the division? It seems to be jealousy and selfish ambition. Plato defined envy as an "ulcer of the soul," and James would probably amplify that to call it a cancer of the community. The jealousy James condemned had generated conflicts that he compared to war and murder.

And what is the remedy? "The fruit of righteousness is sown in peace." In this proverb, James brings together two major themes of this letter. The fruit of righteousness is the practice of which he spoke in last week's passage: active charity toward the needy. The sowing in peace is what makes it genuine. Righteousness is not done for show or as a means of competing with others; it springs from the peace that comes from allowing one's heart to be moved by the needs of others rather than its own passions.

Mark 9:30–37   In each of the three predictions of his Passion, Jesus referred to himself as the "Son of Man," a title that carries at least two worlds of meaning. First, it reminds the reader of Mark 2:27–28, where Jesus taught that the Sabbath was made for man, and that the Son of Man—the human being—was lord even of the Sabbath. The second looks forward to 13:26, where the title "Son of Man" hearkens to a vision from the book of Daniel in which the Son of Man comes on the clouds to receive dominion, glory, and kingship (Daniel 7:13–14). At this stage of the Gospel, no one is looking at Jesus as divine, but their faith in him implies that he is uniquely related to God.

It is this Son of Man—human and something more—who now says he will "be handed over to men" who will kill him. The passive mood of the phrase "be handed over" has clear overtones of God's involvement in all that is going to happen. Whether the disciples found that mysteriously ominous or simply too horrible to contemplate, they were afraid to ask for details. An argument about status provided the perfect escape.

As today's episode closes, we see Jesus, the master teacher, bring his lesson home with a living parable. He picks up a child—a totally dependent person with no status—and proclaims that anyone who receives one like that in his name receives "the One who sent me." The death that Jesus was going toward was politically and physically appalling. Religiously, it was considered proof of the person's God-forsakenness. Jesus, seeing their opinions about rank, declares that God is to be found where they least expect or want to go. The just one will suffer, but God will not abandon him.

---

1 Cf. 2 Tim 4.
2 Cf. Col 1:24.

Connections to Church Teaching and Tradition

- "Through Baptism the lay faithful are made one body with Christ and are established among the People of God. They are in their own way made sharers in the priestly, prophetic and kingly office of Christ" (CL, 9).

- "Through their participation in the *prophetic mission* of Christ, 'who proclaimed the kingdom of his Father by the testimony of his life and by the power of his word,' the lay faithful are given the ability and responsibility to accept the gospel in faith and to proclaim it in word and deed, without hesitating to courageously identify and denounce evil" (CL, 14).

- "The holy people of God shares also in Christ's prophetic office: it spreads abroad a living witness to him, especially by a life of faith and love and by offering to God a sacrifice of praise, the fruit of lips confessing his name[1]" (LG, 12).

Numbers 11:25–29   The book of Numbers recounts events that took place between the Exodus and the arrival at the borders of the Promised Land. In today's reading, the people had been grumbling about a lack of meat. Moses spoke to the Lord and complained that, like a foster father, the burden of caring for them was more than he could bear. God told Moses to gather seventy elders to whom he would give Moses' spirit so they could help him (11:10–15).

The text makes it clear that God bestowed the spirit on the elders, and that they prophesied as a result. Only God could choose to give or to withhold the spirit. When Joshua, Moses' closest assistant, became perturbed about others who prophesied, his complaint was that they did not follow the ritual order, so they should be prohibited from exercising the gift. Moses, more aware than others that the spirit was a free gift, did not cling to status. He not only affirmed the liberty and unpredictability of God's activity, but wished that everyone would be so gifted.

Psalm 19:8, 10, 12–13, 14 (9a)   Psalm 19 has three focal points: creation's testimony to God's goodness, the beauty of God's law, and the human desire to serve God well. In these verses, after praising God's law (*torah*), the psalmist admits that no one, no matter how faithful or vigilant, can be perfect. Even as we strive to be God's servants, we may be blind to our failings. Our only recourse is to turn to God, who will cleanse and guide us.

James 5:1–6   This, the last selection we hear this year from James, withholds nothing in condemnation of the wealthy. In those days, the major forms of wealth were land, precious metals and coins, and luxurious clothing. James mentions all three in this tirade.

James writes in the context of the impending end of the world. He warns the rich that they have stored up treasures for the last days, but the end times that are coming will reverse all their hopes. That which they could have spent on others will not only be rusted, but the money and moth-eaten garments will actually testify against them.

Their land condemns them, too. It has been planted and harvested by unpaid labor. By withholding the poor man's wage, they have become guilty of the hunger, illness, and even death of that worker and his family. The meaning of their entire lives has been nothing but themselves. What more vivid accusation could we find than, "You have fattened your hearts for the day of slaughter"!

Mark 9:38–43, 45, 47–48   The interchange between Jesus and John that opens today's Gospel presents wonderful, subtle twists. First, John explains that the disciples tried, apparently unsuccessfully, to stop someone from using Jesus' name to further Jesus' ministry. Why on earth would disciples not want others to do what Jesus did? Was it because they had not been able to do the same? (Mark 9:14–29). The ironic answer comes from John himself: "because he does not follow us." Here, one of those disciples whom Jesus rebuked in last week's Gospel for haggling over which of them was the greatest unwittingly admits to another status claim: he assumes that he and the rest of them should have followers!

Jesus wastes no time in refocusing the disciples' priorities. If someone performed a mighty deed in Jesus' name, that was a sign of the person's solidarity with Jesus and his ministry. The disciples believe that Jesus is acting with the power of the Spirit of God; therefore, they should recognize that anyone who does the kind of works he does is also graced with power from that same Spirit.

The idea of doing something in the name of Jesus comes up twice in this episode. To do something in the name of Jesus meant either that Jesus directly commissioned them to do that thing, or, at the very least, that they had the intention to work in solidarity with Jesus and his mission. Thus, Jesus says that no one who works successfully in his name can speak ill of him. This is another hard lesson for the disciples: they may walk with and speak quite well of Jesus, but their actions do not meet the criteria for really acting in his name. At the same time, there are others who may not participate in the elite circle or know the precise vocabulary, but their behavior proves that they do act in Jesus' name.

---

1 Cf. Heb 13:15.

Connections to Church Teaching and Tradition

- "The fact that human beings are social by nature indicates that the betterment of the person and the improvement of society depend on each other. . . . Life in society is not something accessory to humanity: through their dealings with others . . . men and women develop all their talents and become able to rise to their destiny" (GS, 25).

- "The intimate partnership of married life and love has been established by the creator and . . . is rooted in the contract of its partners, that is in their irrevocable personal consent" (GS, 48).

- "The building of community with migrants and new immigrants leads to a growing sense of solidarity. . . . Working closely with other advocates . . . the Church can be instrumental in developing initiatives . . . that benefit the most vulnerable members of the community" (SNL, 43).

Genesis 2:18–24   Obviously, with two incompatible creation stories in the first two chapters of Genesis, the purpose of the accounts cannot be to convey a scientific history of creation. This second creation story is far more earthy than the first, where God called the universe into existence by the use of a word. As this account begins, God has already created a man, planted a garden, and turned it over to the man. Then, this attentive God notices that the man is lonely. This is the first time in the creation narrative that God says something is "not good." To remedy the situation, God creates animals, allowing the man to name them. But not one of them was a "suitable partner" for him. The word translated as "suitable partner" can also be translated as "fit helpmate." When we see it that way, we realize that Genesis presents us with the image of a person alone as helpless. To resolve the problem, God puts the man into a sleep so deep that he cannot watch what is going to happen. Then, having created the woman, God presents her to the man, almost like the father of the bride escorting a daughter to her groom. The man expresses his delight as he repeats: this one, this one, this one! Here, we realize that Genesis is teaching theology and anthropology, not history. The point is that it is not good for a person to be alone. Human beings are social by nature. We are created to be partners and helpers one for another.

Psalm 128:1–2, 3, 4–5, 6 (see 5)   As we pray this psalm, we remember that "fear of the Lord" does not connote anxiety. In fact, it is anxiety's opposite. We have fear of the Lord when we are caught up in admiration for God's work, in those times when praise and joy rise up from our inmost being, bursting into adoration or thanks, tears, or even awed silence. Recognizing that this is a pilgrims' song, we can appreciate how people could sing it in joy, blessing one another: "Happy are you!" "May your family be as abundant as a lush vineyard!" "Live to a healthy old age and peace upon us all!" Praying this psalm leads us to recapture the joy of that garden where God created humanity.

Hebrews 2:9–11   This is the first of seven selections we will be hearing from in the Letter to the Hebrews, a work that probably originated as a homily intended to re-inspire Christians whose faith was losing its fervor. The entire first chapter is devoted to describing Christ as the most important word God has spoken to humanity. With manifold allusions to the Old Testament, the author uses traditional language to remind the people of Christ's greatness.

In our selection, the author admits that Jesus was, for a time, less than the angels, and immediately explains why that was so. Jesus chose inferiority to the angels precisely so that he could be one with humanity in all things, including death. Adding an exceptional development to the teaching of Genesis, Hebrews asserts that in the person of Jesus, God became one with humanity to consecrate us, to be brother and helper to us.

Mark 10:2–16 or 10:2–12   In this scene, we find the Pharisees trying to put Jesus in danger or trap him in legalities. The danger came from the fact that John the Baptist had been beheaded over the question of divorce (Mark 6:17–29). While that lurked in the background, rabbis of that day debated the legitimacy of divorce. As so often happened, rather than answer the Pharisees' question, Jesus asked one of his own, and, as usual, caught them in their own trap.

Jesus asked what Moses "commanded." The Pharisees responded by saying what Moses "permitted." Rather than debate the permission, Jesus explained that Moses granted that provision because of the men's hardheartedness. In reality, the law about writing a bill of divorce protected women, proving that they were free to remarry. In addition, the end of the section of the law that they cited indicated that a man had a duty to his wife, not just vice-versa (Deuteronomy 24: 1–4).

Finally, Jesus went beyond the exceptions to the law to talk about God's intent in creation. God created male and female as diverse and interdependent. No relationship on earth is more valuable than that of those whom God has brought together. In Jesus' mind, that applied not just to married couples, but to his disciples and to the whole community, so that they might live as one. According to the plan of the Creator, human beings are created to love and serve one another.

FOUNDATIONS FOR PREACHING AND TEACHING © 2011 Liturgy Training Publications.

Connections to Church Teaching and Tradition

■ "The church has always venerated the divine scriptures just as it has venerated the Body of the Lord, in that it never ceases, above all in the sacred liturgy, to partake of the bread of life and to offer it to the faithful from the one table of the word of God and the Body of Christ" (DV, 21).

■ "God is the foundational reality, not a God who is merely imagined or hypothetical, but God with a human face; he is God-with-us, the God who loves even to the Cross. When the disciple arrives at an understanding of this love of Christ 'to the end,' he cannot fail to respond to this love with a similar love: 'I will follow you wherever you go'" (*Aparecida*, 14).

■ "Charity does not exclude knowledge, but rather requires . . . and animates it. . . . Knowledge is never purely the work of the intellect . . . . if it aspires to be wisdom capable of directing man . . . it must be 'seasoned' with the 'salt' of charity. Deeds without knowledge are blind, and knowledge without love is sterile" (CIV, 30).

Wisdom 7:7–11   The book of Wisdom is probably the last book to be written in what we call the Old Testament. Although it is also entitled "The Wisdom of Solomon," the work was written long after Solomon's death and was addressed to Jews who lived among Greek people who were more impressed with their own philosophy than anything offered by God's Chosen People.

The selection we read today recalls Solomon's prayer for wisdom (1 Kings 3:6–9). We get a sense of how greatly the author values wisdom as we hear the phrases "I prayed" and then, "I pleaded." The kind of wisdom to which this refers can obviously come only from God. Wisdom is more important than power, wealth, health, or beauty. The speaker would choose wisdom even over sight, knowing that with wisdom, one can assign everything else its true and lasting value.

Psalm 90:12–13, 14–15, 16–17 (14)   This is the only psalm in the Psalter attributed to Moses, and it is the opening prayer of the fourth book of psalms. The third book of the psalms (Psalms 73–89) made frequent references to the destruction of Jerusalem and ended with the suggestion that God was rejecting the Davidic dynasty (89:39). Opening a new collection, this psalm pleas for restoration.

The verses we pray are an apt response to the First Reading's proclamation about wisdom. We ask not only to know how to value the days of our lives, but also to learn to appreciate the lessons of times of trial. Our refrain recapitulates the message as we implore God to give us the only thing necessary: the love that gives meaning to life.

Hebrews 4:12–13   Today's verses from the Letter to the Hebrews come at the end of an exhortation to remain faithful and not lose out on salvation as did Moses' people who rebelled in the desert (Hebrews 3:6—4:13). The "word" of God here may be thought of as all of revelation—from creation when the divine word brought everything into being, through the revelation of God's Word in Christ. Thus, divine revelation is alive. It continues and can be encountered again and again through the scriptures. In addition, the word of God, "sharper than any two-edged sword," is a word of judgment that goes beyond superficial appearances and cuts directly to the heart.

Just as the First Reading encourages us to seek true wisdom, this selection from Hebrews calls us to meditate on our appreciation of the word of God. Do we believe in its power? Do we consciously seek an encounter with the living God in scripture? Do we allow that word to judge and guide our daily activities and attitudes? Do we seek the wisdom of the word beyond other values?

Mark 10:17–30 or 10:17–27   As this scene opens, Jesus is on his "way," his journey to Jerusalem. As he moves toward his total self-giving, a man runs to kneel before him. There may be some incongruity in the man's question as he asks what he must do to *inherit* eternal life. The Gospel has just pointed out (10:15) that the kingdom is a free gift. It is received, not earned. Perhaps that is the reason for Jesus' terse answer: "No one is good but God alone."

As their dialogue continues, Jesus reminds the man of the commandments that refer to human relationships, and the man claims to have lived without transgressing them. Then, Jesus looks at him with the discerning gaze that tenderly lays bare the heart. Having searched the man's soul, Jesus invites him to follow him in truly fulfilling the commandments by giving his very self for others. With that, the wealthy man's enthusiasm disappears and he who had run to kneel before Jesus turns away, utterly disenchanted. As the man left, Jesus addressed his followers to underscore the fact that the invitation he had issued applied to them as well as to the retreating rich man.

In the verses preceding this incident, Jesus had claimed that "whoever does not accept the kingdom of God like a child will not enter into it." Here, Jesus teaches that for those who are attached to their wealth, entrance into the kingdom is harder than getting the biggest animal they could imagine through the smallest hole they had ever known. But, he adds, "all things are possible for God." Thus, reliance on God's grace is the way to the wisdom that will free us from whatever might impede our faithful following of Jesus.

Connections to Church Teaching and Tradition

■ "Redemption is offered to us in the sense that we have been given hope . . . . the present, even if it is arduous, can be lived and accepted if it leads towards a goal" (SS, 1).

■ ". . . anyone who does not know God, even though he may entertain all kinds of hopes, is ultimately without hope. . . . Man's great, true hope which holds firm . . . can only be God—God who has loved us and who continues to love us 'to the end,' until all 'is accomplished'[1]" (SS, 27).

■ "Today a choice must be made between paths that lead to life and paths that lead to death.[2] Paths of death . . . are paths that mark a culture without God . . . driven by the idols of power, wealth, and momentary pleasure. . . . Paths of true and full life for all, paths of eternal life, are those traced by the faith. . . . This is the life that God shares with us out of his gratuitous love, for 'it is the love that gives life'[3]" (Aparecida, 13).

---

1 Cf. Jn 13:1 and 19:30.
2 Cf Dt 30:15.
3 Benedict XIV, *Homily in the Eucharist inaugurating the Fifth General Conference of Latin American Bishops* (May 13, 2007), Aparecida, Brazil.

Isaiah 53:10–11 These short verses are found toward the end of the last of the four "Suffering Servant Songs" in Isaiah (52:13—53:12). Using both the voice of God and that of a narrator, the song presents two originally opposite appraisals of the servant and his suffering. In the beginning, the narrator describes an innocent victim whose affliction left him frighteningly marred and finally dead and buried among the wicked. Meanwhile, God's voice presents the victim as "my servant" who will prosper and be exalted. In the beginning, the narrator assumed that the victim must be guilty of some sin fitting his punishment. Eventually it became clear that "it was our infirmities he bore, / our sufferings that he endured" (53:4). In this, the servant can be compared to Moses and the prophets who suffered at and for the sin of their people.

Although the opening line of today's selection sounds exceptionally harsh, the point is not that God is pleased with pain; rather, God is pleased with the faithfulness of the servant in spite of and through the course of his suffering. As the early Church struggled to interpret Jesus' death and Resurrection, this servant song was particularly helpful. It seemed to be a perfect description of how Jesus suffered at the hands of sinful people and bore their guilt, and how God vindicated him and brought salvation through him.

Psalm 33:4–5, 18–19, 20, 22 (22) Psalm 33 is a thoroughgoing song of praise. We begin by praising God's word and works—God's self-revelation to us. Then we recognize that God's justice is expressed in kindness. The next verse reminds us that God's loving gaze is ever upon us, ready to deliver us from all evil. In the final strophe, we proclaim our faith that God is our only source of safety, the only one worth counting on. The refrain we chant sums up and deepens our appreciation of the prayer as we beg for God's mercy and proclaim and promise our trust.

Hebrews 4:14–16 These few verses from the Letter to the Hebrews introduce themes that the author will develop significantly in later parts of the letter. One of the most important of these is the image of Christ as the merciful and final High Priest. The key function of the high priest was to approach the altar of God on the Day of Atonement. He would enter the Holy of Holies with sacrifices on behalf of the people. After the sacrifice he would return wearing a different robe, representing God who was purifying the people. The allusion here is that Jesus' exaltation was his passing into the presence of God with the result that the belief in him, the confession to be held to, would bring salvation from sin.

As the author designates Jesus as Son of God, the emphasis is on divine compassion. The Son of God, far from being aloof, sympathizes with each human creature and, as we proclaimed in the psalm, offers mercy and grace whenever we are in need.

Mark 10:35–45 or 10:42–45 Last week, we heard Jesus promise one hundredfold rewards, along with persecution, to his faithful followers. Now we hear two of the principal disciples make an appeal for even greater rewards and honors with no mention of the suffering. Jesus' reply, "You do not know what you are asking," could hardly have been more pointed. In the verses we skip between these two Sunday Gospel readings, Jesus predicted his Passion for a third time, again to the utter incomprehension of his chosen disciples. Now, in his reply to James and John, Jesus refers to his ultimate self-giving as a cup and a baptism, a strong reminder to the Christian community about the meaning of their sacraments. Jesus then critiqued their understanding of himself and his mission. Following his previous references to the kingdom of God, Jesus now used the rulers of the world as a contrast to the divine. James and John had fallen into the trap of aspiring to be "great ones." What they missed was how their own Lord was leading them and giving them an example. As they were aspiring to the power of the world, Jesus tried to show them that real power, divine power, expresses itself in loving service, in giving oneself for others. Not unlike the rich man of last week's Gospel, the disciples had not yet understood that the only real security and power come from trust in God. Neither wealth nor power can prevent or survive death.

Take Courage, Jesus Is Calling

Connections to Church Teaching and Tradition

■ "The Lord tells us: 'Do not be afraid'[1]. . . . We have no other happiness, no other priority, but to be instruments of the Spirit . . . so that Jesus Christ may be known, followed, loved, adored, announced, and communicated to all, despite difficulties and resistances. This is the best service—his service!—that the church has to offer people and nations"[2] (*Aparecida*, 14).

■ "In daily shared life with Jesus . . . the disciples soon discover two completely original things about Jesus. First, it was not they who chose their master; it was Christ who chose them. Second, they were not chosen for something (e.g., to be purified, learn the Law) but for Someone, chosen to be closely bound up with his Person"[3] (*Aparecida*, 131).

■ "From God's standpoint, faith liberates reason from its blind spots and therefore helps it to be ever more fully itself. Faith enables reason to do its work more effectively and to see its proper object more clearly" (DCE, 28).

Jeremiah 31:7–9 Although much of the book of Jeremiah describes the people's disobedience to their covenant with God and their subsequent exile, Jeremiah's vocation had been described as "to root up and to tear down, to destroy and to demolish, to build and to plant" (1:10). The selection we read today is part of the rebuilding of the people, also called the "Book of Comfort" (Jeremiah 30:1—33:26), which promised a return from exile. What we hear today from the Book of Comfort is an exuberant cry of gratitude for God's restoration of the people. Addressed to a people in exile, refugees scattered "to the ends of the world," it underlines the great contrast between the weakness of the people and God's strength and faithfulness. Their restoration has nothing to do with their merit and everything to do with God's great love. Jeremiah offers us an image of God as a consoler, a shepherd who leads the people to refreshing streams, a road-building father who is careful to see that no one stumbles along the way. We also note that it is the most vulnerable who get special mention: the blind, the lame, and the pregnant women. They have a future for no other reason than having been chosen by God.

Psalm 126:1–2, 2–3, 4–5, 6 (3) This psalm reflects both remembrance of God's saving actions and hope that the same will happen in the future. In recalling the return of the exiles from Babylon, it emphasizes the way God creates something new and wonderful out of disastrous circumstances. Although God's punishment may have been harsh, the people also know the appropriateness of joyous laughter in God's presence. Because their dreams were once fulfilled, they have confidence that God will again restore their fortunes and fill them with joy.

Hebrews 5:1–6 After God instructed Moses to appoint Aaron and his sons as priests, the priesthood became a hereditary office (Exodus 28:1–5, 29:29). Thus, because Jesus was not of the priestly class, the author of the Letter to the Hebrews insists that his priesthood, like Aaron's, was specifically appointed by God. While we can therefore see some similarity between Aaron and Jesus, there is even greater contrast between them. Repeating a citation from Hebrews 1:1–13, which extols Christ's all-surpassing greatness, the author uses a phrase from Psalm 2:7, *"You are my son: / this day I have begotten you,"* insisting that Christ is far more than Aaron: truly God's begotten Son. Finally, we have a citation from Psalm 110:4, *"You are a priest forever / according to the order of Melchizedek."* That same phrase will be cited in Hebrews 6:20, 7:17, and 21. Although there was no "order" of priests in the line of Melchizedek, Hebrews will indicate that Melchizedek ranked over even Abraham, and because no one knew his ancestry, his priesthood was forever (7:3). The point the author makes over and again is that Christ's priesthood is superior to any other; it is eternal and it is God the Father who has given him his glory.

Mark 10:46–52 In the structure of Mark's account of the Gospel, this incident is symbolic of the disciples' slow growth in their understanding of Jesus' mission and message. This is Mark's second account of Jesus healing a blind man. In the first account (8:22–26), the healing took place in two parts; after Jesus' first touch, the man's vision was not clear. In between these two healing incidents, Mark has recounted Jesus' three predictions of the Passion and the disciples' seemingly invincible incomprehension of what he was saying. The implication seems to be that their fear and preconceptions made them blinder than the beggar.

As Mark relates the incident, Bartimaeus hears that Jesus is nearby and begins to call to him for help. By using the title "Son of David," he acknowledges Jesus as a successor to Israel's most important king, the first to whom the words "you are my son: / this day I have begotten you" (Psalm 2:7) were addressed. Although the crowds attempted to silence him, Bartimaeus's hope in Jesus proved more powerful than their objections. The very people who tried to suppress his shouts were sent to tell him to take courage because Jesus was calling him. In his encounter with Jesus, Bartimaeus modeled the faith that the disciples had been failing to attain. Asking for healing rather than money, he responded to Jesus with the insight and courage to become disciple and join him on the fateful road to Jerusalem.

1 Mt 28:5.
2 Cf. EN 1.
3 Cf. Mk 1:17; 2:14.

Connections to Church Teaching and Tradition

- "[The] Beatitudes are taught by Jesus as the foundations for a life of authentic Christian discipleship and the attainment of ultimate happiness. They give spirit to the Law of the Ten Commandments and bring perfection to moral life. That spirit is ultimately the spirit of love. In response to a question from the leader of the people, Jesus taught that love is at the heart of all law" (USCCA, 308–309).

- Purity of heart enables us to see as God sees and accept and love others as our neighbors (CCC, 2519).

- "Eternal life is therefore the life of God himself and at the same time the life of the children of God. As they ponder this unexpected and inexpressible truth which comes to us from God in Christ, believers cannot fail to be filled with ever new wonder and unbounded gratitude" (EV, 38).

Revelation 7:2–4, 9–14   As its name suggests, the book of Revelation is a type of literature in which the author, often writing in the name of a famous person, relates a vision about what is to come, whether in heaven or on earth. Making ample use of symbolism, this type of literature generally speaks to a suffering people, encouraging them to hold fast because God will surely deliver them. In today's reading, John recounts a vision of those who will be delivered in the end times. The number 144,000, rather than being a literal count, is most likely 1,000 times the square of 12 tribes, or perhaps 1,000 times the tribes times the apostles. In addition, the group is described as a great multitude representing every people and nation on the earth.

In response to the question of who these people are, the answer is the cryptic "they have washed their robes and made them white in the Blood of the Lamb." Because their clothing is symbolic of who one is, the author wants us to know that while sharing in the sufferings of Christ, these are the ones who remained faithful, even to the shedding of their own blood. They now rejoice in the presence of God.

Psalm 24:1bc–2, 3–4ab, 5–6 (see 6)   Aptly, this psalm is considered a processional psalm, and we could almost imagine the multitudes approaching the throne, singing it as a victory hymn to the Lamb. It begins by declaring that all creation belongs to the creator. When the psalm speaks of the "mountain of the Lord," it refers to Mount Zion, the location of the temple, and thus of God's special presence. In order to truly enter into the presence of God, one must have pure hands and heart. In other words, one's actions and attitudes must be rooted in love of God and neighbor, not in the vanities of the world. Like the multitudes described in Revelation, these people who long to see the face of God will have a blessed ending to their search.

1 John 3:1–3   John's account of the Gospel speaks more of love than all of the other accounts put together, and, as short as it is, 1 John mentions the word even more than John's account of the Gospel does. Our passage opens with an exclamation: "See what love . . . ." The greatness of God's love is not just an esoteric idea. It becomes palpable in its effects. It actually makes us children of God. According to the theology of John, those who believe in Jesus' name are children begotten by God (John 1:12–13), reborn from above (John 3:3). This is more than simply being God's creatures, or even a Chosen People. According to John, this is the most profound relation to God possible in this life. And yet, there is more.

John goes on to say that what we will be has not been revealed. Now, as believers, we submit our lives to him, imitating the earthly Jesus to the best of our ability. But, the day is coming when we will not simply remember Jesus, nor merely experience what it means to be children of God. In the future, when we see Christ as he is in the glory of the Father, that vision will transform us. Now we strive to imitate him, then we will "be like him." It is almost as if now, as disciples, we make choices in faith. The choice of faith brings us into a unique relationship with God. Because of that, we strive to be ever more like Christ. Now, as Paul says, we see dimly, as in a mirror. Then, when we see the glorified Christ face to face, we will be transformed in ways we cannot imagine (see 1 Corinthians 13:12 and 2 Corinthians 3:18).

Matthew 5:1–12a   In the proclamation of the Beatitudes, we could imagine Jesus describing the very multitudes John described in Revelation, the children of God of whom 1 John writes. Whereas Revelation underlined their number and diversity, and 1 John underlined their unique relationship with God, Jesus talks about the attitudes that lead to their actions.

The people who are the objects of divine favor, the blessed, are those who recognize that they have nothing to bring to God but are dependent on grace for everything. Injustice causes them to mourn, while their desire for right is as strong as hunger and thirst. Hearts fully devoted to God lead them to act with mercy and to sow peace. Their way of living, like that of Jesus himself, will be an affront to powers of domination and thus, like the Master, they, too, will suffer. But even as they have grown in his image, they cannot imagine what awaits them in the end.

Connections to Church Teaching and Tradition

■ "Christian faith has retained the core of Israel's faith, while at the same time giving it new depth and breadth. The pious Jew prayed daily the words of the Book of Deuteronomy which expressed the heart of his existence: 'Hear, O Israel: the Lord our God is one Lord. . . .'[1] Jesus united into a single precept this commandment of love for God and the commandment of love for neighbor. . . . Since God has first loved us,[2] love is now no longer a mere 'command'; it is the response to the gift of love with which God draws near to us. In a world where the name of God is sometimes associated with vengeance or even a duty of hatred and violence, this message is both timely and significant" (DCE, 1).

■ "Reading these sacred texts . . . produces authentic fruits of conversion of heart" (EIA, 12).

■ In their love for one another, the disciples imitate Jesus' love (CCC, 1823).

Deuteronomy 6:2–6   Deuteronomy, the title of which is translated as "second law-giving," reads as if it were three long homilies in which Moses interpreted the law. It is presented as his final message. Our selection from Deuteronomy is a bridge between two discourses. As Moses ends one, he reminds the people to "Fear the LORD," which implies that they should revere and never forget God's greatness. He then goes on to tell them that keeping the law will assure them a long life in a land of "milk and honey," a phrase that implies that the land would be rich with cattle and crops. The centerpiece of today's reading begins with "Hear, O Israel! The LORD is our God. . . ." This is the beginning of the *Shema'*, the prayer spoken by devout Jews every evening and morning, in times of danger and when they are on their deathbed (Deuteronomy 6:4–9).

As the core of the law, the *Shema'* reminds the people that the God who has entered their history is the only God. To love that God with their heart implies that they love God with their intellect, remembering God's great deeds. To love God with the soul means to love him with their affect. To love God with all one's strength means not only with physical strength, but with all they possess as well. Loving God in this way, they will be faithful in every dimension of their personal life. That is the injunction they are to take to heart.

Psalm 18:2–3, 3–4, 47, 51 (2)   This psalm leads us to do just what Moses ordered, to take the law of the Lord to heart, to meditate on it as a sign of God's love. As the psalm praises God's law, it reminds us that rather than being legalistic, the law is a source of wisdom, of joy, of enlightenment; it puts us on the route to justice. As we remember all of that, we joyfully exclaim, "I love you, Lord, my strength!"

Hebrews 7:23–28   Today's passage from Hebrews continues the theme of the absolute superiority of Jesus' priesthood. The author cites three reasons for that: Jesus' singular priesthood is eternal, his self-sacrifice was once-for-all, and he was appointed by God's own oath (see 7:20–21). As a result of that, Jesus is "always able to save" and forever "makes intercession" for those who approach God through him. In that continual priestly role, Christ is not only the high priest representing his own before God, but also the representative of God whose concern for humanity never ceases.

Mark 12:28b–34   The Lectionary's progressive reading of Mark has skipped Jesus' entry into Jerusalem, the curse of a fig tree, the cleansing of the temple, and questions designed to implicate him as an insurrectionist or a heretic. Those readings belong most properly to Lent and Holy Week.

The scribe who asks Jesus about the "first" or greatest of the commandments seems to be motivated more sympathetically than most. Unlike many others, he is genuinely seeking Jesus' opinion (see verse 28a). What we witness here appears to be a conversation about faith between two men who loved their tradition. Replying to the scribe's question, Jesus recited the *Shema'*, something he had presumably done twice a day since he had first learned to pray. Much like a creed, the *Shema'* reminded the people of their special relationship to the one true God. That, of course, helped them maintain their unique identity in times of occupation by foreigners, exile, or other threats to their life as a people of faith. As usually happened, Jesus deepened the scribe's original question. Not stopping with the issue of the first commandment, he immediately added the injunction of Leviticus 19:18b: "You shall love your neighbor as yourself: I am the LORD." Recognizing that reference, Jesus' audience would have immediately understood Jesus' teaching: love of God necessarily expresses itself in love of neighbor.

Upon hearing Jesus' reply, the scribe did something quite unusual in the Gospel: he agreed and added to Jesus' own explanation by repeating the prophetic teaching that care for others is more important than any amount of sacrifice. As the scene closes, Jesus tells the man he is not far from the kingdom of God. Given what has gone before this, especially the Gospel passages we have heard in the past few weeks, that statement seems to have put the scribe ahead of the pain-avoiding, infighting disciples as well as those who clung to their wealth. This is one of the very few moments in which we see Jesus speaking heart to heart with someone who shares and accepts his teaching.

1 Dt 6:4–5.
2 Cf. 1 Jn 4:10.

Connections to Church Teaching and Tradition

■ "Here we consider the various meanings of the word *love* as it relates to both God and neighbor. How important it is for us to understand that love of God and neighbor is truly one great command of Jesus" (DCE, 3, 10–11, 16–17).

■ "Here we find a mandate for the Church and society to care for the needy and the poor as human resources increase. The work of charity calls for a pastoral sense of "who is my neighbor" in the universal Catholic Church, and "who are my brothers and sisters" in the human family" (GS, 9).

■ "This apostolic exhortation of Pope Paul VI emphasizes that the evangelization of the Gospel, including deeds of love and mercy toward our neighbor, are essential for bringing the Gospel to life. We preach the Gospel by our deeds of mercy, compassion, and generous service" (EN, 31).

1 Kings 17:10–16   The end of this passage is unfortunately omitted from the Lectionary. It reads, "[. . .] according to the word of the LORD that he spoke through Elijah" (1 Kings 17:16b). Both Elijah and Elisha are called "man of God." As prophets, they were the mouthpiece of God, revealing messages of divine import and significance. Here, God speaks through the prophet and brings his words to fulfillment, bestowing blessing. We must not take for granted the fact that God is acting here; the prophet is the spokesman, but it is God who acts. Another piece of information brings a touch of color to this passage: the widow's coming from Zarephath suggests that she is a Gentile. Already in these historical books we see the dawning of a universalism in which God extends a hand of compassion and mercy to draw in all people, demonstrating the love of the one who is Creator of all.

Psalm 146:7, 8–9, 9–10 (1b)   Psalm 146 acknowledges and repeats the teaching of the preceding passage: our Creator and God cares for all, the work of divine hands. This psalm expresses so well God's care for the oppressed, the hungry, prisoners, the blind, the stranger, and the widow and orphan (a connection with the First Reading). This stance is understood as divine justice, affirming the right relationship that underlies authentic righteous behavior. When the thwarted plans of the wicked are described at the end of the psalm, it subtly cries out for us to act justly, as God does.

Hebrews 9:24–28   The significance of this passage cannot be understood without a consideration of Leviticus 16, which describes Yom Kippur, the Day of Atonement. Yom Kippur was and still is considered the holiest day of the year for Jews. On this day, the high priest would enter the Holy of Holies with the blood of goats and bulls, and sprinkle it upon the mercy seat. From that mercy seat, God's forgiveness would go out to the four corners of the earth and bring forgiveness and reconciliation with God. This passage in Hebrews tells us that Jesus, our perfect and blameless High Priest, has now taken his own blood and entered the heavenly sanctuary to bring about our forgiveness and reconciliation. He has become the mercy seat of the new law, from which has come our eternal redemption. Another important allusion to the Old Testament is found in the final verse of this passage where it reads, "offered once to take away the sins of many." In the fourth song of the servant in Second Isaiah (read on Good Friday), we find reference to the redemptive death of the servant, which brings about the forgiveness of sins (cf. Isaiah 53:11–12). The author of Hebrews saw Jesus as the fulfillment of both these Old Testament images (the High Priest and the Servant). The author of Hebrews makes the point that this one perfect sacrifice of Jesus need never be repeated, for it has surpassed and completed what the Old Law never envisioned could be accomplished. When Christ appears again, this time it will be to bestow salvation at the end of time.

Mark 12:38–44 or 12:41–44   The Gospel reading marks the third reference to a widow in today's readings. Can we suggest that in each situation (the widow who feeds Elijah, the widow who trusts in God for all her needs, and the widow who gives to God at the temple from her need) that the figure of the widow is employed to teach us something about the path of righteousness? The widow is portrayed in this Gospel passage as one who is neglected by the religious leaders (Mark 12:40), and yet shows us what true religion is all about by her small yet generous gift to the temple treasury. Throughout the scriptures, the biblical authors portray God as caring for the poor. The widow, the orphan, the foreigner, and all who are in need are the concern of God and his people. In the psalms, the king (expected to be God's representative on earth) bears the responsibility of caring for those in need (cf. Psalm 72:1–2, 4, 12–14). The Gospel shows Jesus in this same light, having a heart open to the needs of the poor, bringing them healing of body and consolation of spirit. The religious leaders fail to show or appreciate the kind of compassion expected of God's ambassadors to the poor. Rather, their religious practice is for show and self-aggrandizement. They understand neither their calling nor their deepest responsibility. Earlier in this chapter of Mark's account of the Gospel (12:28–34), Jesus teaches about the great commandment: love of God and neighbor. Does not the widow exemplify this teaching for all to see?

Connections to Church Teaching and Tradition

- "In this Apostolic Letter of John Paul II, one finds the call to a discernment of the 'signs of the times' and the need for personal renewal in the Church and in the hearts of all people as we move toward eternity" (TMA, 36).

- "In reflecting on the end times, the 'mystery of death' takes center stage. When we come to see our lives in relation to eternity, we build a world that sets its heart on things of heaven, with spiritual wisdom" (GS, 18).

Daniel 12:1–3   The book of Daniel in our Catholic tradition is classified as a prophetic writing. In the Jewish tradition, it is part of the *Ketubim*, or "Writings," a wisdom book. That piece of information serves us well in analyzing the text before us. Notice that "the wise shall shine brightly" at the last judgment, while "horror and disgrace" await the others. Daniel, who earlier interpreted dreams and advised the Babylonian king, is here warning the people to live uprightly, for there will come a day of severe reckoning. Wisdom and prudence tell us to live in a manner that acknowledges a day of judgment, when our lives shall be evaluated and a sentence passed. A key point of this passage is its reference to the notion of resurrection. While earlier Jewish thought told only of *Sheol*, the abode of the dead, here we find one of the earliest references to the resurrection of the just, to be later developed in the New Testament.

Psalm 16:5, 8, 9–10, 11 (1)   We do not hear the early part of this psalm, which tells of the psalmist's affirmation and confession of the Lord as his God. With the mention of "false gods," we suggest this psalm reflects some kind of conversion experience on the part of the psalmist; following the God of Israel is a choice of faith which then leads to gratitude and praise. There are several lines of connection between the previous reading and this psalm. In verse 8, "I keep the LORD always before me" is a poetic way of expressing the will and desire to follow God's law; on the day of judgment, God, who knows the human heart, will reward the upright. In verses 9–11, the psalmist refers to both *Sheol* (death) and the "path to life." Though this psalm is not expressing a belief in resurrection, to experience the "abounding joy in [God's] presence" is a way of living uprightly, and righteously coming before God in the Temple.

Hebrews 10:11–14, 18   Last week we saw Jesus portrayed as the new High Priest who has once-for-all completed the act that has brought about the forgiveness of our sins. This was compared to the Day of Atonement where, each year, the high priest would enter the Holy of Holies with the blood of animals that brought about reconciliation of the people with God. Christ has done this by bringing his own blood into the sanctuary not made by human hands, achieving our eternal redemption. This week, the author of Hebrews is making another comparison. By the "daily . . . ministry" of the levitical priests noted in the text, it brings another dimension to the fruitless efforts of sacrifice according to the Old Law. Daily the priests offered sacrifice, but it failed to bring about its hoped-for results. Again, it is Christ whose sacrifice has accomplished the reconciliation that had never been done before; he thus eliminates the levitical priesthood. Christ's once-for-all and single sacrifice, perfected by his total offering, has opened the way for our eternal salvation. The expression "and took his seat forever at the right hand of God" is an expression of the victory won by Jesus' self-sacrifice. These words are found in the opening of Psalm 110, a Messianic psalm, which the evangelists, Saint Paul, and the other New Testament authors used to express the Paschal victory of Jesus through his life, death, and Resurrection. God raised him up and seated him at his right hand.

Mark 13:24–32   The Old Testament prophets spoke of the *Yom Yahweh*, the "day of the Lord," when there would be a reversal of fortunes: the wicked would face shameful judgment and swift destruction, while the poor and the needy who placed their trust in the Lord would be given salvation and blessing. All three of the synoptic accounts of the Gospel conclude the public ministry of Jesus with something akin to the *Yom Yahweh*. One of the distinguishing characteristics of Mark's account of the cosmic upheaval is Jesus' teaching—watch for the signs and know that my word will not pass away. Watching for the signs has given rise to predictions of the final and awesome day; yet Jesus clearly says of that day, "no one knows," but the Father. With all the upheaval that will take place, there is one thing that will remain is God's word: "my words will not pass away." The expression "The Son of Man," drawn from Daniel 7:13, is an image of hope and encouragement. As initially found in the book of Daniel, so also here, Mark is encouraging the early Christians to hold fast to their faith, for in the end it brings them a share in the heavenly and eternal kingdom. Most importantly, they must remain firm and faithful.

Solemnity of Our Lord Jesus Christ the King　　November 25, 2012

Jesus Christ Testifies to the Truth

Connections to Church Teaching and Tradition

- "All God's people, through their Baptism, participate in Christ's offices of priest, prophet, and king" (USCCA, 117).

- "God's people share in Christ's kingly mission, which is to lead others through loving service to them. Jesus came not 'to be served but to serve and to give his life as a ransom for many.'[1] We are called, in imitation of the Lord Jesus, to be people who offer ourselves willingly in service to others. . . . Servant leadership is a responsibility of all God's people within their differing roles and responsibilities" (USCCA, 118).

- Our social duty is to awaken in everyone the love of the true and the good (CCC, 2105).

Daniel 7:13–14　The Son of Man will come on the clouds of heaven. He will receive dominion over all. All nations shall serve him. His dominion shall never be taken away. All this is foreseen by the prophet Daniel. Throughout his ministry, Jesus adopted this title for himself. He seems quite comfortable calling himself the Son of Man, and uses the title to indicate his future glory.

Today, the last Sunday of the church year, we celebrate the solemnity of Our Lord Jesus Christ, King of the Universe. The entire Sunday expresses our belief that Jesus is the ruler of all, the one anointed by God to command all the forces of the universe. The book of Daniel gives us a vision into that future. Throughout his life, Jesus attracted followers. In his dying and rising, he proclaimed the Good News of the Resurrection. In his future coming, he will reveal himself as the Son of Man, the one who possesses all dominion forever.

Psalm 93:1, 1–2, 5 (1a)　The Lord, the Creator, the one who entered into a covenant with Moses—that Lord is king. He wears majestic robes. He is armed. He established the firmament. His throne has been around from time immemorial, and it will continue to last for ages to come. Furthermore, the decrees of this Lord are trustworthy. They are a sign of the eternity of God's power.

Several psalms proclaim the power of God, who entered a covenant with ancient Israel under the title of "Lord." Christians assign this same title to Jesus. On today's solemnity, we sing this particular psalm in a way that links the images of God the Father and God the Son. God the Father created the world and established the covenant; God the Son is Lord of all, the one whose Gospel is trustworthy, and whose kingdom shall last forever.

Revelation 1:5–8　To Jesus Christ belongs all glory and power forever and ever. John says, "he is coming amid the clouds." That sentence from the last book of the New Testament calls to mind a sentence from one of the last books of the Old Testament. In Daniel, in the passage that serves as today's First Reading, the prophet says that the Son of Man will come on the clouds of heaven. Just as Jesus appropriated this title for himself, so the book of Revelation assigns the vision of clouds to Jesus as well. In this one passage we meet prophecy and fulfillment as we are reminded of the words Jesus used to speak of himself.

To drive home the point, the Lord God says in this same passage from Revelation, "I am the Alpha and the Omega." He is the beginning and the end of all things, the one who was and the one who is to come. This passage is cited each year in the Easter Vigil, as the priest inscribes the candle with a cross. This burning light that shatters the darkness of the night symbolizes the risen Christ, the one who rules over all power forever and ever, and even right now.

John 18:33b–37　The kingdom of Jesus is not of this world. He came into the world to testify to the truth, and everyone who belongs to the truth listens to his voice. All this comes to light in the conversation between Jesus and Pilate in the hours before the Crucifixion. John's Gospel makes it clear that Jesus is a king. Even Pilate says it in spite of himself. But apart from the vocabulary, the tone of this passage shows the mastery of Jesus as well. Pilate has worldly authority of Jesus' immediate future, but Jesus has all authority over Pilate and every other temporal claim.

This passage helps us understand what we mean by the title "King" as applied to Jesus. To a contemporary society in which kings are held in low esteem, the word carries a sense of entitlement and caste. But the kingship of Jesus is not of this world. We all yearn for a ruler who will take responsibility for society, whose own goodness will influence the goodness of others, who will contain evildoers and rescue the poor. Jesus Christ is the ideal ruler, and we have given to him the throne of our hearts.

1 Mt 20:28.

The Roman Missal

Starting on the First Sunday of Advent of this year, November 27, 2011, we will begin to use new words at Mass as we implement the English translation of the third edition of *The Roman Missal*. Homilists and catechists will be called upon to provide formation to parishioners as they grow in their use and understanding of these new words. The following homilies have been provided to you in order to help you help your parish through this time of transition.

All homilies come from Preparing Your Parish for the Revised Roman Missal: Homilies and Reproducibles for Faith Formation © *2011 Archdiocese of Chicago: Liturgy Training Publications, 3949 South Racine Avenue, Chicago IL 60609; 1-800-933-1800; www.LTP.org. Excerpts from the English translation of* The Roman Missal © *1973, 2010, International Commission on English in the Liturgy Corporation (ICEL).*

Homily Introducing the New Translation

By John Mark Klaus, TOR

Starting on the First Sunday of Advent of this year, November 27, 2011, we will be hearing and saying some new words at Mass. This is because we will begin to use the English version of the third edition of *The Roman Missal*. The Bishops have been working on this translation of *The Roman Missal* since Pope John Paul II announced a revision of the Missal in 2000.

No significant changes have occurred in the Mass since the Mass began to be prayed in the vernacular after the Second Vatican Council. Because of this, you are probably wondering how this translation will affect the way we celebrate the Mass in our parish.

One thing that has not changed is the structure of the Mass. There still will be two major parts of the Mass, the Liturgy of the Word and the Liturgy of the Eucharist. Our postures—sitting, standing, kneeling, singing, listening, proclaiming, and praying at Mass—will also be the same. What will change are some of the words we hear, some of our responses, and some of the parts of the Mass that we sing. With these changes, we as a parish will be more conscious of how and what we are praying during the Mass as a community.

Change is hard on all of us, and perhaps some of the responses may sound different for a while until we adjust. The priest's parts will also change, so we need to be patient with each other.

Most importantly, we will pray that we remain open to the work of the Holy Spirit within our Church.

Homily on the Gloria

By Daniel Merz, SLL

This homily was written for the Midnight Mass for the solemnity of the Nativity of the Lord, reflecting the scriptures for that Mass (Isaiah 9:1–6, Titus 2:11–14, and Luke 2:1–14). It may be adapted to be used at another time.

The scriptures in today's Mass especially emphasize the words *appearance* and *glory*. We hear these words from Isaiah (9:1), Titus (2:11, 13), and Luke (2:9, 14). Throughout Advent, we refrain from singing the Gloria, except on the feast of Our Lady of Guadalupe and the solemnity of the Immaculate Conception of the Blessed Virgin Mary, precisely to heighten our anticipation of the appearance of glory on this night. The Gloria is the song of the angels, and its words flow out as both commentary on, and response to, the appearance of the Lord of glory on this Christmas night. Let's ponder for a moment what the revised translation of the Gloria has to teach us.

The first change we will hear with the revised translation of the Gloria comes in the second line of the hymn. We have been singing, "peace to his people on earth" but will sing, "peace to people of good will." The phrase "good will" is new. The Church has always stressed the importance of the will, both human and divine. When our human will is ordered to the divine will, it is a "good will," and consequently, we will experience true peace. When Jesus "appeared" in the flesh, he taught us what it looks like when a human will is in perfect communion with the divine will.

Five verbs follow, flowing from this good and peaceful will (*praise, bless, adore, glorify, give thanks*). Conformed to Christ, "we praise" (God is wonderful in the gift of this child.), "we bless" (God is good and deserving of love for appearing to us in this way.), "we adore" (This appearance is worthy of awesome reverence.), "we glorify" (by living this mystery and letting it draw us closer to God), and lastly, "we give God thanks for his great glory" (ultimately in the Eucharistic Prayer). The current translation only mentions three of these verbs, but each of the five reveals a different response to this appearance of God's glory in our midst.

Our hymn proceeds to remind us of the unique glory that appeared on this night. The revised translation has restored the phrases "Only Begotten Son" and "Son of the Father," phrases that had been combined into "only Son of the Father." The modifier "begotten" is important, because, though the Father has many children both by creation and by adoption, he has only one Son who was begotten from before the world began, and who is born for us on this night.

Lastly, the revised translation brings out the movement of Jesus, first toward us and then toward God. The hymn first states, "You take away the sins of the world," an action focused on us. That action is followed with "receive our prayer." The hymn continues, "you are seated at the right hand of the Father." The translation we have been using follows this phrase with "receive our prayer," but the original version follows it with "have mercy on us." Seated at the right hand of the Father, Jesus has already ascended with our prayers. His purpose now is to intercede on our behalf for God's mercy. In this, of course, is the culmination of the glory that first appeared on earth as a little child. Following his life, his suffering, and death, he rose and ascended in full glory to the right hand of the Father. This is the definitive glory of our great God. The light of the Christ child, and of this holy and splendid night of peace and good will, must come to fruition in the radiance of the risen and ascended Christ.

Shortly, in this Eucharist, we will join in that upward movement of Christ to his Father. In his Word, he has come to us, and we must offer our prayers to him. In the Eucharistic Prayer, we will ascend with Christ to the right hand of the Father, where he is interceding for us. Let us open our hearts to this glory that our spirits might not remain only intent upon the child before us, but be raised with him to the heavenly throne of God.

Homily on the Creed

By Daniel Merz, SLL

With the revised translation of *The Roman Missal*, it might be helpful to take a look at some changes in the translation of the Creed. First, why do we even say the Creed during Mass? There are two main reasons. The Creed serves as the key for understanding the entire Bible, Old and New Testaments—like a condensed version of the Bible. This is why it comes at the end of the Liturgy of the Word. Any understanding of scripture—including that made during homilies—must be in agreement with the Creed. Secondly, it serves as a marker or guide for the Communion that will soon follow. The Creed is our communion in the faith that enables us to share in Communion in the Eucharist. It serves as key and summary of the Word, as well as introduction to, and criterion for, Communion.

One of the first changes in the revised translation of the Mass texts that the assembly will pray will be at the start of the Nicene Creed. Instead of stating, "We believe" as we start the Creed, members of the assembly will say, "I believe." The first liturgical use of the Creed was at Baptisms, and still today, whenever we celebrate a Baptism, we profess the Creed. As a representation of our faith, the Creed is most appropriate to Baptism, which brings others into our faith. The words of the Creed give us the opportunity for individual ownership of this faith. It's similar at Mass. Each of us must profess individual ownership of the common faith that is necessary for sharing Holy Communion as a Church: "I believe."

In the first part of the Creed, we profess God the Father as Creator. He is "maker of heaven and earth, / of all things visible and invisible." God is the maker of what is visible, such as the earth and the stars and you and me; he is maker not only of "unseen" things (as the former translation has it), but also of "invisible" things, such as angels. He is also maker of what is invisible, such as our immortal souls. The main point of the second part of the Creed is our affirmation that Jesus Christ is both divine and human. The same man who became flesh, "incarnate of the Virgin Mary" (in other words, who received our human nature from her), and who suffered death on the cross—this man is also "God from God, Light from Light." John's first letter tells us that God is light (1 John 1:5–7), so Jesus is divine light. The holy ones, the saints, dwell in this light. They dwell in the presence of this eternal light, in the presence of Jesus. Thus, we pray that our deceased loved ones may dwell forever in this light.

The most striking change in the Creed is the phrase that Jesus is "consubstantial with the Father." We used to say, "one in Being with the Father," which is just as difficult to say. Consubstantial refers to the core substance of who Jesus is; this core substance is the same core substance of who God the Father is. This is the most important word in the Creed. It professes specifically that the divinity of Jesus and the divinity of the Father is one and the same, without saying that Jesus is the Father, or vice versa (kind of like how ice and steam are both H_2O without being the same thing). *Consubstantial* is an important word; it was fought over by theologians and bishops for centuries as they sought the best word to clarify this great truth about Jesus. It deserves our respect and attention. The Creed goes on to profess faith in the Holy Spirit and the Church. The former translation stated, "we acknowledge one baptism," whereas, now it states, "I confess one Baptism." Our job is not simply to acknowledge Baptism, but to confess our faith in its saving power. Similarly, we no longer "look for the resurrection of the dead" as though it were lost, but rather we "look forward" to it, as something that fills us with hope and expectation.

Today, let's be mindful of how this Creed opens up for us the correct understanding of the Bible, and just as importantly, how it calls us to communion in faith so that we can approach this altar to receive Holy Communion, the Body and Blood of our Lord, human and divine, consubstantial with the Father in his divinity, and consubstantial with you and me in his humanity.

Homily on the Lamb of God

By Daniel Merz, SLL

"Behold the Lamb of God, / behold him who takes away the sins of the world."

With the revised translation of *The Roman Missal,* the priest will say these words as he holds up the consecrated host just before Holy Communion. This change in the words of the Mass is a slight one from the previous translation "This is the Lamb of God / who takes away the sins of the world." With these words, the priest takes on the role of John the Baptist whose function then, as now, is to point to Christ, who is just as capable of taking away our sins in this Eucharist as he was some two-thousand years ago as the sacrificial lamb on the cross.

It is interesting that the liturgy puts this quotation from John the Baptist adjacent to the words "Blessed are those called to the supper of the Lamb," which alludes to Revelation 19:9. The lamb is the most frequent image for Christ in the book of Revelation, and, perhaps more significantly, the "supper of the lamb" in Revelation refers to the wedding feast of Christ and his Bride, the Church. What is interesting is that, in a passage a little beyond the one quoted above from the Gospel according to John, John the Baptist calls himself the friend of the Bridegroom, and then later is beheaded because he protested the illicit marriage of King Herod. The beauty is that the Baptist, who was a celibate, gave his life defending the sanctity of Marriage. The liturgy delights in this type of wordplay. Eucharist is the foretaste of the heavenly wedding feast, and so we have a celibate priest speaking the words of the celibate John the Baptist to the Bride of Christ, the Church—you, the assembly—and pointing to Christ, the Bridegroom. The previous translation stated, "Happy are those called," but the revised translation states that those who are called are "blessed." Regardless of whether we feel happy or sad when we come to church, we are all "blessed" in being called to Holy Communion with our Bridegroom.

As we continue to look at the liturgy, we see that the assembly's response to the priest just before Holy Communion comes from Matthew 8:8 and Luke 7:6–7. The revised translation is more faithful to the scripture that underlies this prayer. Many may never have realized that they were quoting the words of the Roman centurion in Luke's account of the Gospel. The centurion had asked Jesus to heal his servant, and when Jesus agreed, saying that he would come to the house, the centurion replied, "Lord, I am not worthy to have you enter under my roof; only say the word and my servant shall be healed." Jesus responds to the centurion's words by saying that never in all of Israel had he found such faith, and he heals the servant from a distance. The liturgy asks us to call to mind the faith, humility, and reverence of this centurion, who sought the healing power of Jesus, but felt unworthy to have Jesus come under the roof of his house. The Christian who approaches the altar should have the same faith, humility, and reverence in preparing to receive the Holy Eucharist under the "roof" of our body. Just as the roof is the external shelter for what is most important to us as social beings—our family—so too is our body the "roof" or external shelter for that which is most precious to us as individuals—our soul.

The Church places three scripture readings side by side in the liturgy, and communicates so much with so little. We are reminded of the mutual support that celibates and the married can provide for each other. We are reminded that our Communion derives from the sacrifice of the Lamb who has taken away our sins. We are reminded that this banquet meal is a foretaste of the heavenly wedding feast. We are reminded that in coming to Holy Communion, we are to have the attitude of the centurion in Luke's account of the Gospel, a man of faith, humility, and reverence. And we are reminded that we are also in need of healing, just as the centurion's servant was. In this Eucharist, may we indeed find the healing and forgiveness we need and the eternal love and commitment of the Bridegroom, whom we need above all else.

Abbreviations Key: Books of the Bible

The following abbreviations are used for the books of the Bible cited in the text.

Gen	Genesis	Song	Song of Solomon	1 Cor	1 Corinthians
Ex	Exodus	Wis	Wisdom	2 Cor	2 Corinthians
Lev	Leviticus	Sir	Sirach	Gal	Galatians
Num	Numbers	Isa	Isaiah	Eph	Ephesians
Deut	Deuteronomy	Jer	Jeremiah	Phil	Philippians
Josh	Joshua	Lam	Lamentations	Col	Colossians
Judg	Judges	Bar	Baruch	1 Thess	1 Thessalonians
1 Sam	1 Samuel	Ezek	Ezekiel	2 Thess	2 Thessalonians
2 Sam	2 Samuel	Dan	Daniel	1 Tim	1 Timothy
1 Kings	1 Kings	Hos	Hosea	2 Tim	2 Timothy
2 Kings	2 Kings	Joel	Joel	Titus	Titus
1 Chr	1 Chronicles	Am	Amos	Philem	Philemon
2 Chr	2 Chronicles	Jon	Jonah	Heb	Hebrews
Ezra	Ezra	Mic	Micah	Jas	James
Neh	Nehemiah	Zeph	Zephaniah	1 Pet	1 Peter
Tob	Tobit	Zech	Zechariah	2 Pet	2 Peter
Jdt	Judith	Mal	Malachi	1 Jn	1 John
Esth	Esther	Mt	Matthew	2 Jn	2 John
2 Macc	2 Maccabees	Mk	Mark	3 Jn	3 John
Job	Job	Lk	Luke	Jude	Jude
Ps	Psalms	Jn	John	Rev	Revelation
Prov	Proverbs	Acts	Acts of the Apostles		
Eccl	Ecclesiastes	Rom	Romans		

Abbreviations Key: Major Church Documents

The following is a list of documents that are referenced in the Connections to Church Teaching and Tradition section on the scripture background pages. Full texts of the documents can be found in *Vatican Council II: Volume 1: The Basic Sixteen Documents* and *Vatican Council II: Volume 2: More Post Conciliar Documents* (Austin Flannery, ed.), on the Vatican Web site (www.vatican.va), on the United States Conference of Catholic Bishops Web site (www.usccb.org), or online by typing the English or Latin title into a search engine.

AA	Second Vatican Council, *Apostolicam Actuositatem*
AG	Second Vatican Council, *Ad Gentes Divinitus*
Aparecida	Fifth General Conference of Latin Bishops (CELAM), *Documento Conclusivo de Aparecida*
CCC	Interdicasterial Commission for the Catechism of the Catholic Church, *Catechism of the Catholic Church*
CIV	Pope Benedict XVI, *Caritas in Veritate*
CL	Pope John Paul II, *Christifideles Laici*
CSDC	Pontifical Council for Justice and Peace, *Compendium of the Social Doctrine of the Church*
CSL	United States Conference of Catholic Bishops, *Communities of Salt and Light*
CU	Synod of Bishops, *Convenientes ex Universo*
DCE	Pope Benedict XVI, *Deus Caritas Est*
DOP	Pope John Paul II, *Message of His Holiness Pope John Paul II for the Celebration of the World Day of Peace*
DV	Second Vatican Council, *Dei Verbum*
DVI	Pope John Paul II, *Dominum et Vivificantem*
EDE	Pope John Paul II, *Ecclesia de Eucharistia*
EIA	Pope John Paul II, *Ecclesia in America*
EN	Pope Paul VI, *Evangelii Nuntiandi*
EV	Pope John Paul II, *Evangelium Vitae*
GCD	Sacred Congregation for the Clergy, *General Catechetical Directory*
GDC	Sacred Congregation for the Clergy, *General Directory for Catechesis*

GIRM	Congregation for Divine Worship and the Discipline of the Sacraments/United States Catholic Conference, *General Instruction of the Roman Missal*
GMD	United States Conference of Catholic Bishops, *Go and Make Disciples: A National Plan and Strategy for Catholic Evangelization in the United States*
GS	Second Vatican Council, *Gaudium et Spes*
JDDJ	Lutheran World Federation and Pontifical Council for Promoting Christian Unity, *Joint Declaration on the Doctrine of Justification*
JM	World Synod of Bishops, *Justicia in Mundo*
LG	Second Vatican Council, *Lumen Gentium*
MD	Pope John Paul II, *Mulieris Dignitatem*
MF	Pope Paul VI, *Mysterium Fidei*
OHWB	United States Conference of Catholic Bishops, *Our Hearts Were Burning Within Us: A Pastoral Plan for Adult Faith Formation in the United States*
PDV	Pope John Paul II, *Pastores Dabo Vobis*
PO	Pope Paul VI, *Presbyterorum Ordinis*
PT	Pope John XXIII, *Pacem in Terris*
RCIA	Congregation for Divine Worship and Discipline of the Sacraments, *Rite of Christian Initiation of Adults*
RH	Pope John Paul II, *Redemptor Hominis*
RM	Pope John Paul II, *Redemptoris Mater*
RMI	Pope John Paul II, *Redemptoris Missio*
RP	Pope John Paul II, *Reconciliatio et Paenitentia*
SC	Second Vatican Council, *Sacrosanctum Concilium*
SCA	Pope Benedict XVI, *Sacramentum Caritatis*
SNL	United States Conference of Catholic Bishops and Conferencia del Episcopado Mexicano, *Strangers No Longer: Together on the Journey of Hope*
SS	Pope Benedict XVI, *Spe Salvi*
SWJCB	Liturgical Press, *Selected Works of Joseph Cardinal Bernardin: Homilies and Teaching Documents*

TEE	United States Catholic Conference, *To the Ends of the Earth: A Pastoral Statement on World Mission*
TMA	Pope John Paul II, *Tertio Millennio Adveniente*
USCCA	United States Conference of Catholic Bishops, *United States Catholic Catechism for Adults*
UN	International Commission on English in the Liturgy, *Universal Norms on the Liturgical Year and the General Roman Calendar*